The More I Know,
The Less I Understand

The More I Know, The Less I Understand

Young Researchers' Essays on Witnessing Auschwitz

Auschwitz-Birkenau State Museum
in Oświęcim, 2017

This publication was made possible partially thanks to the financial support
of the Consulate General of the Republic of Poland in Vancouver.

This book was published due to the financial support
of the Memorial Foundation for the Victims of Auschwitz-Birkenau.

Cover designed by
Ellyn Hill

Photo on the cover by
Cameron Corea

Language editing and proofreading:
Jasmine Spencer

Editorial board:
Dr. Jacek Lachendro, Dr. Piotr Setkiewicz, Dr. Bożena Karwowska,
Adelina Hetnar-Michaldo, Marta Berecka

Edited by:
Dr. Bożena Karwowska, Anja Nowak

Layout:
Iza Witowska

Drawings by former prisoners and documents:
Collections and Archives of the Auschwitz-Birkenau State Museum

ISBN 978-83-7704-202-1

*In memory of Stanisława Kawalec (née Biernacka)
and Prof. Henryk Kawalec,
and All Others who perished*

Contents

Piotr M. A. Cywiński

Place of Memory.
Place of Learning. Place of Reflection.

Primarily through the efforts of survivors, the space of Auschwitz-Birkenau became, after the war, a Place of Memory. With time it became a symbol of the entire Shoah, as well as many other tragedies caused by Nazi Germany. It has become the symbol of all failures and downfalls in human history. To use the metaphorical expression of Heinz Thilo, a German SS officer and physician in Auschwitz, it became the "anus mundi." Today, millions of visitors, mostly young people, become acquainted with this space, and through this encounter they learn about history and the human tragedies of that time. They also have a unique and challenging opportunity to reflect on the essence of human behavior, the limits of freedom and the susceptibility of humanity to hate and demagogy. We strongly believe that, unfortunately, such deep reflection remains necessary even today.

Auschwitz can be encountered in a number of ways. Most visitors opt for guided visits, choosing between general or study tours. However, there are a growing number of projects that demand significant direct engagement from their participants. Such projects offer their participants a rare opportunity for reflection and a chance to explore in depth those things that Auschwitz can teach us about humankind. This collection of essays is the fruit of such a project initiated by The University of British Columbia and carried out with the academic and educational support of The International Center for Education about Auschwitz and the Holocaust and The Research Center of the Auschwitz-Birkenau State Museum. These essays are a record of the participants' reflections and deepening knowledge gleaned from their encounter with Auschwitz. They may help to shape one's own way of approaching this particularly sensitive topic. They can be used to prepare others for a visit to Auschwitz or as part of an educational program. Finally, they can inspire personal reflection. I hope that the efforts of this determined and committed group of Canadian students, as represented by this collection of essays, becomes a common good to be shared with others, a means of disseminating memories, encounters and reflections about Auschwitz and the essence and limits of humanity.

Bożena Karwowska
Anja Nowak

Introduction

The book presented here is comprised of a selection of essays that undergraduate students from the University of British Columbia (Vancouver, Canada) wrote as a part of an intensive research seminar, *Witnessing Auschwitz*, in the years 2014, 2015 and 2016. This seminar includes two weeks of lectures, study tours, discussion panels, workshops and consultations at the Auschwitz-Birkenau State Museum as part of a full month that each group of students spends in Poland. However, preparations for the seminar start earlier, with a course titled *Representations of the Holocaust*, which all of them take in Vancouver.

Peter Hayes, a prominent Holocaust scholar, warns educators that "making dreadful developments intelligible runs the risk of seeming to lend them a kind of intelligence or even justification" and he quotes a French proverb: "to understand all is to forgive all".[1] Teaching and learning about the Holocaust should thus refrain from creating a false sense of understanding. It is our belief that instead, it should build an educated non-understanding on the basis of the scarce and incomplete historical documents available to us, and on various multidisciplinary notions and approaches. The teaching goals of this undertaking are to help students come to terms with confusing and often conflicting information, to become accustomed to the puzzlement created by incomplete knowledge about the Holocaust and to become more self-aware about the human need to judge.

---

1 Peter Hayes, "Introduction", *How was it possible? A Holocaust Reader*, Lincoln and London: University of Nebraska Press, 2015, p. xiii.

In the introductory lecture of the course we show students a copy of a sketchbook with drawings portraying the life of Auschwitz prisoners. This sketchbook was found on site at the camp in 1947 and published for the first time in 2011.[2] While discussing the importance of this testimony, students eventually come to the realization that the victim who hid these "drawings in the bottle" was actually trying to reach out to them personally. To avoid the language barrier, the message comes in pictures, and it was hidden and preserved for a future generation. Thus, from the very beginning of the course, we very strongly emphasize that students are to learn about the Holocaust, but that they must also carry out this message and find their own ways of becoming what we call proxy witnesses. In line with these goals we emphasize that one of the reasons for studying the Holocaust is the persistent lack of closure and a constant need to examine and re-examine our knowledge about this dark period in human history.

Holocaust education in many countries is currently built around survivors and their willingness and ability to share stories with the next generation. This, for rather obvious reasons, is not a sustainable educational model. As Holocaust educators we must thus ask ourselves how to teach about the Holocaust when there are no more survivors to share their stories. This is the question we seek to answer in the collaboration between the University of British Columbia and the Auschwitz-Birkenau State Museum as we continue to develop and implement this innovative educational program. In our model of multidisciplinary inquiry, students from various departments study issues related to the Holocaust in the context of the social responsibilities of researchers and professionals. The program follows a non-linear approach; it is structured around various issues connected with Auschwitz, the German Nazi concentration and extermination camp, rather than retracing a linear sequence of historical events. In a similar manner, our students' research is centered around a certain topic of interest to them: a circumstance or aspect of the camp that sparks their academic curiosity.

2   Agnieszka Sieradzka, *Szkicownik z Auschwitz = The Sketchbook from Auschwitz*, Oświęcim: Państwowe Muzeum Auschwitz-Birkenau, 2011.

This new model based on multidisciplinary undergraduate research focuses on introducing students to conceptual tools and on fostering the development of critical thinking, instead of simply relying on the transmission of historical facts and personal stories. It stresses first and foremost an analytical and critical education, including awareness of the importance of ethical and respectful language. During the seminar in Poland students come into contact with the best researchers and educators in the field, who share their knowledge and expertise with the group and help students to develop their own research interests. At this point, the students gain their academic independence, working on questions that arise from their knowledge.

The sketchbook with which we start the lectures does not offer a happy ending, but it demonstrates an unparalleled faith in humanity. In the midst of unimaginable horror, witnessing the disappearance of the European Jewry and the cruelty of the SS, somebody believed that the German Nazi system would ultimately not succeed in changing traditional values, that people would still understand what was right and wrong, good and bad. And that one day we would follow the sketches, trying to learn more and trying to tell the story of what happened. We want our students to be guided by the same faith in humanity in their quest to become proxy witnesses.

The essays you will find in this book are the result of a long journey. Coming from various backgrounds, personal as well as academic, all of our students invested an incredible amount of time and dedication into learning about the camp and the crimes committed here. They presented themselves with a most difficult learning process, struggled with the immense challenge of this topic and the human fates it is comprised of and still found the dedication and intellectual strength to pursue their academic inquiries. In the preparatory course back in Vancouver, we guide students through a process that encompasses dealing with emotions - outrage, sadness and many other stages of powerlessness. Being here on site, the place touched all of us deeply, and we turned our emotions into an intellectual response and a great need to share and to educate others, to keep the stories alive.

Our students' work is as multi-faceted as the young people who participated in the program: each of our authors is a lens that makes visible a different facet of this site and the events that took place. Together with our colleagues from the Museum we believe that historical knowledge is a necessary background for every study of the Holocaust, regardless of their specific disciplinary approach. Our students learned about the history of this site during lectures, workshops, study tours and seminars. At the same time, academics, educators and members of various departments of the Museum supported our students in developing their own questions and interests, taking the young people seriously in their ambition and their capacity to learn and to contribute to an academic exchange.

As editors, we did not want to interfere with the students' own individual voices, and at the same time editorial and academic work with students is naturally varied. Some topics made it easier to challenge students and ask for several revisions and additions; in other cases students' essays gave academics involved in the editorial processes an opportunity to add supplementary information in footnotes. Such additions as these footnotes feed into an important stream of historical background knowledge and allow us to address even more aspects of the students' chosen topics without affecting the unique voices available in the students' essays. In this way, we also direct interested readers to additional sources. You can read these "two voices" as an embodiment of the substantial exchange, between two generations of academics and educators, that has taken place and that will continue to take place over the years to come. These additions are not meant to be corrective; rather, they show the points at which the research editors found opportunities to open up additional paths, to complement or deepen certain perspectives, opening the book to a variety of readers, including educators and researchers.

It takes a village to raise a child and it takes many people and institutions to raise in young people such a strong need to share what they learned and to educate others about the Holocaust. After the *Witnessing Auschwitz* seminar, many of our students have created opportunities to speak to their peers and communities in Canada and abroad; they have committed themselves to volunteer work, initiated education workshops at schools, decided to pursue graduate programs in the field of Holocaust or Genocide studies, given talks, published articles, written their theses and been socially engaged in manifold ways. Their engagement with the topic sparked in them a need to pass on their knowledge, to share their experience and their commitment. This publication is another wonderful opportunity for their dedication and intellect to unfold, and for them to share what they have learned with a wider audience. It is also our way of thanking all those without whose help this would not have been possible.

From the first talks with Alicja Białecka (Auschwitz-Birkenau State Museum), Dr. Janet Giltrow (Faculty of Arts, UBC) and Katherine Beaumont (UBC Go Global) on the educational cooperation between The University of British Columbia and the Auschwitz-Birkenau State Museum, the Consulate General of the Republic of Poland in Vancouver and the three consecutive Consuls General – Mr Krzysztof Czapla, Dr. Krzysztof Olendzki and Mr Marcin Trzciński – have continuously and generously supported the project. Also Marek Stankiewicz deserves a very special thank you for being with us from the very inception of the project through to every step of our long journey. Thank you as well to Michael Messer for his invaluable support over the years. The *Witnessing Auschwitz* seminar would not be possible without significant funding by the UBC Faculty of Arts Research Abroad (ARA) awards, the administrative support of UBC Go Global and the tireless and caring help of Shareen Chin.

The program of the seminar, designed with the crucial cooperation of Marta Berecka (Educational Projects) and the kind encouragement of the Director of the International Center for Education about Auschwitz and the Holocaust Mr Andrzej Kacorzyk, would not be the same without the continuous support of the Auschwitz-Birkenau Museum's Research Center, including that of the editors of this new kind of project, Dr. Piotr Setkiewicz and Dr. Jacek Lachendro, along with the Museum's many other departments.

Graduate students from the University of British Columbia were able to accompany the seminar thanks to the generous support of the Holocaust Education Committee of the Faculty of Arts, which also supported several undergraduate students both in Poland and in Vancouver. A special thank you for the support of graduate assistants goes also to Prof. Markus Hallensleben.

Before the seminar papers took the shape of the texts in this book, they were presented during three consecutive *Witnessing Auschwitz* conferences at UBC. We would like to thank Nina Krieger and the Vancouver Holocaust Education Center for their organizational cooperation and for providing students with various platforms to share with others what they learned during the seminar. We are grateful to Prof. Geoffrey Winthrop-Young for being a part of the conferences and helping to make them an academic gathering of both students and faculty.

The book owes a lot to Adelina Hetnar-Michaldo, who seamlessly and graciously coordinated the work on its publication. Special thanks also go to Asia (Aja Jade) Beattie for her inexhaustible dedication to this book project. A sincere thank you to all our contributors, including students, academics, artists and editors, for their continuous interest and willingness to push on, developing and refining their ideas and bringing all this to life. The cover of the book was generously supported by Robert Płaczek, and the entire book took its final shape thanks to the invaluable advice and generous help of Jadwiga Pinderska-Lech and the publishing department.

Thanking everybody would require many more pages so - we extend our thanks to every single person and institution contributing to the learning experiences of students during their research in the Auschwitz-Birkenau State Museum.

At the end - there were two people whose enthusiasm made it impossible to doubt that the project would be successful. Bill Levine and Risa Levine - we thank you for a lot. Actually, for everything.

Maria Dawson

The Roles of Food in the Development and Implementation of Nazi German Policies: A Case Study of the General Government

Food is a fundamental necessity for human life. Abraham Maslow in his now-famous hierarchy of needs qualified access to food as one of the most basic requirements that must be fulfilled before an individual can consider any other aspects of life and happiness. While this theory in its details is fiercely debated, it highlights the crucial nature of food in human lives. By extension, there is significant potential for food to be used as a tool of power, control and destruction. Psychologists, nutritionists, anthropologists and historians all have different ways of examining food and the role of food in society. By utilizing the tools of each of these fields, especially through a historical lens, this paper will examine the role of food in Nazi policy with a case study of the Nazi German occupied region of the General Government in Poland during the Second World War. In Nazi German policies food played a wide range of roles, an example of which will be examined, focusing on economic policies in the General Government region of occupied Poland and food deprivation and starvation as tools for implementation of the extermination programs within the Auschwitz-Birkenau concentration camp.

Economics and Overpopulation

Agricultural and industrial food production in occupied Poland, and the failure of those industries to meet Reich standards of efficiency of production, were amongst the most pertinent justifications for the relocation of Poles upon the commencement of the German occupation. The displacement and extermination of European Jews and Poles was in part a decision justified not by social policy but instead by supposed pragmatic considerations of perceived overpopulation and suffering labor productivity.[1] The economic systems of Eastern Europe and Germany functioned on contrasting principles and practical decisions. Germany's economy was more focused on high-efficiency and mass production with the intention of maximizing national wealth, while the Polish economy was more agrarian in general and more locally focused, often with trade interactions not stretching beyond the local.[2] The Polish agriculture market was based on a model in which there was very little, if any, surplus in production.[3] This economic system of self-sufficiency within Polishe villages did not meld well with the Nazi German economic model. For the Third Reich government, a reduction in population in the General Government region was seen as being critical for increased productivity in the region in order for the economy to be more reflective of Nazi German ideals.[4] Connections between poverty and the economic model in use in Eastern Europe were also drawn; correspondingly, as many of the Ostjuden were in lower economic brackets, the Nazis argued that their elimination was also a means of reducing poverty.[5]

German spatial planners and economists determined that overpopulation was the primary problem preventing the General Government region

---

1 Götz Aly and Susanne Heim, "The Economics of the Final Solution: A Case Study from the General Government," *Simon Wiesenthal Center Annual*, 1988, 5, pp. 3-48.

2 Ibid.

3 Ibid. **[ED]** In addition to overpopulation and the fragmentation of farms, the greatest impacts on the low level of productivity in Polish agriculture were the Great Crisis in the years 1929-1935 and the general decline in food prices on the world market. In addition, for political reasons, Germany introduced high tariffs on imports of Polish grain, wood and coal. As a result, when the end of 1930s saw the development of industrial production, improvement in agriculture followed more slowly and with delay.

4 David Cesarani, *Holocaust: Critical Concepts in Historical Studies Vol. II*, London: Routledge, 2004, p. 141.

5 Ibid., p. 142.

6 Aly and Heim, "The Economics of the Final Solution," p. 8.

from achieving a correct economic order.[6] The label of "overpopulated" was designated to a region if the calculated potential productivity of the land was higher than the actual productivity or was based on the level of unemployment.[7] The Nazis assigned the label of overpopulated to a region when the calculated potential productivity of the land was higher than the actual productivity, or when there was a high rate of unemployment.[8] The logic was the following: for the Nazis overpopulation meant a reduction of the amount of space available for agricultural development. This assumption translated into a formula that calculated the portion of a region available for food production using the number of people living in a given area and the cost of living.[9] The equation implied that in places where the available land for agriculture was limited, and the cost of living was already relatively low, a reduction in population would improve production.[10] Converting the population into an abstract factor entailed the possibility to see it as a neutral variable that could be managed without regards to any ethical considerations. As Götz Aly and Susanne Heim explain: "The actual function of this formula lies in it being abstracted from its substantive content and thereby suggests the possibility that individual factors can be manipulated . . . Thus expressed in manageable terms, population size became a magnitude that was, alongside others, variable at will".[11]

The Nazi Germans believed that the issue of overpopulation could be resolved with the removal or elimination of the Jewish population from the General Government territory.[12] The portion of the region's population that was Jewish was approximately equivalent to the percentage by

---

7 Ibid.
8 The original formula, as quoted by Aly and Heim was: "The space available for food (Nahrungsraum, or N) equals the size of the population (Volkszahl, or V) times the cost of living (Lebenshaltung, or L). In abbreviated form: N = V x L". Ibid.
9 Ibid.
10 Ibid.
11 Ibid.
12 Ibid.

which the population would need to be reduced in order to achieve the desired population count in the eyes of the Nazi authorities.[13] Thus, the Germans drew a link between economic development and the elimination of the European Jewry.[14] This is important to acknowledge and review for the sake of understanding the political role of food, separate from its physiological role.

Starvation

In order to understand the uses and abuses of food control by the Nazis during the Holocaust, it is essential to also understand the basic physiology of starvation and the history of food control within the regime. The history of intentional starvation as a means of murder by the Nazis goes back to the early days of the Third Reich. Starvation was introduced as the first method to be used in the T-4 euthanasia program on disabled individuals, chosen because it was "passive, simple, and natural," according to historian Michael Berenbaum.[15] Thus starvation as a method of mass extermination, while a more indirect method than others that were utilized, was an integral part of Nazi extermination plans from the onset of the era of the Third Reich. In addition to starvation's use as a method for intentional killing in the pre-war years, according to an Army journalist, the prisoners in the concentration camps were on a "deliberate starvation diet".[16]

There are a number of levels on which starvation occurs; as Jack Shepherd observes, "the reality of the process of starvation is that rarely does

---

13 Ibid.

14 Ibid. [ED] This view, however, was criticized by many other historians (for example: Michael Wildt) who emphasized that Aly in his economic approach ignores the role of anti-Semitism in the context of population policy in occupied Poland and extermination of the Jews.

15 Michael Berenbaum, *The World Must Know: The History of the Holocaust as Told in the United States Holocaust Memorial Museum,* Boston: Little Brown, 1993, p. 64.

16 Ibid., p. 189.

a food supply completely and abruptly disappear."[17] Instead starvation occurs to varying degrees, with a "prolonged period of caloric deficit" causing "semistarvation," which results in both physical and mental deficits that are often permanent.[18] In order to categorize and quantify levels of starvation the medical and international communities have had to create standards of measurement. The lowest level of starvation occurs with the loss of 5 to 10 percent of an individual's body weight and typically does not incur a loss of bodily function. The second level occurs with a loss of 15 to 35 percent of body weight, and if this occurs amongst the general population it is classified as a famine. The final and most severe level of starvation is when 35 to 40 percent of body weight is lost, and this is "invariably fatal."[19]

There are a large number of nutrients that are necessary for sustaining human life. For example, a body must be able to build its own proteins and enzymes, which are mostly protein-derived. Without these, metabolism cannot take place, and starvation at the cellular level occurs.[20] Metabolism and some other biochemical reactions also require micronutrients.[21] These are nutrients that, although only being required in small quantities, are essential for continued sustenance of life, the deficit of any given one can be equally devastating to macronutrient depravation.[22]

Food Production in KL Auschwitz-Birkenau

Agriculture played an integral role in many Third Reich decisions, from the treatment of Soviet citizens upon the German invasion in 1941, to the

---

17 John Butterly and Jack Shepherd, *Hunger: The Biology and Politics of Starvation*, Hanover: Dartmouth College, 2010, p. 58.
18 Ibid.
19 Ibid.
20 Ibid., p. 65.
21 Examples of such micronutrients include: vitamins A, C, and D, albumen, niacin, riboflavin, thiamine (aka vitamin B), and magnesium, the insufficiency of all were recognized within the ghetto.
22 Ibid., p. 71.

justification for the relocation of hundreds of thousands of individuals across Eastern Europe, to the role of Auschwitz-Birkenau concentration camp in broader Nazi German industry and economic conditions. Heinrich Himmler, the chief of the SS and the man responsible for the oversight of concentration camps, had the intention for Auschwitz-Birkenau to become "the largest agricultural station in Eastern Europe," where experiments relating to food production would take place; as well, a vast number of farms would exist as part of the camp complex.[23] Thus in the summer of 1940, just after the first transport had arrived to the camp in June, the first agricultural work detail was created.[24] Besides farming, Auschwitz-Birkenau also had its own slaughterhouse and dairy that were utilized for the production of food intended for consumption by prisoners as well as by SS personnel, and in some cases to be sent out of the camp to other regions of Reich territory.

Food produced in the concentration camp was made with the intention of being fed to both prisoners and German personnel, specifically the SS at Auschwitz-Birkenau and soldiers on the front line. Between the food produced for the prisoners and for the Nazis there was an evident and intentional discrepancy in the quality of the food. There was also discrepancy in the means of production. For example, sausages produced for the SS were made in a room separate from that where sausages produced for prisoners were made.[25] In addition, these sausages were noted as having a higher caloric count and fat content than those for prisoners, and the production process used proper techniques for preservation, a luxury not

---

23 Łukasz Martyniak, "Schlachthaus und Molkerei (The History of the KL Slaughterhouse and Dairy)," *Auschwitz Studies*, 2014, 27, p. 1. [ED] Apart from grain, agricultural production SS in the areas adjacent to Auschwitz also included the cultivation of the plant known as Taraxacum kok-saghyz, containing at its roots a certain amount of natural rubber. In Harmęże they also bred angora rabbits in order to obtain the wool used to produce textiles. Thus, only a part of the ground from the camp farms could be used to feed prisoners.

24 Ibid., p. 1.

25 Ibid., p.5.

afforded to the food of prisoners.[26] The lesser quality of preservation of sausages allocated for prisoners made the meat more prone to contamination and bacterial growth that would result in disease. In part as a result of the higher quality of meat afforded to the SS, theirs was the primary source of smuggled meat into the camp.[27] In order to smuggle meat out of the work detail any stolen food needed to be compensated for, as the SS kept close track of the amount being produced. This could be done by adding water to the sausage mix is order to replace the stolen volume.

The Nazis confiscated the land on which the slaughterhouse was constructed from the Polish citizens before it was designated for use by the Auschwitz concentration camp.[28] Construction on the land began before the commandant of Auschwitz had gained official possession of the territory, indicating the importance of food for the functioning of the Reich. It is also indicative of the influence of the camp's leaders in the specific region.

Food Consumption in KL Auschwitz-Birkenau

Food and nutrition within the camp cannot be understood through broad generalizations of experience. For different prisoners who were in the camp at different time periods their experiences with food varied widely. It has been determined that with only the minimum provisions allotted to every prisoner within the camp through official means, it was possible to survive no longer than three months. In an essay by Rolf Keller, malnutrition is cited as one of the three primary reasons that of the 10,000 Soviet Prisoners of War sent to Auschwitz-Birkenau in the fall of 1941, fewer than 10 percent were still alive five months later, in March of 1942. The other two reasons were the "brutal treatment" they received

---

26 Ibid., p. 9.
27 Ibid. [ED] Similarly, the bread was baked in the camp bakery with moldy flour and contained worthless extras (such as chopped chestnuts). Łukasz Martyniak and Bohdan Piętka, "Piekarnie obozowe w KL Auschwitz," *Zeszyty Oświęcimskie*, 2013, 28, pp. 112-118.
28 Ibid., p. 2.

and outright murder committed by SS.[29] In order to survive longer than this, prisoners would need to either hold a position within the camp that would grant them greater rations and require less physically demanding work, or they would have to acquire food through alternate means.

One example of a means of acquiring additional food was to "organize". This was the term used for obtaining items not issued officially within the camp. An example of this was that those working in the kitchen or within the network of food production; they would smuggle food out of their workplace to either consume themselves or trade for other commodities on the black market that existed within Auschwitz-Birkenau. Additionally, those who worked in what was referred to as "Canada," the area in which the belongings from newly arrived transports were sent, were able on occasion to smuggle food as well as other items that could either be consumed personally or traded with fellow prisoners. Smuggling was a risky endeavor, one that would result in harsh repercussions if a prisoner was caught.

Within Auschwitz-Birkenau the majority of prisoners who worked within the food complexes of the camp and its subcamps were Poles, despite the fact that especially in the final year and a half of the camp's operation the large majority of the prisoner population was Jewish.[30] This may be attributed simply to the fact that food production complexes were established in the early months of the camp's operation when most prisoners were there as political prisoners. This however does not stand up to scrutiny as more subcamps were created over time, as the camp's population was growing to its eventual peak around 100,000, and more

---

29 Rolf Keller, "Racism versus Pragmatism: Forced Labor of Soviet Prisoners of War in Germany (1941–1942)," *Forced and Slave Labor in Nazi-Dominated Europe: Symposium Presentations*, Washington, D.C.: Center for Advanced Holocaust Studies United States Holocaust Memorial Museum, 2004, p. 118.

30 [ED] However, in the second half of 1944, at least in some agricultural sub-camps of Auschwitz, there were more Jews than Poles. For example, in September, 1944, in Wirtschaftshof, only 18 percent of the prisoners in Birkenau were non-Jewish. Andrzej Strzelecki, "Podobóz Wirtschaftshof Birkenau," *Zeszyty Oświęcimskie*, 2016, 29, p. 107.

food was necessary. It is possible that these positions were given to political prisoners as the effort for extermination was focused on Jewish people and these jobs were considered of higher quality, officially often including shelter, and unofficially the potential for acquiring additional food. Relatedly, in the second half of the camp's operation some prisoners were permitted to receive packages from outside the camp, including food. Jewish prisoners were never granted this privilege, thus again indicating the targeted nature of starvation even within the confines of Auschwitz.

To a certain extent, the diet of prisoners was influenced by where the transports arrived from. Some of the food procured from the luggage of new arrivals was sent out into the Reich, but some remained within the camp. Based on this the diet of prisoners was altered over the years of the camps operations. In addition, diet could be a means by which inmates could infer where transports were arriving from without having interaction with new arrivals, based on what foods were being introduced for prisoners. Rudolf Vrba elaborates on this in his memoirs, when he mentions that the prisoners knew transports were arriving from Hungary because of the influx of sausages.

Food in the Warsaw Ghetto

The Warsaw ghetto provides an example of starvation and systematic restriction to access to food that is important to examine in conjunction with starvation studies in concentration camps. It is important to recognize that starvation was not isolated to concentration camps, and in fact was in some cases arguably more rampant in the Jewish ghettos established by the occupying Nazi forces. In addition, those individuals who did survive life within the Warsaw ghetto were sent, with few exceptions, to concentration camps. Thus it is crucial to understand that individuals were arriving at the concentration camps from a variety of conditions.

In Poland, calories were rationed for the three demographic groups, as defined by the Nazi Germans. Jewish people were allotted less than 200 calories daily. Polish people were allotted approximately 700 calories while

German nationals were allotted over 2500 calories. In the Warsaw ghetto specifically, even with smuggling, the daily calorie intake of residents was seldom greater than 1,100.[31] In 1941 and 1942 more than ten percent of the inhabitants in the Warsaw ghetto died, a total of over 80,000 individuals.[32] These deaths were the result of a combination of factors, not least of all starvation and overcrowding; the ghetto took up 2.4 percent of the city's land and held 30 percent of its population. As well, disease ran rampant as a result of the first two factors.[33]

The phenomenon of starvation, as well as methods of recovery, are difficult issues for scientists to study and understand because of the ethical implications that any human study would have. As a result, the examination and observation of residents in the Warsaw ghetto in 1942 and of prisoners of concentration camps after liberation in 1945 provide some of the rare observational data on starvation.[34] Additionally, within the Warsaw ghetto physicians began in February of 1942 to conduct studies on hunger and the related diseases after they recognized the unique opportunities to answer certain medical quandaries, and continued to do so until July of the same year.[35] This is also why today we have a relatively large amount of data on starvation in the Warsaw ghetto.

Food restriction and systematic starvation in the Warsaw ghetto is important to study not only for the extreme nature with which intentional starvation was carried out on a massive scale, but also for the

---

31 Berenbaum, *The World Must Know*, p. 74. [ED] For additional information see also: Barbara Engelking and Jacek Leociak, *The Warsaw Ghetto: A Guide to the Perished City*, New Haven and London, Yale University Press, 2009, for example pp. 255-258, 280-292, 304-311and 477-478.

32 Roman Mogilanski and Benjamin Grey, *The Ghetto Anthology: A Comprehensive Chronicle of the Extermination of Jewry in Nazi Death Camps and Ghettos in Poland*, Los Angeles: American Congress of Jews from Poland and Survivors of Concentration Camps, 1985, p. 57.

33 Berenbaum, *The World Must Know*, p. 74.

34 Butterly and Shephered, *Hunger*, p. 56.

35 Myron Winick, ed., *Hunger Disease: Studies by the Jewish Physicians in the Warsaw Ghetto*, New York: John Wiley and Sons, Inc., 1979, pp. 3-4.

role this ghetto specifically played in furthering the understanding of starvation and the development of post-war international standards of human rights.

Post-War Ramifications

Starvation was incorporated by the United Nations into the Convention for the Prevention of Crimes of Genocide in December of 1948 as one of the defining components of what constitutes genocide. They defined what constitutes genocide as, in part, an action "deliberately inflicting on the group conditions of life calculated to bring about its physical destruction," which has since been interpreted to include denial of access to food.[36] This decision acknowledged the specific role of starvation in the Nazi German extermination efforts, the degree to which starvation is able to decimate a population and the necessary breadth of the definition of genocide. Subsequent UN documents have either implicitly or explicitly addressed hunger and starvation and the basic rights of all people to food.[37]

With regard to instances of mass famine or starvation in a variety of locations and time periods, the decision of external parties to provide aid is often too late in coming. This is largely because potential donors ask for quantitative evidence of the crisis, usually in the form of a death toll.

36 "Convention on the Prevention and Punishment of the Crime of Genocide, December 9, 1948," *United Nations Treaty Series*, No. 1021, p. 280.

37 Article 11 of the 1966 *International Covenant on Economic, Social, and Cultural Rights* includes the right of every individual to both "adequate food," and "to be free from hunger." In 1974, the World Food Conference, endorsed by the General Assembly, recognized the "economic and social implications" of increasing imbalance between the world's food producers and food consumers. The General Assembly's 2008 resolution, "The right to food," reaffirmed previous UN commitments to eradicate hunger. "International Covenant on Economic, Social, and Cultural Rights, New York, 16 December 1966," *United Nations Treaty Series*, vol. 993, no. 14531; World Food Conference, *Universal Declaration on the Eradication of Hunger and Malnutrition*, 17 December 1974; General Assembly resolution 63/187, *The right to food*, A/63/430, 18 December 2008.

This means that the crisis has to be well under way in order to elicit an international response. While denial of a crisis' occurrence and delays in realized action play a role in prolonging the wait for aid, the demand for quantifiable data demonstrating the need for aid is the primary source of delay.[38] It is important to note that these statements were made primarily with regards to famines in the latter half of the twentieth century, but they are also pertinent to the study of the Holocaust and the international response to reports of starvation within the concentration camps, as well as broader conditions.

Conclusion

Food plays a role in human life and interaction beyond its simple physiological importance on an individual basis, from the conception of ideological policies supported by, or even arguably rooted in, agricultural concerns to the systematic deprivation of food and essential nutrients within specific populations based on ideological policies. The complexity of these roles are crucial to examine in studying the frameworks used for the displacement of hundreds of thousands of people in Nazi German occupied territory and the means of extermination used against, primarily, Europe's Jewish population.

38 Butterly and Shepherd, *Hunger*, p. 139.

Joe Liu

Deciphering Business Relationships in Nazi-German Occupied Europe: Business Ethics in Dealing with Morally Questionable Regimes

Introduction

From gradually gaining power in the 1920s to the mass liquidation of the ghettos and concentration camps, economic issues had always been at the forefront of the German Nazi party's blueprint for domination. It was an integral part of its national socialist agenda to have ample control over the means of production and distribution of resources. Businesses were encouraged and compelled to work with the state to advance its power and reach. Household names like Bayer (known as IG Farben in the Nazi era,[1] a company that systematically exploited concentration camp prisoners), Hugo Boss (the main supplier of Nazi party uniforms; the company's profit grew exponentially during Nazi rule and used forced labor in the process), Volkswagen (created by Nazi's German Labor Front in 1936; the *People's Car* project was an attempt to boost the economy) and many more all benefitted in various ways from Nazi policies.

One of the fundamental purposes of Holocaust studies is to educate and prevent similar mistakes and oversights from happening in the future. The issue of business ethics is therefore an interesting lens to look through in the study of the Holocaust. [2] What does it mean to conduct business

---

1 [ED] Bayer was a part of IG Farben, one of its three major "founding companies" in 1925 (along with Agfa and BASF). After the war, when IG had been dissolved, Bayer became independent again.

2 My participation in the *Witnessing Auschwitz* seminar was possible thanks to the generous financial and academic support of the UBC Sauder School of Business. I am especially grateful to Dr. David Silver for his help, encouragements and invaluable suggestions and comments on an earlier version of the chapter.

ethically in exceptional times? How do business ethics theories apply in such a unique context? The discussion so far has focused on whether particular companies are responsible for aiding the Holocaust. Instead, this paper attempts to answer the above questions and aims to lay out frameworks for businesses to take note of in extraordinary circumstances, especially when working with questionable regimes.

Legacy Business Ethics Frameworks Are Difficult to Apply

The issue of corporate social responsibility and business ethics is an age-long debate with varying thoughts, ideas and theories from philosophers of all disciplines. Two prominent doctrines from two renowned economists describe what are widely considered the most influential foundations of the business ethics discussion, although they take two opposite approaches. Milton Friedman argues that the only responsibility a company should have is to increase its profits and maximize shareholder returns within societal rules. If the decision makers of a company decide to act on their own social conscience and divert away from the profit-maximizing goal, it is essentially taxing the firm's shareholders unfairly without democratic due process to determine which social improvements should be invested in. Friedman warns that this leads to totalitarianism.[3] In contrast, Edward Freeman's stakeholder theory states that a company has the duty to not only maximize returns for its shareholders, but also take into consideration the well-being of its other stakeholders, including employees, customers, society, the environment, the government and so on. Both frameworks have their merits and flaws with many debatable aspects, but one particular facet that these theories often fail to address is that of business ethics in extraordinary circumstances. Friedman's shareholder doctrine stresses the belief that it is good for businesses to stay

---

3 Milton Friedman, "The Social Responsibility of Business is to Increase its Profits," *The New York Times Magazine*, 13 September 1970.

"within the rules of the game" and "engage in open and free competition without deception or fraud".[4] This idea collapses when "the rules of the game" are inherently corrupt and "open and free competition without deception or fraud" is systematically impossible. Freeman's theory suffers similar issues due to the ambiguous definition of "stakeholders". In a world where groups of people are marginalized as subhuman, their interests can be easily disregarded and overlooked as non-stakeholders. There is simply arbitrary rule or force drawing the line between "stakeholders" and "non-stakeholders", particularly in desperate times.

Europe during World War II, particularly in Nazi Germany, was caught in precisely the kind of event in which such social constructs and the rule of law fell apart and no longer applied. The frameworks described above fail to explain or assess the ethics (or lack thereof) of Nazi Germany and its collaborating businesses' exploitation of millions of individuals; further, they lack any provision of guidance for companies in such circumstances to act. It would be a serious breach of morality to say that a company in German-occupied Europe during WWII was ethical because it maximized shareholders' return while following the "rules", or to say that a business was unethical because it failed to consider the welfare of the government as a stakeholder in its acts.

This paper therefore explores the relations between businesses and Nazi dictatorship and aims not necessarily to judge past business actions as ethical or unethical. Instead, this paper, in examining several cases of businesses' involvement in the exploitation of the situation, of concentration camp prisoners, and groups targeted during the Nazi era, aims to shed light through a historical perspective on the proper ways of conducting business in extraordinary circumstances. One of the most significant distinctions we need to make here is that there is a difference between direct responsibility for the atrocities committed during wartime and exploitation of the situation despite knowledge of the atrocities.

---

4 R. Edward Freeman, *Strategic Management: A Stakeholder Approach*, Cambridge: Cambridge University Press, 2010.

Many discussions regarding business activities during wartime and dictatorships address the question of whether or not the wrongful actions or events would have even been possible without business involvement. I would argue that this is irrelevant when discussing the ethics of doing business; such is a futile illusion where business actions are judged by the end ahead of the means. Nevertheless, looking at several cases of business involvement during the Holocaust, it is apparent that this manner of thinking is prevalent in a number of assessments.

The Case of IBM

In Edward Black's book *IBM and the Holocaust*, he claims that one crucial development of technology that allowed Nazi Germany to facilitate the Holocaust was a data and information keeping system that enabled Nazi authorities to collect and record census data that was later used to track and capture Jews and "undesirables". Black argues that without the assistance of IBM's technology through its German subsidiary Dehomag, the Holocaust would not have been possible. He writes, "from the very first moments and continuing throughout the 12-year existence of the Third Reich, IBM placed its technology at the disposal of Hitler's program of Jewish destruction and territorial domination".[5] It is well known that IBM's Hollerith machine was widely used by Nazi authorities to collect identification data, schedule concentration camp transports and carry out camp operations;[6] what's more, IBM had supplied tabulators, key punchers and various other machines to Dehomag before Germany declared war against the United States in 1941. Some evidence outlined by Black has also pointed out that even after IBM lost official control over Dehomag, IBM remained a main supplier to Dehomag by using various subsidiaries

---

5 Edward Black, *IBM and the Holocaust: The Strategic Alliance Between Nazi Germany and America's Most Powerful Corporation*, New York: Crown, 2001, p. 79.

6 Dr. Piotr Setkiewicz, personal communication, 19 May 2015.

in Europe under the name Watson Business Machine. This activity makes it clear that IBM retained their intentions to continue to operate and profit in the German market throughout the war period.

Opponents of Black base their argument on the claim that IBM was simply unaware of the political climate in Germany from 1933 to 1941 and that regardless, even without IBM's technology and supplies, Nazi Germany authorities would have found another way or another supplier to carry out systematic identification and the mass extermination of "undesirables". In his review of Black's book, historian Henry Turner Jr. of Yale University writes, "Black fails to produce evidence that IBM was aware its machines were being used for genocidal purposes while the United States was at war with Germany. Nor does he prove that the machines were essential to the Holocaust".[7]

Distilling this excerpt into two parts, the question boils down to awareness and the impact of IBM on the persecution of Jews. While awareness is an important element in determining the ethics of doing business with a questionable regime, it would be incredible to say that IBM was completely unaware of the situation in Germany at that time. With the anti-Nazi protest in New York in 1933, the passing of Nuremberg Laws in 1935 and the approximately 120,000 German-Jewish emigrants to Western Europe and the Americas from 1933 to 1939,[8] ample signals and hints of Jewish persecution were transmitted internationally and, as such, IBM ought to have examined its business relationship with the Third Reich more cautiously.

The second question relating to Turner Jr.'s quotation is whether IBM's technologies were essential to the Holocaust. Richard Bernstein of the New York Times echoed on a similar note with a hint of ridicule: "Is Mr. Black really correct in his assumption that without I.B.M.'s technology,

---

7   H. Turner Jr., "Reviews of Books: IBM and the Holocaust: The Strategic Alliance between Nazi Germany and America's Most Powerful Corporation by Edwin Black," *The Business History Review*, 2001, 75(3), p. 637.

8   United States Holocaust Memorial Museum, "Refugees," 20 June 2014, web, http://www.ushmm.org/wlc/en/article.php?ModuleId=10005139, accessed 25 July 2015.

which consisted mainly of punch cards and the machines to tabulate them, the Germans wouldn't have figured out a way to do what they did anyway?"[9] From these quotations, it seems that an excessive portion of the effort made in inquiring into the role IBM played in Nazi Germany with respect to the Holocaust surrounds hypothetical questions as to what might or might not have happened if the Nazis did not have access to IBM's technology. In terms of business ethics, "if I don't do it, somebody else will"[10] is a futile question to focus on. It is important for a business, when it comes to the ethics of dealing with morally questionable clients, to follow strict guidelines such that, if misuses of the products are highly plausible, the business must follow up with either more due diligence or establish that refusal of service is warranted. This is especially important when the nature of the business and its products can be easily exploited. In IBM's case, none of the above guidelines were employed.

Although Black's claim that IBM was the main facilitator of the Holocaust and the mass persecution would not have been possible without the company's technology is somewhat overstretched, it is simply not the issue to be concerned with in the process of investigating a historical case of business ethics. At the same time, it is also true that the absence of concrete, explicit evidence showing that IBM was "fully aware" of the situation in Nazi Germany makes it especially difficult to judge. However, in this day and age, where information technology is more advanced than ever, lack of awareness is no longer a valid excuse for a company to claim ignorance in dealing with dubious regimes. Even though in IBM's case it was entirely legal on the surface for the firm to do business in and with Nazi Germany until 1941[11] (which according to the Friedman Doctrine

9   Richard Bernstein, "I.B.M. and the Holocaust: Assessing the Culpability," *The New York Times*, 7 March 2001, web, http://www.nytimes.com/2001/03/07/arts/07BERN.html, accessed 4 July 2015.

10 Ronald A. Howard and Clinton D. Korver, "Draw Distinctions: Overcoming Faulty Thinking," *Ethics for the Real World: Creating a Personal Code to Guide Decisions in Work and Life*, Boston: Harvard Business Press, 2008, p. 43.

11 Donald W. Mccormick and James C. Spee, "IBM and Germany 1922–1941," *Organization Management Journal*, 2008, 5(4), pp. 208-213.

would be entirely ethical since no rule was broken and it was a profit seeking venture), a line should have been drawn once immoral acts were instituted by the Nazis as they gained power.

The Case of Crematoria Manufacturers

Having established that one key to address faulty behaviour in doing business with totalitarian or authoritarian regimes is "awareness", it is nevertheless incredibly hard to prove explicitly. Very few companies, if any, would ever declare in literal words that they conduct operations immorally, at least not until after the fact. The main manufacturer of crematoria of various concentration camps, Topf & Söhne, is a case that demonstrates the company's awareness, which can serve to provide guidance for current businesses when they assemble information in their due diligence process,[12] thereby avoiding pitfalls.

Topf & Söhne, which perhaps needs no introduction to those familiar with the Holocaust, was the major builder of immovable crematoria inside various concentration camps, especially in Auschwitz where the company supplied 46 out of a total of 66 ovens throughout the Nazi's concentration camp network.[13] There is little dispute about Topf & Söhne's involvement and its knowledge of the mass murder of the camp prisoners during the Holocaust, so it is not necessary here to regurgitate once more. However, there are lessons to be learnt from the interaction and cooperation of the crematoria manufacturer and the Nazi authorities. Using the case of Topf & Söhne as a precedent, companies are urged to think critically in both operational and legal senses in order to avoid supporting morally corrupt clients executing atrocities with their services and products.

---

12 Assuming companies perform due diligence on their clients already by default, regardless of the degree of depth. So I say "in their due diligence process" instead of "with due diligence process" as the latter signifies that due diligence process did not exist previously.

13 Robert McGinn, "Sixteen Case Studies of Ethical Issues in Engineering," *The Ethically Responsible Engineer*, Hoboken: John Wiley and Sons, 2015, p. 138.

In Rudolf Höss's memoir, later named *Death Dealer*, the Auschwitz camp commandant recited the way multiple corpses were crammed into an oven for cremation.[14] Detailed instruction of mass cremation was provided by Topf & Söhne themselves to camp authorities in September, 1941.[15] Nevertheless, Ernst-Wolfgang Topf, the managing director of the firm, claimed during his trial that he had no knowledge of the use of the crematoria. Although extremely unlikely, let us assume that Topf was indeed unaware of the purpose of the crematoria but nonetheless provided instructions for cremating multiple bodies. The most relevant question now is how companies can safeguard the use of their products without explicitly knowing how they are being deployed.

In order to mitigate the risk of aiding crimes, the company must ask itself before providing designs or instructions: (1) whether such designs or instructions are standard industrial practices, and (2) why would a client want such designs or instructions for their products and/or services. In Topf's case, cremating multiple bodies in one cremation chamber was an extremely unusual practice (conventionally, bodies were and are cremated individually out of respect for the dead and their families so that they can collect "pure" ashes); it was also illegal according to the *German Cremation*

---

14 Rudolf Höss and Steven Paskuly, *Death Dealer: The Memoirs of the SS Kommandant at Auschwitz*, Buffalo: Prometheus Books, 1992.

15 Deborah Lipstadt, M. MacLaughlin, and D. Leshem, *Auschwitz-Birkenau Crematoria: Civilian Ovens Comparison*, web, http://www.hdot.org/debunking-denial/ab4-civillian-ovens-comparison/, accessed 10 January 2017. [ED] The instruction refers to "regular" use of a crematoria. There is no doubt that by installing a new type of crematoria in Nazi concentration camps, the "Topf" company implicitly accepted a high mortality implied by them, namely, several dozen corpses a day. However, this can be explained by the conditions of war and epidemics of infectious diseases. But more significant in this regard was the conference in August, 1942, when, representing the company engineer, Prüfer agreed to provide four new crematoria for Auschwitz, which were to have a theoretical ability to burn more than four thousand corpses a day. It is obvious that such a great number of deaths in the camp could not have resulted from "natural" causes. Nevertheless, Prüfer did not protest because such an agreement would bring considerable profits not only for the company but also for him personally.

Act of 1934 and the *Regulation of Implementing the Cremation Act of 1938*.[16] When the request for designs or instructions to cremate multiple bodies was made, Topf & Sons, if it was not aware of the ultimate purpose, should have critically examined why these atypical functions were needed as well as determined whether this request was legal in the first place. Companies in similar situations should evaluate these abnormal requests critically by asking why and how instead of simply reducing the issue to a profitability function of revenue minus cost in its offer tendering and decision making processes.

In addition to the issues outlined above, the locations of the crematoria were also suspect. German law at the time mandated that crematoria could only be built near cemeteries.[17] As experts in the cremation industry, Topf & Söhne should have known the legal aspects of cremation. When the firm was contacted to build crematoria in the concentration camps by the Nazi government, it should have been alarmed that there might be malevolence involved due to the illegal nature which the crematoria were evidently to be used; certainly, when a government or authority is willingly breaking the laws that it itself established, it is a hint that they are not acting in good faith. Companies that undertake work with governments must look out for traces of hypocrisy in order to avoid supporting ill-intended public actions. (SS commander Heinrich Himmler justified the illegal building of crematoria within the concentration camps by declaring it a national security issue.[18] This is eerily similar to how many governments today avoid transparency to the public.)

---

16 Gesetz über die Feuerbestattung (Cremation Act), 1 RGBI § 3-9, 1934.Verordnung zur Durchführung des Feuerbestattungsgesetzes (Regulations of Implementing the Cremation Act), 1 RGBI § 1000-13, 1938.

17 Dr. Piotr Setkiewicz, personal communication, 19 May 2015.

18 Ibid.

Ethical Companies During the Second World War?

In the context of World War II and Nazi Germany, it is difficult to fully determine whether or not a business was proactively ethical or unethical in German-occupied Europe. The reason is simple: no company within the Nazi' sphere of influence would openly condemn and/or refuse to participate in the exploitation and extermination of the oppressed in fear of retaliation or forced takeover by the state. Therefore, similar to gauging the unethical by proxy above, there are certain traces that we can look for in order to hypothesize ethical decisions made by companies.

For example, the systemic round up of forced laborers provided an ample supply of human resources for companies to profit from during Nazi rule. When the war began and the economy started to boom due to wartime demand, these labor forces should have been fully utilized. However, such was not always the case and often there would be idle prisoners with no work to do[19] although the use of forced laborers would have been immensely profitable for manufacturers.

Many firms have cited reasons for not using forced labor, such as product quality and low capacity. From this standpoint, speculation can be made that some companies indeed did disagree with the exploitative policies at that time, but used these other reasons to avoid directly declining offers from the state. Nonetheless, the general attitude of the companies that refused forced workers remains uncertain, and further research should be done on this topic.

Reconciliation and Moving Forward

As discussed in this paper, lack of concrete, explicit evidence summarily makes it very difficult to prove any level of consciousness in connection to

---

19 Ibid.

the various businesses involved in the operations of concentration camps and the extermination of the oppressed during World War II. There is considerable plausibility in many cases, but incomplete or partial evidence cannot, and should not, be the material that we use to judge because judgments made in haste would be just as dangerous as leaving suspects unaccountable. Endless debate and attempts to somehow "prove" accusations in a black and white manner may very well be fruitless and unproductive.

Because the Holocaust is one of the most researched historical events in modern days, there is an abundance of factual accounts and records of the situations that businesses experienced during that time. Thus we can leverage and examine these experiences to formulate best practices in response to these situations. Instead of devoting our efforts to debates regarding what could have been or would have been, the discussion of business ethics in the context of historical events should be redirected to outlining behaviours that are at no time acceptable and providing frameworks to respond to extraordinary situations since this would be far more extensive in and effective at providing guidance in a forward-looking, useful manner.

John Denault

The Gladiators of Auschwitz: Boxing Within the Camp

The title, concerning boxers and the "gladiators of Auschwitz", is meant as an invitation for speculation and for provoking thought. I chose it to relate conceptions of boxing within the camp to something already existing in societal consciousness and present in contemporary transnational cultural memory. In fact, gladiators within Roman society and boxers within the Auschwitz death camp occupied a similar niche within their "communities". In ancient Rome, gladiators, despised as slaves, were redeemed only in victory; as were the Jews and political prisoners who were forced to participate in the games of their SS overseers. Both were to perpetrate violence in order to entertain the spectators. Many gladiators and boxers were chosen for their roles because of their potential entertainment value, based on their bodily characteristics – on how big they were, or how small and malnourished. Boxer and gladiator alike were selected for their ability to kill or their ability to die. Gladiators who rose to fame were entitled to the "privilege" of access to medicine and food, as were some of the Auschwitz boxers. Those who won garnered the respect of their spectators, who rewarded them for their performances. In Auschwitz, successful boxers were working in better kommandos and had access to better food, and thus had a better chance to survive. Defeat could end in death, which according to witnesses' accounts occurred frequently. Those who fought within gladiatorial combat were occasionally commemorated, and figuratively speaking, also were the boxers within testimony. Those who perished in both "arenas" are remembered as part of something much larger – a system leading to a destruction, with individuals only emerging through survival or witnesses' testimonies. This essay is my personal attempt to commemorate the boxers who existed within Auschwitz by making you, the reader of this text, aware of their existence. The purpose of this paper is to add their lives and testimonies to the diverse and tragic narrative that is Auschwitz.

The Holocaust was a manifestation of incomprehensible violence. Its organization demonstrates the most inhumane actions humanity has ever perpetrated. As a zone in which law was suspended, Auschwitz was a site wherein limitless manifestations of human capability found free range, demonstrating human ability to inflict unbridled violence on fellow human beings, yet also the range of adaptability present in each individual. Of the approximately 1.3 million people deported to the camp, over 200,000 survived.[1] Although Auschwitz, existing outside the realm of traditional societies, was a factory of death, it also developed its own institutions including medical facilities (apart from the "medicinal facilities" which were used for experimentation), and its own social order, albeit one that was constantly subject to change with the exception of a ceaseless meting out of arbitrary acts of violence. As such, those deported to Auschwitz were severed from their pre-camp self. Those unable to adapt were unable to survive, a common enough happenstance that gave way to prisoners coining the term "Musselmen", or muslims.[2] Violence, murder and abuse were foundational features that structured the camp's hierarchy. At the helm were the SS (which included Germans, Austrians and Volksdeutsche[3]); beneath them were the prisoners, where social order was determined through

---

1   [ED] According to estimations by Dr. Franciszek Piper around 220,000 – 230,000 survived the camp. Approximately 95% of them were transferred to other camps where a part of them perished. Franciszek Piper, "Auschwitz: How Many Perished Jews, Poles, Gypsies. . .," Kraków: Poligrafia ITS, 1992, pp. 51-52.

2   [ED] Glosary to the *Voices of Memory* series (Auschwitz-Birkenau Museum Publishing House) explains the term "Muselmann" as "prisoner in state of extreme mental and physical exhaustion". To learn more about about the term please read Giorgio Agamben, *Remnants of Auschwitz; The Witness and the Archive*, transl. Daniel Heller-Roazen, New York: Zone Books, 2002, pp. 41-86.

3   [ED] In the spring of 1943 there were about 150 Ukrainian guards in Auschwitz; fifteen of them deserted at the beginning of July, and two weeks later the Ukrainian company was disbanded.

nationality, strength, intelligence and the ability to perpetrate violence. The SS gave preferential treatment to those who could speak German and they therefore often designated to German criminals the position of camp kapo. Those below them were subject to cruel and brutal treatment, though some prisoners had better conditions than most: those working in camp facilities such as the kitchens, hospitals, and offices, musicians playing in the Auschwitz orchestras, as well as inmates with athletic ability.

Three sports found favour within Auschwitz: boxing, wrestling, and football.[4] Among the very few methods of survival, boxing was one.[5] Not all boxers were considered equal; at the top of this particular hierarchy German boxers ranked first and Polish boxers second. Although Slavic peoples were regarded as inferior, those who could box were seen as superior to the rest and this favour was granted in direct, tangible ways. For example, a Polish boxer, Tadeusz Pietrzykowski, was given the option of signing the Volksliste as SS officials assumed that their athletic prowess could only be explained by these boxers being of German descent. This would have allowed such boxers to leave the camp and be granted German citizenship. However, Pietrzykowski refused to become a citizen of the Third Reich. In 1943 he was transported to KL Neuengamme where, thanks to his exceptional skills, he continued his "boxing career". German boxers would fight for prestige, Polish boxers for food and the ability to resist oppression within the camp. Jewish boxers, existing at the bottom of the hierarchy, fought for increasing the chances of survival: if they lost a match, they might be executed; if they won, they received food and favour, and they increased their odds for surviving the camp.[6]

---

4 [ED] In Auschwitz sports activity was tolerated by the SS. However, it was usually limited to functionaries or prisoners in so called good kommandos who performed relatively light work, most often indoors, as well as to well-built prisoners who, despite being in the camp, kept their strength, or to prisoners who were professional boxers and used technique to knock down their competitors. Matches (bouts) were usually organized for the entertainment of the SS and the functionaries.

5 Alan Scott Haft, *Harry Haft: Auschwitz Survivor, Challenger of Rocky Marciano*, Syracuse: Syracuse University Press, 2006, pp. 56-57.

6 Ibid., p. 67.

Salamo Arouch, an exceptional Jewish boxer, fought over 200 fights and survived two years in Auschwitz. He claimed that he only survived the camp because he practised "a manly art",[7] which he compared to "cock-fighting" as the matches were done bare-knuckled and ended only after one challenger could no longer fight. The winner would receive extra rations and placement in a lighter work kommando; the loser might be executed.[8] Though Arouch managed to survive the camp, his entire family died, as did over 95% of the people from his region, Salonika.[9] Boxing saved Salamo Arouch's life, as it did other Jewish boxers', including the French-Jewish Sim Kessel, the Polish-Jewish Moshé Garbaz and the Polish-Jewish Harry Haft.

According to memoirs by Sim Kessel,[10] he was caught attempting to escape Auschwitz, yet managed to survive. He and four other Polish inmates attempted to walk out of the camp. They were caught and returned, and summarily sentenced to execution. Kessel was sentenced to hang but the rope broke during his "execution". He was then taken to be shot. When he was escorted by a man named "Jacob", he mentioned that he was a boxer, and according to Kessel his life was spared.[11] Jewish boxers used their talents in order to survive, pummelling opponents in order to receive food and favor. For Jewish boxers, matches well fit the profile

---

7 Phil Berger, "Boxing: Prisoner in the Ring," *The New York Times: Sports World Specials*, December 18, 1989, section C, page 2, column 3.

8 Susan Schindehette, Jack Kelley, et al. "Boxer Salamo Arouch's Death Camp Bouts End in a Triumph of the Spirit," *People Magazine*, 33.7, 19 February 1990, web, http://people. com/archive/boxer-salamo-arouchs-death-camp-bouts-end-in-a-triumph-of-the-spirit-vol-33-no-7/.

9 Ibid.

10 [ED] It is difficult to confirm all facts from Sim Kessel's story on the basis of saved testimonies and documents. The story partially seems to be composed of various facts that really happened in Auschwitz; however, other prisoners were involved in them. To learn more please read Carolina Franzen "Holocaust Survivors' Memoirs - Difficult Questions" in this volume.

11 Ira Berkow, *Counterpunch: Ali, Tyson, the Brown Bomber, and Other Stories of the Boxing Ring*, Chicago: Triumph Books, 2014, pp. 154-155.

of Primo Levi's "grey zone"[12] because, though these men utilized their talents for the purpose of "sport", they were aware that the consequences of winning directly correlated with the possible death of those defeated.

Pugilism served to provide some semblance of pre-camp life for both those fighting inside the ring and those watching the fights; temporarily, sports, even violent ones, removed inmates from the horrors of Auschwitz.[13] For the athletes, practising their sport was a form of escape and of resistance. Within the ring – but only within the ring – prisoners were not only allowed but encouraged to knock out their German overseers, with German SS officers betting on Polish fighters such as Tadeusz Pietrzykowski.[14] Pietrzykowski survived the war and also garnered the respect of camp authorities, from the kapos to the SS men. After his first match against Walter Dünning, a professional boxer turned criminal who weighed in at 70 kilograms, while Pietrzykowski weighed in at just 45, Dünning rewarded Pietrzykowski with bread and margarine, claiming he was happy to have boxed a true fighter. Another kapo, Otto Küsel, a spectator and boxing enthusiast, rewarded Pietrzykowski with work in the stables, claiming he could not be worked too hard as his strength was better spent boxing.[15] In another match, an SS guard named Karl Egersdörfer placed 1,000 marks on Pietrzykowski and upon his win, told the boxer that he could have anything he wanted.[16] Pietrzykowski requested food, demonstrating the continuous need in which inmates existed; in return, he received five kettles of soup, which he distributed amongst his friends.[17] As mentioned before, he was even asked by senior SS officers if

12 To learn more about the Primo Levi concept please read Carlo Halaburda's text on the grey zone in this volume.

13 Andrzej Rablin, *Auschwitz-Birkenau Museum Testimony*, APMA-B Statement Collection, vol. 101.

14 Ibid.

15 Tadeusz Pietrzykowski, *Auschwitz-Birkenau Museum Testimony*, APMA-B Statement Collection, vol. 88.

16 Marta Bogacka, *Bokser z Auschwitz losy Tadeusza Pietrzykiego*, Warsaw: Demart SA, 2012, pp. 90-91.

17 Ibid.

he wanted to sign the Volksliste, which would have resulted in his release. He refused, stating with a touch of irony that he was not worthy of such a distinction, but later said he needed to stay in order to save his friends.[18]

Boxing saved Pietrzykowski's life, and after his first bout, the SS organized a series of other bouts for their personal entertainment. He was not pleased to serve the blood-lust of the Germans, but he did enjoy competing, and in turn, defeating Germans. Every victory Pietrzykowski had in the ring against a German was a victory for the Polish people. Pietrzykowski stated that though boxing provided him with a means of survival, he also simply enjoyed being able to practice his art form against true athletes. He rarely took pleasure in the physical act of violence, with the exception of his fight against the German kapo known as the "Pole-Killer" (his name unknown). Pietrzykowski took such pleasure in massacring this opponent that he nearly killed the kapo.[19] After the bout, SS physician Friedrich Entress took Pietrzykowski to the hospital where he was injected with Typhus, probably in retaliation for his performance. After suffering from the infection began, his fellow prisoners took care of him in the hospital and helped him to survive.[20]

Interactions between Pietrzykowski and the SS were complex, as certain guards sought to assist him, whereas others sought to destroy him. Due to the nature of Auschwitz, guards had limited moralities, capable of justifying almost anything. Those who supported him had benefitted in some way or another from his performances, just as those who punished him had private agendas. His match with the "Pole-Killer" came to the attention of the camp Gestapo, who launched an investigation, the result of which determined the call for his execution. The Gestapo were tasked with finding potential threats to the regime, and identified groups and individuals not sanctioned within the Nazi ideals. Pietrzykowski, due to his performances and wins over Germans, was probably deemed an enemy of the state. However, SS guards had their own motivations outside

18 Ibid.
19 Ibid., p. 92.
20 Ibid., pp. 92-93.

the scope of party lines. In fact the Neuengamme deputy commandant, Albert Lütkemeyer himself, led him out of Auschwitz. Before the war Lütkemeyer was a boxing referee and met Pietrzykowski in one of the tournaments. In 1943, during the visit in Auschwitz, he recognized the Polish boxer and arranged his transfer to Neuengame.[21] As Pietrzykowski departed the camp, his first opponent, Walter Dünning, gave him a pair of real boxing gloves as a gift.

Pietrzykowski made use of the privileges granted him through boxing not only to his own benefit, but to help his friends as well. For example, while working in the SS staff buildings, Pietrzykowski planted lice infected with Typhus within the collars of SS officers, allegedly resulting in four dying from the infection.[22] Further, by allying himself with other Polish inmates, especially those of notoriety, Pietrzykowski demonstrated his resistance to other inmate observers: Pietrzykowski was close acquaintances with both the talented painter and Olympic skier, Bronisław Czech, a member of the Polish Underground,[23] and with Father Maksymilian Kolbe, a priest who gave up his life in place of another man who was selected for death. Kolbe was a Polish Franciscan who established his friary at Niepokalanów. At the beginning of the war the friary provided shelter for Poles and Jews expelled by Germans from western Poland. Father Kolbe assisted in protecting and sheltering them prior to his arrest in February of 1941.[24] As Poland was a predominantly Catholic nation, Pietrzykowski held an immense respect for Kolbe, and, "taking advantage of the fact his position allowed him to move more freely, Pietrzykowski would give Kolbe bread in order to help keep him alive".[25] Pietrzykowski was not the only boxer who helped others. As another brief example, there

---

21 Ibid., p. 96.
22 Hermann Langbein, *People in Auschwitz*, Petaluma: University of Northern California Press, 2004, p. 240.
23 Bogacka, *Bokser z Auschwitz*, p. 80, p. 99.
24 Patricia Treece, *A Man for Others: Maximilian Kolbe, Saint of Auschwitz*, New York: Harper and Row, 1982, pp. 91-93.
25 Ibid., p. 98.

was the Jewish boxer Herztko "Harry" Haft, who saved his brother from perishing within Auschwitz.

Hertzko Haft, later known as Harry Haft, was a Polish Jew who, prior to the outbreak of the Second World War, was living in Bełchatów. Born into a poor family, Haft was accustomed to hard work and limited food.[26] Due to his impoverished circumstances and the existence of several youth gangs in his home city of Bełchatów, from an early age, Haft had been a fighter. Over the span of six years (1939-1945) he would be transported from camp to camp in various locations in occupied Poland, spending almost two years in Auschwitz. First held in labor camps around Poznań and Strzelin, Haft was deported to Auschwitz subcamp Neu-Dachs in Jaworzno on September 2, 1943.[27] Before the arrest the Haft brothers had been involved in illegal smuggling rings around Bełchatow, enabling them to maintain access to wealth and adequate food.[28] At the time of his deportation to Auschwitz, Haft was still a strong man and eventually he was taken on to steal for a German officer, whom he referred to as Schneider.[29] Haft was caught stealing for Schneider, but did not relinquish his name during the interrogations, which included rigorous beatings and torture. This resulted in Schneider's trust in him and his recognition of Haft's exceptional capability of fighting. Thus the officer trained Haft as an "entertainer", namely as a boxer decimating his opponents for the entertainment of the spectators.[30] Among Germans Haft was mostly known as "the Jew Animal". His brother, Peretz, was transported to Auschwitz from Łodz later, presumably in 1944.[31] By that time Haft was already protected by Schneider, who believed that Haft would be his advocate in the event of the German defeat.[32] Harry used this to help his brother in any

---

26 Haft, *Harry Haft*, p. 11.
27 Reinhard Kleist, *The Boxer: The True Story of Holocaust Survivor Harry Haft*, London: SelfMadeHero, 2014, p. 186.
28 Haft, *Harry Haft*, pp. 20-21.
29 The true identity of Schneider is not known.
30 Ibid., p. 60.
31 Ibid., p. 58.
32 Ibid., p. 55.

possible way. He shared his food with Peretz and arranged for him work in an easier kommando. When his brother was working in the coal mine, he was responsible for linking together the coal carts to the trains leaving the camp. While working, Peretz broke his foot and Harry ensured that he was not sent to the gas chambers, but to the hospital, where he was well taken care of and recovered.[33] In January of 1945, Harry and Peretz were sent on a death march, beginning with walking to a train station bound for the Flossenbürg concentration camp.[34] The food they received prior to their deportation help them to survive, because within the Flossenbürg concentration camp, food was non-existent, and inmates began resorting to cannibalism.[35] After a series of deportations and marches, the two brothers managed to find work and food that helped them to regain their strength. On their final death march, Harry heard a series of gunshots, and fearing execution, escaped. Peretz feared he would be killed during the escape, and chose to remain in the marching group of prisoners.[36]

After liberation, Harry and his brother were reunited in Poland. Haft, although not a professional boxer prior to the Auschwitz camp, became one later, in the United States after the war. His strength and affinity for fighting became his saving grace under the supervision of Schneider in the confines of Auschwitz. He used his talents to save himself and his brother, proving that his fighter's will was essential in his survival.

On the surface, the boxers' affinity for violence might appear remarkably similar to that of the kapos, who also brutalized in order to survive. Yet, key differences frame these two shows of violence differently. In boxing, both sides could fight back, block and defend themselves; when a kapo beat a prisoner the prisoner could do little but take the beating. The kapos acted under their own volition within the construct of the camp hierarchy. The SS and officers were vastly outnumbered by inmates, and the creation of the kapo was an effective means of reducing the operating

33 Ibid., p. 59.
34 Kleist, *The Boxer*, pp. 186-187.
35 Haft, *Harry Haft*, pp. 70-71.
36 Ibid., p. 76.

costs and manpower of the facilities. The SS chose inmates who were violent criminals; their choices were based on these criminals' propensity to commit violence. The role of the kapo as a functionary was that of an enforcer, to force the will of the SS and camp regime upon the inmates who were below them, utilizing violence as a necessary means of imposition. Boxing provided a structured space for violence; kapos' capacity for violence was boundless under the authority of the guards and officers of the SS. Further, though both boxers and kapos survived by essentially violent means, kapos beat and murdered inmates in order to maintain their positions, which helped them to survive; boxers practised their sport and in turn received better treatment. That said, it is important to acknowledge one core difference, which was for Jewish boxers, because the sport pit them against their opponents in a severe dichotomy between life and death, both of which were to be dealt out according to the results of the match. The differences between violence as exercised by boxers and kapos is noted in survivor testimonies, with a preferential difference in favour of the boxers, whose display of violence against kapos was accepted, even encouraged, by their fellow inmates. Put differently, while both boxers and kapos survived by way of violence, the general ethos among camp inmates for each of these groups of people survived with them, continuing on through written accounts delineating those who exerted violence *against* the Nazi Germans, from those who exerted violence *for* the Nazi Germans.

Boxing served as a release for both the boxers and the witnesses. It was an opportunity to lash out against the war, to vent unadulterated emotion into an act of violence that would not necessarily result in punishment. For the boxers, it was a method to strike out against the injustices which they continuously faced; doing so proved that the Übermensch were not superior,[37] and provided hope to the inmates by showing that their enemies could be defeated.

37 Ibid., p. 95.

Melody Cheung

Artist and Witness:
Conversation Through Forbidden Art

Art is the culmination of complex interactions between imagination and "aesthetic attitudes".[1] Historically, viewers have analyzed art from an aesthetic point of view in both its meaning and its worth.[2] However, in the 20th and 21st centuries, the "deconstruction of subjectivity" began to influence art theory.[3] Yet, art made during the Holocaust[4] cannot be analyzed using only traditional Euro-Western theories of art. The extreme circumstances of the Holocaust led to the production of unique pieces of prisoner-created artwork that act as both dialogue and testimony. More specifically, these art pieces are categorized into four main groupings by the Auschwitz-Birkenau Memorial and State Museum:[5] private aesthetic use, works commissioned for the German Lagermuseum,[6] works

1 M. W. Rowe, "The Definition of Art," *The Philosophical Quarterly,* 1991, p. 272.
2 Christopher Williams, "Modern Art Theories," *Journal of Aesthetics and Art Criticism,* 1998, p. 377.
3 John Haldane, "ART THEORY: AN HISTORICAL INTRODUCTION," *The Art Book,* 12(3), 2005, p. 31.
4 I am grateful to Agnieszka Sieradzka (Collections) for introducing me to the art created in the camp, as well as for her encouragement, suggestions and support.
5 [ED] Agnieszka Sieradzka, "Art at Auschwitz Concentration Camp," *Auschwitz-Birkenau Memorial and Museum E-Learning,* web, http://lekcja.auschwitz.org/en_18_sztuka/.
6 [ED] The Lagermusuem was established in Auschwitz main camp in the fall 1941. Its aim was to amass valuable objects collected by the SS in and around the town of Oświęcim, or taken from the luggage of people deported to the camp. It also amassed a collection of pieces of art made by prisoners. Read more about the Lagermuseum in: Sieradzka, "Art at Auschwitz Concentration Camp," http://lekcja.auschwitz.org/en_18_sztuka/.

made post-World War Two and Forbidden Art, which were "works made secretly in concealment from the SS, showing the *truth* about life in the camps".[7] The truth about the camps is a contentious subject because each prisoner's experience was so individual unto themselves. Yet, this is why Forbidden Art lends such a striking testimony; its existence substantiates its own individual agency and authenticity in the context of the group. Art portraying camp life outside of Nazi sanction was illegal, yet prisoners created Forbidden Art. Although the styles, skill-level and subject matter of Forbidden Art types differ greatly from one another, a great deal of its importance lies in its subjects rather than its aesthetics. Furthermore, its importance lies in the fact that the prisoners themselves recorded Auschwitz and its horrors from their own points of view.[8] Whilst it might be simpler to label the Holocaust an aberrant case existing on the fringes of extremity, this would illegitimate Forbidden Art.[9] Rather than excluding the Holocaust from analysis, it is necessary to study it as a reminder of human possibility at its best and worst limits. This is applicable to the pieces that have survived the Holocaust and points to the legitimacy of continued analysis of the Holocaust.

The artworks that I will be examining include the thematic of space at their core. The physical space represented in Forbidden Art is important because it creates an aesthetic and symbolic space where the illegal artistic representations of the camps become a "communal conversation" that transpires between the artists and the viewers.[10] This essay does not claim to encapsulate a single methodology as to how to read and react to Forbidden Art, but to explore a dimension of the relationship

---

7   "Works of Art," *Auschwitz-Birkenau Memorial and Museum*, web, http://auschwitz.org/en/museum/historical-collection/works-of-art/, accessed 19 June 2015.

8   Philip Rosen and Nina Apfelbaum, *Bearing Witness: A Resource Guide to Literature, Poetry, Art, Music, and Videos by Holocaust Victims and Survivors*, Westport: Greenwood Press, 2001/2002, p. 134.

9   Mark Ward, "The Ethic of Exigence: Information Design, Postmodern Ethics, and the Holocaust," *Journal of Business and Technical Communication*, 24(1), 2009, p. 72.

10   Ward, "The Ethic of Exigence," p. 69.

between artist and viewer and the ethical implications behind them. The conversation that happens between artist and viewer in Forbidden Art is an important one to pursue because of the subversive intention with which prisoners created their work. Such work gave prisoners a forum for testimony in which agency and authenticity shine through. Through these pieces, the prisoners have asked viewers of their works to look into and beyond their artworks and to bear witness. In bearing witness, the viewer moves past passivity and into an exchange that layers meaning and allows the prisoners, whose voices the Nazis had silenced, to be heard.

Forbidden Art in Context: An Overview

Art is an expression through which artists can create space with the inclusion or exclusion of certain elements. Spatiality in art exists in the physical parameters of the art but also through the creation of art itself. As Miranda Ward writes, "form is itself a kind of expression".[11] It is an opportunity for conversation. However, it is crucial to understand that art is also created in the eyes of the viewer. Through the space and context viewers occupy, they process art and layer meaning from their own experiences. In this way, art is itself a process in which the ebb of time creates and recreates meaning through the people it affects. This meaning is extraordinary in works made during the Holocaust as it gives voice to the victims in a visual manner. In terms of visual representations of the Holocaust, I will focus on art created during the existence of the Nazi German concentration and extermination camp Auschwitz, which existed on Polish soil during the years 1940-1945. Through this discussion, I will explore the role of physical space represented in Forbidden Art and how it creates a different kind of space that initiates a conversation between artist and audience.

11 Miranda Ward, "The Art of Writing Place," *Geography Compass*, 8(10), 2014, p. 758.

In order to further contextualize the Forbidden Art that prisoners created in the camps, it is necessary to first frame the space and time prisoners inhabited. Many prisoners who created art were members of the educated group in Polish society termed inteligencja; the Nazis typically assigned them to work groups that more easily had access to materials needed in the making of visual representations.[12] People like Franciszek Jaźwiecki[13] and Mieczysław Kościelniak[14] were professionally trained artists, their skills working in their favour in the day-to-day survival of the camp.[15] That being said, these same people risked their lives to record the camps. Reasons for creating these pieces varied. For example, portraitist Jaźwiecki wrote in his memoirs that he drew "to find a moment of happiness" and that "every time [his] work was taken from [him]... the

12 Piotr Setkiewicz, Personal interview, 15 May 2015.
13 [ED] Franciszek Jaźwiecki graduated from the Kraków Academy of the Fine Arts in 1933. On December 1, 1942, he was deported to Auschwitz where he was assigned prisoner number 79042. He was employed first in the potato room and then in the camp painting workshop. On March 12, 1943, he was transferred to Gross-Rosen concentration camp; on April 22, 1943, to Oranienburg; and on July 22, 1944, to Halberstadt (a sub camp of Buchenwald concentration camp). In May 1945, he was liberated during the evacuation of the sub-camp. Jaźwiecki made portraits of his fellow prisoners in all these camps. At the Auschwitz-Birkenau State Museum there is a collection of 114 portraits made by him. To learn more about Franciszek Jaźwiecki's portraits see: Sieradzka, "Art at Auschwitz Concentration Camp," http://lekcja.auschwitz.org/en_18_sztuka/.
14 [ED] Mieczysław Kościelniak studied at the Kraków Academy of Fine Arts in the years 1931-1936. On May 2, 1941, he was deported to Auschwitz and given the prisoner number 15261. He worked in various Kommandos including, among the others, camp workshops and the printing press. Collaborating with Lagermuseum, he painted numerous portraits, landscapes, genre scenes and greetings cards on orders from the SS. He also worked illegally making numerous sketches depicting life in Auschwitz. On January 18, 1945, he was transferred to Mauthausen concentration camp and then to sub-camps Melk and Ebensee. He was liberated on May 6, 1945. To learn more about Mieczysław Kościelniak's work see: Sieradzka, "Art at Auschwitz Concentration Camp," http://lekcja. auschwitz.org/en_18_sztuka/.
15 Agnieszka Sieradzka, "Examples of Illegal Art from the Auschwitz Museum Collections," Forbidden Art: Illegal Works by Concentration Camp Prisoners, Oświęcim: Auschwitz-Birkenau State Museum, 2012, pp. 88, 91.

greater was [his] effort and stronger the will to start another picture".[16] Others drew in order to record the daily horrors of the camp. It was not without great risk that artists made representations of the camp because there were severe consequences for being caught in producing, hiding and/or smuggling out "illegal" art.[17] Even so, these people created in the face of the "organized power" of the camp and, in doing so, subverted the objective of the organized power in creating "stable framework[s] of social structures"[18] that worked vigilantly to dehumanize the people imprisoned there.

Furthermore, the art produced was a statement in and of itself. The Third Reich tried very hard to cultivate a very particular image of the camps and therefore expressly made illegal art depicting the camp in an unsavoury light.[19] This is where Forbidden Art made in the camp plays an important role in undermining the goals of the Third Reich.

Wolfgang Sofsky writes about the power the Nazis exerted through the space of the camp. This power was exerted in part to organize people into neat constructs of existence; thus as Sofsky writes, camp-power had to constantly "legitimate itself, [it was]... a weak power".[20] In the case of Forbidden Art, its existence is in itself its power. It is something that was not meant to be, yet it exists and continues to occupy time and space. This is one of the many reasons that the artists who created these pieces are important actors in the Holocaust narrative. For this reason, the next section will highlight how the artist plays a role in the representation of physical space in Forbidden Art and how this, in turn, creates a figurative space for the artist to express their testimony and creates space for other victims to be heard as well.

---

16 Jolanta Kosiec, *Suffering and Hope: Artistic Creations of the Oświęcim Prisoners*, Warsaw: K. Miarki W Mikolowie, 1989, p. 3.

17 "Works of Art."

18 Wolfgang Sofsky, "The Order of Terror: The Concentration Camp," trans. William Templer, Princeton, N.J.: Princeton University Press, 1997, p.18.

19 Agnieszka Sieradzka, *Szkicownik z Auschwitz = The Sketchbook from Auschwitz*, Oświęcim: Państwowe Muzeum Auschwitz-Birkenau, 2011, p. 5.

20 Sofsky, "The Order of Terror," p. 21.

The Artist's Representation in Forbidden Art

The meaning in Forbidden Art has been a contentious subject because of how individual it is to each person. Each prisoner navigated the camp in an intensely different way, which is reflected in the different pieces that artists created. However, these differences are what Miranda Ward argues to be valuable about individual narrators. Although she writes about verbal depictions of place in her works, her ideas can be used to describe Forbidden Art as well. A singular artist represents a "multiplicity and individuality" of narratives because their personal narratives allow the possibility for other individual narratives to exist in the same space.[21] The possibility for individual representation to allow space for group representation means that space can act as a framework for the intention of the artist without excluding the group.[22] The individual permits and even informs the possibility of the group.

As Monika Herzog and Christianne Hess contend, it is important not only to know and engage with the pieces that exist, but also those that no longer exist or were destroyed.[23] For instance, the space that *is* represented can act as a reminder of what is not there. In doing so, the individual artist gives context to the possibility of what the spatial organization of the camp meant to them and offers insights, for those who were not there, into how they may have navigated this space. Take, for example, the works of the unknown author of the *Sketchbook from Auschwitz*.[24] In many of

---

21 Ward, "The Art of Writing Place," p. 761.

22 Julia Kellman, "Telling Space and Making Stories: Art, Narrative, and Place," *Art Education*, 51(6), 1998, p. 36.

23 Monika Herzog and Christianne Hess, "'Resistant Material': Drawings and Other Artifacts of the Ravensbruck Memorial's Collections," *Forbidden Art: Illegal Works by Concentration Camp Prisoners*, Oświęcim: Auschwitz-Birkenau State Museum, 2012, p. 37.

24 [ED] A collection of drawings made in the camp by an unknown prisoner, probably a Jew, with the initials MM. Two functions of Auschwitz, those of a death camp and of a concentration camp, were presented in the drawings. In 1947 the collection was found on the grounds of Auschwitz Museum and Memorial. To read more see: Sieradzka, "Art at Auschwitz Concentration Camp," http://lekcja.auschwitz.org/en_18_sztuka/.

this author's works, spatial perspective is carefully used to construct the scale of operations in the camps. In *Sketchbook from Auschwitz*, a sketch that depicts a new transport of people arriving at the camp by railway uses lines of perspective to emphasize the dimensions of the camp and its operations. The perspective used can be seen by viewers as an intentional feature by the artist to give context as to the enormity of the events happening. Furthermore, in creating the physical representation of the camp, the artist creates space for both their own voice to be heard as well as others'. Sieradzka suggests that the author of the sketchbook knew exactly what they were doing, recording the camp in order to preserve these "unprecedented events" for future generations.[25] Another example of how Forbidden Art creates context is the work titled *Marching Out of Abbruch* by Wincenty Gawron.[26] [PICTURE 1] In this piece of artwork, Gawron illustrates a scene in which gun-wielding guards are herding faceless prisoners to an unknown point in the distance. What is immediately striking about Gawron's piece is how many prisoners there are and how orderly they are. Gawron has drawn them in neat rows with all the prisoners in step with each other. In the creation of this piece, Gawron creates a statement of contrast. The context he gives is of the order that existed in the camp, all the while in a place where law and order were arbitrarily created at the whim of those who had power. This represents the idea that it is possible to "make sense of a reality... both chaotic and orderly".[27] The role of personal representations of the negotiations of physical space is an important one because it creates context, which can then act as a

25 Sieradzka, *Sketchbook*, p. 12.

26 Wincenty Gawron, *Marching Out to Abbruch*, Oswiecim: Auschwitz-Birkenau State Museum, 1942. [ED] Before the war Wincenty Gawron studied at the Warsaw Academy of Fine Arts. On April 5, 1941, he was deported to Auschwitz where he received the prisoner number 11237. He was employed in various *Kommandos*; among others, in a sculpture workshop. He produced letter openers, ornamental boxes, landscape woodcuts and drew caricatures or portraits of SS-men and prisoners. On May 16, 1942, he escaped from the camp. See Sieradzka, "Art at Auschwitz Concentration Camp," http://lekcja.auschwitz.org/en_18_sztuka/.

27 Ward, "The Ethic of Exigence," p. 69.

platform from which the voice of the artist and other silenced victims of the Holocaust can be heard by the outside world for all time.

Moreover, Forbidden Art authenticates experience. The presence of the artists in the authenticity of time create a space for testimony. Rather than the removed analysis of scholars or experts, the ordinary eye is giving witness to extraordinary events and authenticated in their testimony. After all, it was prisoner-artists who recorded and memorialized the camp through their own eyes.[28] Borrowing from Miranda Ward's idea of how language has constructive power in creating specific narratives, so too does art have power in creating powerful personal narratives.[29] Art functions in distinctive ways, in which the intimacy of the narrative is "grounded in particularities of each location"; but art also creates a bridge by which testimony can transcend spatial-temporal limits.[30] In this way, individual pieces of art can act as a podium where voice is given back through the constructive power of space in art. The previous example of Gawron's artwork is an instance of this as it testified to the conditions of the concentration camp and portrayed Auschwitz in a way that the SS had expressly forbidden. Other pieces, like one by Zofia Stępień,[31] [PICTURE 2] show intimacies and humanity from the brief moments of respite that existed despite the suffocating conditions of the camp. Stępień's work shows a woman kneeling and praying by the infamous fences in the women's camp in Birkenau. The fences, however, are not the largest nor the most striking feature in the piece as the Virgin Mary takes up more than

---

28 Rosen and Apfelbaum, *Bearing Witness*, p. 134.

29 Ward, "The Art of Writing Place," p.757

30 Kellman, "Telling Space and Making Stories," p. 38.

31 Zofia Stępień, *Prayer*, Oswiecim: Auschwitz-Birkenau State Museum, 1943. [ED] Zofia Stępień-Bator was deported to Auschwitz on March 1, 1943, and received prisoner number 37255. In the camp she started drawing portraits of her fellow prisoners; she also made decorative greetings cards. In January 1945, she was transferred to Ravensbrück concentration camp, then to Neustadt Glewe (one of Ravensbrück sub-camp) where she was liberated in May, 1945. To learn more about portraits by Zofia Stępień-Bator, see: Sieradzka, "Art at Auschwitz Concentration Camp," http://lekcja.auschwitz.org/en_18_sztuka/.

half the page. What this shows is Stępień's ability to testify to what was important to her and perhaps what gave her strength. In Forbidden Art, the intention of the artist is key. Each stroke of a pencil was tantamount to a death sentence because of the harsh punishments the SS issued to those prisoners whom they caught.[32]

In the works of the *Sketchbook from Auschwitz*, it can be extrapolated that the prisoner-artist had expressly intended these works to stand as testimony, as evidenced by the location and condition in which the artist-prisoner hid the sketchbook. A former prisoner, who was working as a watchman on the grounds of Auschwitz Museum and Memorial, later found the *Sketchbook from Auschwitz* inside a bottle and under the foundations of a barrack in sector BIIf in Birkenau.[33] These works reconstruct the space of the camp from an individual perspective in a way that testified to the humanity that still existed in the camp. Furthermore, they are also a reminder of the possibility of other testimonies that may or may not have survived: the existence of something also suggests that, inversely, there exists a lack of something else. Perhaps then, the physical space of art can simultaneously act in a way that allows the viewer to see through the artist's perspective, as well as act as a gateway into the gaps in knowledge. In the Gawron work, faceless male prisoners march. From this glimpse into the conditions of the camp, other questions may arise, such as where they were marching, and to what fate. Similarly, a portrait of what appears to be a guard beating an unidentified prisoner calls to mind similar questions of what is there and not there.[34] [PICTURE 3] The creator of this sketch, Kościelniak, has simplified the drawing so that the background is not shown. Perhaps this was made in haste or it was a deliberate action. Whichever it was, it does show that which Kościelniak thought was important enough to record because this is what he chose to draw first. The power dynamics that existed in the camps were complex

32 Sieradzka, "Forbidden Art," p. 91.
33 Sieradzka, "Sketchbook," p. 7.
34 Mieczyslaw Kościelniak, "Done," Oswiecim: Auschwitz-Birkenau State Museum, 1943.

and difficult, if not impossible, for the modern eye to understand, but they are significant nonetheless. In essence, Kościelniak testifies that this was something that happened and was something that was important enough to record and remember. For this to be remembered is an entrenchment of its history and of identity in the Holocaust. As Lenia Marques and Greg Richards argue, art is a representation that becomes part of "the collective identity of places".[35] It is important to note that they speak of identity and not memory. Through this kind of place-based art, identity allows the singular voice to enlighten a wider spectrum whilst at the same time not becoming lost in said spectrum. Rather than speaking *for* victims, the artist and their identity *speak up* for the victims. In doing so, Forbidden Art has the opportunity to act as a podium for other prisoners.

Prisoner-artists created these works in opposition to the greater system and, in this way, their voices act in contrast to the dehumanizing system of the camps. Whilst the likes of Mengele and Himmler dehumanized and clustered people into indistinguishable groups and numbers, the artist-prisoners who created Forbidden Art acted in a space of reclamation. This reclamation is made possible by the agency of the individual artist creating their works. Philip Rosen argues that one of the reasons artists created their works was to shed light, for the rest of the world, on what was happening in the camp.[36] In doing so, they did something else as well: they helped reclaim their own agency as individuals. Moreover, they also became agents in reclaiming the humanity of other victims and prisoners of the camp by capturing their likeness in art. Through the artists' statements of individual reclamation of agency, the collective group can also partake because the individual does not preclude the possibility of the group. Stępień's sketch of the woman praying to the Virgin Mary is an example of this. If prayer was important enough for Stępień to portray then it could have also been important for others as well. It also shows

35 Lénia Marques and Greg Richards, "The Dimensions of Art in Place Narrative," *Tourism Planning and Development*, 11(1), 2014, p. 4.
36 Rosen and Apfelbaum, *Bearing Witness*, p. 134.

that Forbidden Art was created in contrast to the exterminatory nature of the camp in death and dehumanization. For Stępień, it had to do with the portrayal of prayer. For others, like Franciszek Jaźwiecki, it was through portraits they made of individuals in the camp. The art prisoners created in the camps in turn created testimonies to the travesties of Nazi design, as well as of the ability of prisoners to dissent. In their individual pieces, artists created a space of reclamation in which dehumanization is refused and individual voices are allowed to be heard and become a rich part of the collective narrative of the Holocaust.

The Viewer as a Witness to Art

The question of what the relationship is between the viewer, the artist and Forbidden Art still remains. Though this relationship is at times intensely personal, it is also worth examining from an academic standpoint. To discuss these questions, it is pertinent to reflect back on the creators of these pieces. The intentions of creators of camp-made, illegal art lead to questions regarding responsibility. Herein lies the importance of the viewer of Forbidden Art: as Miranda Ward remarks, there is a distinctive relationship in which the author, the work, the spatial-temporal place and the viewer interact.[37] In this, the representations of space and individual testimony have the power to affect viewers. This is one of the reasons that viewers of Forbidden Art have responsibility: viewers play a role in art's continued existence and effect because the audience becomes part of the conversation and discourse of the Holocaust. The viewer has the power to choose whom to understand and gives voice to their interpretations of art. In prisoner-created art, the viewer has the opportunity to interact within and through the space of art to try to understand the intentions of the artist. Though seeking the true intentions of the artist may seem difficult if not impossible, it is in the very act of interpretation of Forbidden

37 Ward, "The Art of Writing Place," p. 763.

Art that the continuation of the conversation happens. Additionally, the perception of the viewer may include an acknowledgement of the agency that the artist possesses. At the same time, perceptions become extant because of the agency of the individual viewer. In viewing these art pieces, the viewer creates a conversation with the artist' perspectives. It is an opportunity for the viewer to move beyond seeing and into the act of witnessing, an act which "battles against oblivion and indifference".[38]

By moving past just viewing, the ethical implications of witnessing must be discussed in reference to representations of space in Forbidden Art because this kind of representation asks the viewer to actively engage in the work as testimony by seeing as the artist saw, by interpreting what is included within the space of representation and by interpreting what is excluded. That being said, it would be relatively easy to fall into moralistic preaching regarding the actions that the witness should take in light of what they have seen. Viewing Forbidden Art is not a call to arms per se; rather, it is a call to see such pieces as authoritative testimony. Forbidden Art asks the viewer to move past the experience of viewing art for pleasure and on to something Sue Tait defines as bearing witness. Instead of passively witnessing, bearing witness asks the viewer to engage in the works and "perform responsibility".[39] Tait emphasizes that bearing witness is a "transmission of moral obligation" where the ultimatum of the artist is not "exhausted by the concept of truth".[40] Instead, creators of Forbidden Art portray that which they have experienced and the viewer is asked to "bear witness" to the trauma that prisoners experience, interlacing it with their own narratives.[41] From this, bearing witness can also prompt an opportunity where the agency and humanity of the victims is given back to them through the witnesses' understanding of intentionality and agency of the artists. Through this understanding, witnesses also create

38 Sue Tait, "Bearing Witness, Journalism and Moral Responsibility," *Media, Culture and Society*, 33(8), 2011, p. 1223.
39 Ibid., p. 1221.
40 Ibid., p. 1227.
41 Ibid..

ethical understandings of the victims of the Holocaust that are portrayed in Forbidden Art. Rather than just viewing pieces of art, witnesses view art with justness that stems from the ethical framework within which understanding of Forbidden Art is built. It is a process in which layering of meaning occurs as the viewers own "experiences, impression and knowledge" create a "polyvocal" space.[42] This polyvocal space is one in which multiple generations can converse without spatial-temporal limitations. Through the theoretical space created by Forbidden Art, the conversation about the Holocaust and the ethical conversations that happen between the past and present can persist.

Conclusion

Today, the Auschwitz-Birkenau Museum and Memorial houses over 2000 works made by concentration-camp prisoners.[43] Even with this many surviving works from the camp, still more were destroyed deliberately or by the test of time. Artists working under extreme conditions and in constant danger of punishment created Forbidden Art and as such this canon of art exists beyond the regular parameters of art theory and moves into the space of testimony. The existence of Forbidden Art has its value in and functions as a form of testimony in which its subversive nature lends power to the deliverance of agency to the artist and their fellow prisoners. Moreover, the power of Forbidden Art also acts as a bridge over which the prisoner-artists ask the viewers to come into conversation in an ethical manner: to bear witness to the nature of the Holocaust and to the highly personal truths in their art.

Forbidden Art asks the viewer to become a witness and, in doing so, to become part of continuing the narrative. What prisoner-artists ask of the witness is the rejection of passivity. In conversing about and with

---

42 Ward, "The Art of Writing Place," p. 763.
43 Sieradzka, "Forbidden Art," p. 85.

the creators of Forbidden Art, the witness transcends the boundaries of time and space. In doing so, "space" becomes more than its physical manifestation; it becomes a dialogue through which the events of the Holocaust are not limited to photographs frozen in time or numbers typed on a sheet of paper. The physical and conceptual space created in Forbidden Art demands of the witness of agency, continuing the Holocaust narrative in an ethical manner that refuses the complacency of history. Perhaps at its core, then, Forbidden Art creates a space where the conversation that happens between witness and artist is a continuous demand in which each individual is asked to value the stripped-down humanity that exists in Forbidden Art. Art acts as powerful testimony because of its implicit humanity. It calls upon the witness to understand the inherent complexity of the artist. It asks the witness to recognize the dignity and authority of the artists' personal narratives. Ultimately, as the space represented in Forbidden Art is shared, over time it epitomizes the transcendent nature of human life. As Tadeusz Borowski writes, "the faces of our parents, friends, and the shapes of objects we left behind - these are the things we share. And even if nothing is left to us but our bodies . . . we shall still have our memories and feelings".[44] If nothing else, Forbidden Art demands of the witness something both complicated and extremely simple: to share in the memory of the Holocaust and to continue its narrative ethically.

44 Tadeusz Borowski, *This Way for the Gas, Ladies and Gentlemen*, London: Penguin, 1976.

PICTURE 1

Wincenty Gawron, *Marching Out to Abbruch*, Poland, 1942.

Auschwitz Birkenau State Museum Collections, PMO-I-2-1525_D-2

Zofia Stępień, *Prayer*, Poland, 1943.

Auschwitz Birkenau State Museum Collections, PMO-I-2-0885_B

Mieczyslaw Kościelniak, *Done*, Poland, 1943.

Auschwitz Birkenau State Museum Collections, PMO-I-2-0223_B-2

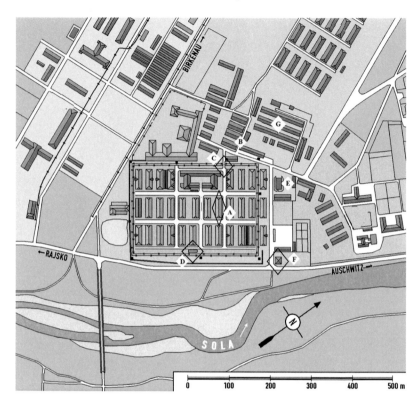

A   Barrack 15 – where the FK lived
B   the buildings where the fire equipment and engines were kept
C   the main gate to the camp
D   the swimming pool behind block 6
E   Crematoria I
F   Commandant Höss' house
G   Workshops

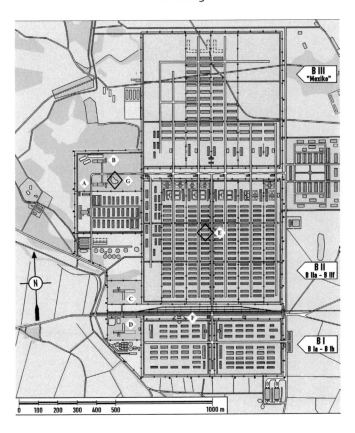

A   Crematorium IV

B   Crematorium V

C   Crematorium III

D   Crematorium II

E   The secluded barracks of some Sonderkommando members

F   The water reserves next to the ramp/path to crematorium II and III

G   The water reserve used to fight the fire of Crematorium IV; the red dotted line denotes the path the Feuerwehrkommando entered Birkenau from Auschwitz

Mieczysław Kościelniak „Powrót z pracy" / „Return from work", Poland 1950.

Auschwitz-Birkenau State Museum Collections, PMO-I-2-159

PICTURE 7

DOCUMENT NO. 3680 - PS CONT'D.

Abschrift.

SS-Wirtschafts-Verwaltungshauptamt, Oranienburg, den 4.1.43
Amtsgruppe D - Konzentrationslager,
DII/1 53 Ma./Hag.

Betrifft: Verwertung der abgeschnittenen Menschenhaare.

An die
Kommandanten der KL
Buchenwald, Dachau, Flossenbuerg, Mauthausen, Neuengamme,
Ravensbrueck, Sachsenhausen, Natzweiler.

Die Errichtung einer Werkstaette zur Verarbeitung der abgeschnittenen Maennerhaare der Haeftlinge in einem der KL laesst sich aus technischen Gruenden zurzeit noch nicht verwirklichen. Die anfallenden Haare muessen daher an einen bestehenden Verwertungsbetrieb abgeliefert werden.
Die bis jetzt dort gesammelten Schnitthaare sind deshalb baldigst an die Firma

Alex Zink Filzfabrik AG. Roth b. Nuernberg,

zum Versand zu bringen. Die Haare sind mit RM -.50 je kg in Rechnung zu stellen. Die Betraege sind in der Reichskasse zu vereinnahmen. Der Versand hat porto- bzw. frachtfrei zu erfolgen.
Die mir jeweils zum 5. eines jeden Monats einzusendenden Meldungen ueber die Menge des gesammelten Schnitthaares sind weiterhin einzureichen. Dabei ist die Menge des an die Firma Zink abgesandten Schnitthaares mit anzugeben. Die gesammelten Mengen sind laufend an die Firma Zink abzusenden.

gez. Maurer | Der Chef des Amtes D II.
F.d.R.d.A. | gez. Unterschrift
gez. Unterschrift | SS-Obersturmbannfuehrer
SS-Hauptscharfuehrer u.
Stabsscharfuehrer

101/R kg netto 1/F.43 "A CERTIFIED TRUE COPY"

- 3 -

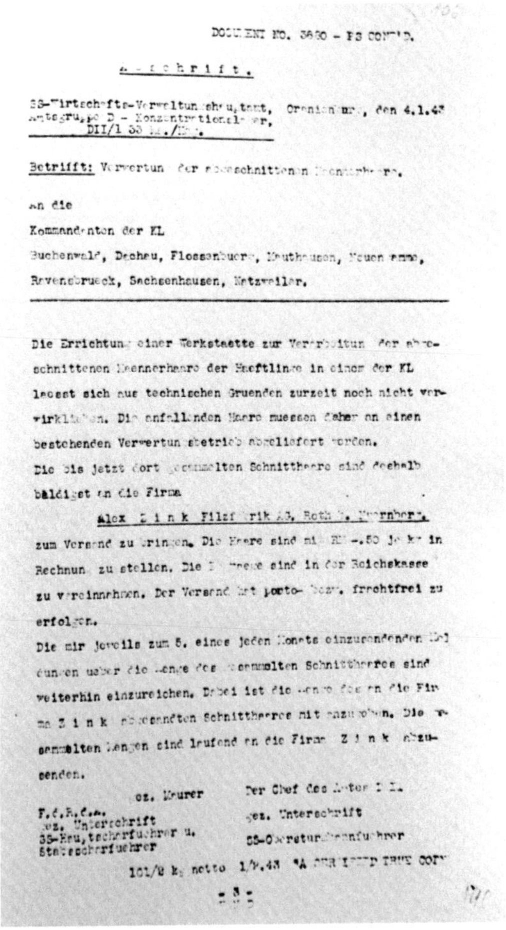

Letter from The Head of the Main Reich Economic and Administrative Office to the Commanders of Concentration Camps regarding the collection, price and further usage of Victims hair. Dated Jan 4 1943.

Copy provided through Dr. W. Płosa,
Head of Archives at the Auschwitz-Birkenau State Museum.

Sara Brewster

The Feuerwehrkommando
of Auschwitz-Birkenau

The infamous gates of Auschwitz welcomed prisoners with the information Arbeit macht frei [work makes one free]. However, for far too many of the prisoners in Auschwitz freedom came only in the form of death.

Prisoners' work was exploited to further the German economy. In the camp, prisoners were placed in work groups [kommandos], two of which will be highlighted here for their involvement in the revolt in Crematorium IV in Birkenau at one in the afternoon on October 7, 1944. The first kommando, the Sonderkommando,[1] assisted the SS in operating the gas chambers and crematoria: they escorted and loaded people into gas chambers, extracted and transported the human bodies from the crematorium, took all valuables (hair, gold teeth, etc.) from the corpses and burned the remains.[2] Due to their knowledge and in view of the tasks that members of this working group performed, the Sonderkommando were divided from the general prisoner population of Birkenau. In this isolation, they planned, organized and carried out their ambitious goal

---

1 The information provided here is based on Dr. Igor Bartosik's lecture on Sonderkommando (translated by Bożena Karwowska), in the *Witnessing Auschwitz* seminar, University of British Columbia, 23 May 2016. See also Adam Wilma and Igor Bartosik, *I Was at the Auschwitz Crematorium: A Conversation with Henryk Mandelbaum, Former Prisoner and Member of the Sonderkommando at Auschwitz*, Oświęcim: Auschwitz-Birkenau State Museum, 2011.

2 [ED] It is crucial to understand that they were chosen to do the job by SS-officers and they had to obey their orders.

of rebelling against their imprisoner, the German SS.[3] It is noteworthy to add here that their actions in fact testify against popular misconceptions of a "passive Jewish" victim.

The second kommando, the Feuerwehrkommando[4] [fire work group, or fire brigade], was made up of mostly of Polish prisoners[5] who were to protect the camp's wooden buildings from fire as well as the entire camp from burning in the event of an airstrike. The SS also housed members of this kommando separately in a block inaccessible to the rest of the general prisoner population in Auschwitz. The Sonderkommando, the Feuerwehrkommando and all the prisoners within the barbed wire of Auschwitz and Birkenau existed in a space that operated outside of normal law.[6] However, each commando was created on the basis of rules and laws (or a lack thereof) of different political spaces. The Sonderkommando emerged precisely out of this state of exception and functioned to obliquely lessen the burden of the SS officers as well as to assist them with their mass killings; the Feuerwehrkommando emerged out of the Nazis' need to protect the SS enterprise and, though a clear contradiction, to insure it according to the rules of the outside world.

3　See Igor Bartosik, *Bunt Sonderkommando: 7 października 1944 roku*, Oświęcim: Auschwitz-Birkenau, 2014.

4　Bohdan Piętka, "The fire brigade Kommando (Feuerwehrkommando) at KL Auschwitz," *Auschwitz Studies 26*, Oświęcim: Auschwitz-Birkenau, 2012, pp. 179-198.

5　[ED] Feuerwehrkommando was thus created during "the Polish period" of the camp, when the majority of prisoners were Polish. Since the first transports consisted mostly of Polish prisoners, they also form a majority of "old numbers". To learn more about the "Polish" and "Jewish" periods of Auschwitz please see Franciszek Piper, "The Political and Racist Principles of the Nazi Policy of Extermination and Their Realization at KL Auschwitz," *Auschwitz: Nazi Death Camp*, Oświęcim: Auschwitz-Birkenau State Museum, 2011, pp. 11-20.
　　[ED] In the years 1940-1942 Auschwitz was a concentration camp and in the years 1942-1944 it was predominantly a death camp for the Jews from all over Europe.

6　[ED] As Giorgio Agamben explains, the zone behind the barbed wires was created as a space of exception, and was possible only because of a suspension of the normal state's laws. In his essay "What is a Camp," the Italian philosopher writes: "*The camp is the space that opens up when the state of exception starts to become the rule. In it, the state of*

The creation of the Feuerwehrkommando came out of necessity to protect the massive SS enterprise that was Auschwitz (and later on, in 1942, Birkenau). The Nazis particularly needed insurance against fire as most of the factory buildings in Auschwitz were wooden. On May 2 (or April 10[7]) 1941, an insurance broker, Mr. Plints from Allianz Insurance, visited Auschwitz and inspected "all [possible] sources of fire" under the watch of an SS guard. The broker noted that Auschwitz had "fire-fighting arrangements", which probably referred to fire-extinguishers; watercolor paintings designed by artist employed prisoner Władysław Siwek illustrated how to extinguish a fire.[8] Alfred Sacks, another Allianz insurance broker who visited in January, 1942 to renew the policy, concluded his evaluation with positive recommendations, concluding that Auschwitz

exception, which was essentially a temporal suspension of the state of law, acquires a permanent spatial arrangement that, as such, remains constantly outside the normal state of law" (253). This space of exception was a phenomenon that Primo Levi named "the grey zone", explaining that Nazi Germany stripped its victims of innocence and, in using prisoners to assist in the extermination of other prisoners, blurred the lines between victims and perpetrators. However, the space on the other side of the barbed wire, with the camp administration and the SS guards who oversaw the camp, was governed by laws – those of martial law in Germany and in occupied Poland. And while the prisoners operated in the zone of exception, the SS ran its economic enterprise according to the laws and customs of the Reich. This means that the two commandos were created out of and according to rules of different zones. See Giorgio Agamben, "What is a Camp?" *The Holocaust: Theoretical Readings*, ed. Neil Levi and Michael Rothberg, Boston: Houghton Mifflin Company, 2008, pp. 252-256.

7   The visit occurred on May 2 and the insurance policy was backdated to April 10. Gerald Feldman, *Allianz and the German Insurance Business: 1933-45*, New York: Cambridge University Press, 2001, p. 411. See also *"Das 'Wagnis Auschwitz',"* *Der Spiegel*, June-July 1997.

8   Fire-fighting arrangements are translated by the Allianz's book as "fire-extinguishers" and the article assigns Hoss' order to Władysław Siwek as given just before the visit by Allianz. Wladyslaw Siwek's watercolors depict how to extinguish fires in the prisoner blocks. Within these drawings are instructions on how to use a fire extinguisher. Piętka, "The fire brigade," pp. 179-198. In my opinion [ED], Sack may refer to either, or both, of these to make up the "firefighting arrangements".

was under "constant military supervision, there is perfect order and cleanliness" with "no risk of fire".[9]

After the brokers' visit, Allianz insured Auschwitz for an annual fee of 1360.95 Reichsmark. The insurance provided protection for the factories, warehouses and timber stocks, valued at 581, 400 Reichsmark, including clean-up, should a fire occur.[10] Allianz maintains (as of 1997) that Auschwitz' insurance policy number, A908506, only covered the SS factories, and never the camp itself; however, it is important to add that at KL-Plaszów (near Kraków), their insurance policy additionally covered the prisoner barracks.[11]

Seemingly, the "fire-fighting arrangements" Sacks cited in his spring visit were sufficient for Auschwitz because a formalized Feuerwehrkommando is not mentioned until late 1941. According to Sigmund Sobolewski, the camp authorities assigned twelve men, including himself, to form the Auschwitz Upper Silesia Feuerwehrkommando on December 27, 1941. The brigade was made up of the so called "old number[s]",[12] those who were among the first transports to Auschwitz, starting in June, 1940, when the prisoner population consisted mostly of Polish "political prisoners". Eventually, the Feuerwehrkommando expanded to include twenty-seven men and three fire-engines.[13] The members of the Feuerwehrkommando were organized into three brigades of eight or nine men so that a brigade

9   "Das 'Wagnis Auschwitz'," p. 58.; Feldman, *Allianz*, p. 411.
10 "Das 'Wagnis Auschwitz'," p. 58; Feldman, *Allianz*, p. 412.
11 "Das 'Wagnis Auschwitz'," p. 54, p. 60.
12 Piętka, "The fire brigade,", p. 188. Of the 34 known Feuerwehrkommandos (with known numbers), 26 had numbers less than twenty-five thousand; one Sigmund Sobolewski (no. 88) was a part of the first transport to Auschwitz. The name "old number" comes from this period as they were the prisoners who survived Auschwitz the longest.
13 Roy D.Tanenbaum, *Prisoner 88: The Man in Stripes*, Calgary: Calgary University Press, 1998, p. 141. *Prisoner 88: The Man in Stripes,* is Sigmund Sobolewski's memoir as told to Roy Tanenbaum. In the first transport to Auschwitz, (when he was 17), Sobolewski held several jobs in the camp, including a brigade leader on the Feuerwehrkommando. Sobolewski survived the Sonderkommando revolt of October 7, 1944, and ultimately survived the camp. The biography continues past the camp and tells Sobolewski's story of life in Canada and Holocaust Education efforts.

could always be in the barrack, ready to respond. However, according to archival documents, Rudolf Höss, the commandant of Auschwitz, issued the official order to form the Firekommander and came up with the "official" fire alarm procedure only on March 4, 1942.[14] Höss' order set the Feuerwehrkommando as responsible for dealing with all fires, not only within Auschwitz and Birkenau, but also within a fifteen kilometre radius of each camp.[15] The order also outlines the different kinds of alarms which would sound in the Feuerwehrkommando members' block in case of fire. For a fire inside the camp, the alarm would ring in a trio of long rings, about fifteen sets per minute.[16] Between its inception and 1944, the Feuerwehrkommando attended to several fires, including a blaze in the women's barracks in Birkenau, and a workshop after it was damaged by an air raid.[17]

The two kommandos were brought together in the events of October 7, 1944, when the fire commando was called in to respond to a fire at Crematorium IV, which was the result of the Sonderkommando's revolt. Though the revolt occurred sooner than the Sonderkommando members planned it, it would be difficult to classify it as spontaneous. With the German army loosing on the Eastern front, the prisoners of Auschwitz knew that there was the possibility of the SS considering or even planning a mass liquidation of the camp population if/when the Soviet Red Army approached the camp. A few months before the liberation of Majdanek, on July 22, 1944, during the twenty-four hour "Fall Harvest Action", the SS murdered twenty-thousand Jewish prisoners. The knowledge of what happened in November, 1943, in Majdanek (near Lublin, in German-occupied Poland), travelled with prisoners transported from there to Auschwitz. Knowing this, the Sonderkommando prepared themselves for the likely mass liquidations or transports deep into the Reich. The Sonderkommando (and others) knew that they would likely die if they were to resist. To make sure

14 Piętka, "The fire brigade," pp. 194-195.
15 Ibid.
16 Ibid.
17 Piętka, "The fire brigade," pp. 183-184.

that at least part of their knowledge survived, several members of the Sonderkommando buried notes and testimonies between 1943 and 1944, and illegal photos were taken and smuggled out in August, 1944. Additionally, Alfred Wetzler and Walter Rosenberg-Rudolf Vrba[18] carried Zyclon B canister labels and detailed information pertaining to the operations of the crematoria. These testimonies and eye-witness accounts were, as Filip Müller explains, the contingency plan in case the revolt failed.[19] However, they also knew that, to refer to Ester Wajcblum's words: "thousands may die, but some will survive. We must not allow the murder of a million in secrecy. It is our duty to try and make possible a massive escape".[20] To members of the Sonderkommando, death was nearly unavoidable, but the choice to die in a revolt was favoured over death in the gas chamber. The plans were intended to reach other prisoners of Birkenau as well and they were to join following the Sonderkommando's revolt.

Before the end of its operation, Birkenau, however, became the site of the largest mass liquidation of people (Hungarian Jews) in its history. Filip Müller in his memoir writes that in May, 1944, the Nazis placed SS-Hauptscharführer Moll in charge of the crematorium.[21] Sigmund Sobolewski recalls that the preparations for the murder of one hundred thousand Hungarian Jews "led every member of the detail, no matter what class or walk of life, and even the worst people, to urge that this game be stopped at last".[22] By October, 1944, the transports from Hungary were nearing an end and the members of the Sonderkommando feared that the end of Auschwitz was near and the scenario known from Majdanek highly probable.

To plan a revolt as ambitious as that of the Sonderkommando required months of preparation. The revolt was intended to firstly kill the SS guards

18 [ED] Rudolf Vrba was registered in the camp as Walter Rosenberg.
19 Filip Müller, *Auschwitz Inferno*, London: Routledge, 1979, p. 143.
20 Roy D. Tanenbaum, *Prisoner 88: The Man in Stripes*, Calgary: Calgary University Press, 1998, p. 274.
21 Müller, *Auschwitz Inferno*, p. 128.
22 Thomas V. Maher, "Threat, Resistance and Collective Action: The Cases of Sobibór, Treblinka and Auschwitz," *American Sociological Review* 2010, 78.2, pp. 252-272, p. 265.

of crematorium IV and V and burn their bodies. Then, secondly, using the SS' arms and uniforms, the members of the Sonderkommando would liberate crematorium II and III and continue to the nearby camps (that is, the men's, women's, etc.).[23] In addition, the Sonderkommando members placed a high level of importance on destroying the tools of mass destruction, the crematoria – not so much the buildings, but the ovens in particular.[24] According to Filip Müller's autobiography, one of the inspirations for the revolt was the unnamed Jewish woman brought to Birkenau in one of the transports, and who, in October, 1943, shot SS Unterführer Schillinger.[25] The members of the Sonderkommando wondered what a large group of armed men could do if a "weak, single" woman, armed only with a pistol, caused so much panic among the SS guards. However, it took a considerable amount of time to make the necessary connections, to gather supplies, and to form a plan. All this indicates beliefs and information[26] regarding any kind of regularly scheduled liquidation of the Sonderkommando members to be highly questionable. There are several accounts of Sonderkommando members working in this kommando for years, as well as being liberated from Birkenau.[27] [28]

---

23 Bartosik, "Sonderkommando," lecture.; Müller, *Auschwitz Inferno*, pp. 144-146.

24 Bartosik, "Sonderkommando," lecture.

25 [ED] See http://auschwitz.org/en/history/resistance/prisoner-mutinies/. See also Tadeusz Borowski's short story "The Death of Schillinger" and Haya Bar-Itzhak, "Women in the Holocaust: The Story of a Jewish Woman Who Killed a Nazi in a Concentration Camp: A Folkloristic Perspective," *Fabula*, 50(1-2), 2009, pp. 67–77.

26 [ED] See description of the Sonderkommando in Primo Levi's explanation of what he termed the "grey zone" in his *The Drowned and the Saved* (1986) and Miklós Nyiszli, *Auschwitz: A Doctor's Eyewitness Account*. See also Piotr Setkiewicz, *Voices of Memory 6: The Auschwitz Crematoria and Gas Chambers*, Oświęcim: Auschwitz Birkenau State Museum, 2011.

27 While it is now known to be false, the idea that the Sonderkommando were liquated every few months was first told in Miklós Nyiszli's book *Auschwitz: A Doctor's Eyewitness Account*: one of the first published accounts of Auschwitz-Birkenau (1946). See also Igor Bartosik, *Bunt Sonderkommando: 7 Października 1944 Roku*, Oświęcim: Auschwitz-Birkenau, 2012, p. 4.

28 Müller, *Auschwitz Inferno*, p. 146.

As Geheimnisträger, the bearers of secrets, the Sonderkommando members were secluded from the rest of the camp population, but to carry out a task at this scale, they needed assistance from other prisoners. In order to destroy the ovens of crematorium IV, they had to make connections with women who worked outside the camp at the Weichsel-Union-Metall-werke. As far as historians are able to establish,[29] four Jewish women were involved in this operation. Ester Wajcblum and Regina Safirsztajn, who worked at the Union in the gunpowder-kommando, smuggled out gunpowder in spoon-sized amounts in special pockets in their uniforms. Ala Gertner, an office worker at the Union, passed the gunpowder to Róża Robota, who worked in the Canada warehouses. She was responsible for sorting clothing and sent the gunpowder to the Sonderkommando in their laundry carts. With this gunpowder, Sonderkommando members were able to create grenades and rig the crematorium to explode upon a signal from the camp resistance. In fact, the October 7 revolt resulted in the death of two SS guards (ten more were injured) and the destruction of crematorium IV at the cost of 450 Sonderkommando members' lives.[30] The revolt impacted all prisoners, but only the Feuerwehrkommando members witnessed firsthand the SS's brutality and the Sonderkommando members' bravery.

Despite the Sonderkommando's and Feuerwehrkommando's different locations and roles within Birkenau and Auschwitz respectively, members of both kommandos shared some similar experiences as they were all promienten prisoners,[31] meaning that they were in a position of privilege that allowed the prisoners to gain favour from SS guards who would, for instance, turn away as the prisoners "organized"[32] (Lagersprache, or camp

---

29 Isabel Wollaston, "Emerging from the Shadows: The Auschwitz Sonderkomman-do and the 'Four Women' in History and Memory," *Holocaust Studies*, 20(3), 2014, pp. 137-170.

30 A total of about 250 Jews died fighting, including mutiny leaders Załmen Gradowski and Józef Deresiński. Another 200 were killed in revenge of the revolt.

31 Primo Levi writes about "prominent prisoners" in his book *The Drowned and the Saved*.

32 [ED] Life in Auschwitz 1 (the main camp) is depicted from the point of view of a prisoner

language for steal) food, medicine and material goods. Additionally, the Sonderkommando members could shower more frequently than other prisoners, and the Feuerwehrkommando members were issued two pairs of quality boots.[33] According to Edward Sokół, a Feuerwehrkommando member, "[they] suffered no hunger" and "no one was beaten".[34] However, according to Sigmund Sobolewski, another Feuerwehrkommando member, "the difference between a prominente... [and] an average prisoner" was the "same difference between being caught in a hurricane or a volcanic eruption; life as a prominente [was] better, but only by comparison".[35] Nevertheless, the position of privilege did not exclude prisoners from the harsh rules of the camp. One of the SS doctors chose Ryszard Dacko to have his legs injected with a substance as part of a medical experiment. The SS used members of the brigade, including Edward Sokół, to find and beat prisoners who were hiding instead of reporting to work.[36] Life inside the camp was irrational and any attempt to explain it within rational terms is impossible as the rational terms require comparison to normal life, a comparison the camp does not allow.[37]

The fire the Feuerwehrkommando attended was on October 7, 1944, around one in the afternoon, and was the result of the Sonderkommando's revolt. Sobolewski recalls that he was lying in bed, reading old letters from his mother when the fire alarm sounded. The Feuerwehrkommando members in Auschwitz, Block 15,[38] quickly sprang into action. As ordered by Höss' 1942 decree, the first brigade immediately left their block and ran through the camp's gate to collect their fire-fighting gear. The gear (two thousand metres of hose, a helmet, gas-mask, axe, fireman's belt and

in Tadeusz Borowski's short story "Auschwitz our home." In her *Smoke over Birkenau*, Severyna Szmaglewska gives a definition and examples of what the term "organize" meant in the camp, especially in chapter 3, "Delousing Day," p. 66.

33 Piętka, "The fire brigade," p. 182.
34 Piętka, "The fire brigade," p. 187.
35 Tanenbaum, *Prisoner 88*, p, 177.
36 Piętka, "The fire brigade," p. 184.
37 Ibid., p. 130.
38 At the beginning they were housed in blocks 19, 9 (24) and at the end 15.

ropes for each prisoner[39]) was stored outside of the barbed wires, in cupboards next to the fire-engines in the garage of the Commandant's office (located opposite the Blocksführerstube, at the entrance with the Arbeit macht frei gate [B on the Auschwitz map]). More gear was held in another garage neighbouring a joinery workshop [G on the Auschwitz map]. In his memoir, Sobolewski recalls the chaos there: the SS men running about, donning their black helmets, which foreshadowed the events unfolding in Birkenau. The Feuerwehrkommando members gathered their gear and boarded the fire-engine. According to Edward Sokół's testimony, an SS guard (possibly their SS Hauptscharführer Engelschall) drove through the gate next to the Commandant's office (and house).[40] The second brigade followed.[41] [PICTURE 4]

From Auschwitz, the first brigade drove to Birkenau, and, once there, drove up the long road separating sectors BII from BIII (Mexico). Crematorium IV and V were in a protected access zone and this meant that anyone wanting to enter needed special permission, and this included the Feuerwehrkommando, under SS supervision. According to Sobolewski, even SS Hauptscharführer Engelschall's authority and presence did not allow the Feuerwehrkommando and their engines into the zone. However, in Sobolewski's words: "the crematorium engulfed in flames spoke for itself". By the time the first brigade was finally allowed through the gate,[42] the second brigade arrived, and they could proceed without delay.[43] The fire-engines and Feuerwehrkommando members arrived at the burning crematorium IV, and the Feuerwehrkommandos began their Aktion.

Both Sokół and Sobolewski begin their testimonies of the revolt by describing the abject horror of the blood-soaked ground which greeted

---

39 Ibid.
40 Piętka, "The fire brigade," p. 183, p. 189.
41 Map by: HEROMAX, "Auschwitz-Birkenau," *Wikipedia*, web, https://commons.m.wikimedia.org/wiki/File:AUSCHWITZ-BIRKENAU.png, Creative Commons Attribution Share-Alike 3.0 Unported license, modified by Sara Brewster, 7 July 2016.
42 Tanenbaum, *Prisoner 88*, p. 270.
43 Piętka, "The fire brigade," p. 189.

them as they entered the crematorium space. The SS was systematically murdering the Sonderkommando members. Simultaneously, with the "speed and efficiency of a professional brigade", the Feuerwehrkommando members got to work.[44] Under the watch of SS Hauptscharführer Engelschall, they set up their equipment. However, the members of the Feuerwehrkommando sabotaged the SS orders, lending a hand to the Sonderkommando members' plans and allowing the crematorium to burn further. The water pump failed to start when SS Hauptscharführer Engelschall ordered Mieczysław Zakrzewski, the Feuerwehrkommando member in charge of operating and maintaining the pump,[45] to begin pouring water. Only when Engelschall drew his gun and aimed at Zakrzewski did the pump begin to work. By the time the water hit the blaze, the roof had begun to collapse.[46] Crematorium IV was destroyed, in part by the Feuerwehrkommando member's lack of immediate action.

In order to fight a fire such as crematorium IV, the Feuerwehrkommando members needed water. There were several water reservoir locations in Auschwitz and Birkenau. In Auschwitz, there was a large reservoir behind barrack six [D on Auschwitz map]. There were more in Birkenau, namely, two along the road dividing sectors BI and BII and one next to crematorium IV [F and G, respectively, on Birkenau map]. Aside from serving their intended purposes of being available for fire protection and fulfilling insurance requirements, the reservoirs were sites of propaganda, temptation and punishments. In Auschwitz, the water reservoir was designed as a swimming pool. According to Sigmund Sobolewski, the pool was used twice, both times for propaganda purposes. First, a film was shot of the Feuerwehrkommando members training, and second when the SS ordered an "Olympic champion from Czechoslovakia" to perform dives for the Red Cross' visit.[47]

---

44 Ibid.
45 Tanenbaum, *Prisoner 88*, p. 271; Bartosik, *Bunt Sonderkommando*, p. 21.
46 Tanenbaum, *Prisoner 88*, p. 271.
47 Ibid., pp. 249-250.

The reservoirs in Birkenau, between sectors BI and BII, were also located near the selection platform. The second Birkenau reservoir was next to crematorium IV. SS Hauptscharführer Moll would make prisoners play "leap frog" (probably Lagersprache for "treading water") in the water until they drowned of exhaustion.[48] This reserve was also used as a place to dispose of the ashes from the crematoria as well as the location where the Feuerwehrkommando members drew their water. The water reservoirs played various roles in the Nazis' "purposeful unpredictability"[49] at Auschwitz-Birkenau.

After forty-five minutes of fighting the blaze, the Feuerwehrkommando was ordered to leave the crematorium zone. At this point, the SS had either sent away or had killed the remaining Sonderkommando members. The Feuerwehrkommando members and their SS supervision left the "enclosure through the opening [they] made at the start of the fire-fighting action".[50] From there, they briefly re-entered the area beyond the barbed wire, the road between the two sections of Birkenau and the larger space between the two camps of Birkenau and Auschwitz. Edward Sokół described the main camp after the Feuerwehrkommando returned as a place on full alert; none of the prisoners slept that night.[51]

This was not the Feuerwehrkommando's first fire alarm, but it would be the last for the Polish Feuerwehrkommando members. On the 24th of October, 1944, German prisoners from Auschwitz[52] replaced them, transferring them to KL Sachsenhausen (in Oranienburg, Germany).[53][54] [PICTURE 5]

48 Müller, *Auschwitz Inferno*, p. 128.
49 Tanenbaum, *Prisoner 88*, p. 249.
50 Piętka, "The fire brigade," p. 190.
51 Ibid., pp. 191-192.
52 [ED] According to Bohdan Piętka, the German prisoner who replaced the Polish one were not from KL Auschwitz but from KL Sachsenhausen.
53 Piętka, "The fire brigade," p. 184.
54 Map by: HEROMAX, "Auschwitz-Birkenau," *Wikipedia*, web, https://commons.m.wikimedia.org/wiki/File:AUSCHWITZ-BIRKENAU.png, Creative Commons Attribution Share-Alike 3.0 Unported license, modified by Sara Brewster, 7 July 2016.

The nightfall of October 7, 1944 marked the end of 450 Sonderkommando members' lives and the beginning of the end of the crematoria in Birkenau. The Feuerwehrkommando members who lived through the day retained their memory and bore witness, not only regarding the actions of the SS, but of the Sonderkommando members' bravery. The Sonderkommando members also bore witness, albeit in advance, by smuggling photographs of the crematorium and writing (and burying) their testimonies. The narrative of the events leading up to and including October 7, 1944 includes the story of two work groups who came together under tragic circumstances, and together, through action (Sonderkommando), and inaction (Feuerwehrkommando), they destroyed one of the most lethal tools of the Holocaust.

Riley Hass

Resisting the Concentration Camp: The Stories of Selected Escapees from Auschwitz-Birkenau

In the various forms of texts from Auschwitz, stories of prisoners physically escaping the camp are a common reoccurrence. Most people, if not all, thought about physically escaping from the camp, but only a few went forward with the task. As one can assume there were countless obstacles and limitations personally as well as systematically, making an escape very complex.[1] Hermann Langbein said that anyone who wanted to resist the camp had to "look for like-minded people" to succeed.[2] With each coming day new obstacles within the camp and outside would arise, making escaping the hardest form of resistance in Auschwitz. The physical escapes from Auschwitz are some of the most important forms of resistance against captors because those who escaped were the exception to the rule of imprisonment; they gave inspiration to the rest of the camps, overcame the camp system and some were able to share their stories to the rest of the world, exposing the operations of Auschwitz. These

---

1 [ED] In order to limit the possibility of escapes SS men created special security and alarm systems. They also victimized brutally the captured escapees to discourage their fellow prisoners from escapes. See more: Jacek Lachendro, "Escapes of Prisoners from Auschwitz," Auschwitz-Birkenau Memorial and Museum E-Learning, web, http://lekcja.auschwitz.org/en_15_ucieczki/. See also: Piotr Setkiewicz, "The Fencing and System for Preventing Prisoner Escapes at Auschwitz Concentration Camp," *The Architecture of Crime: The Security and Isolation System of the Auschwitz Camp*, Oświęcim: Auschwitz-Birkenau State Museum, 2008.
2 Hermann Langbein, *People in Auschwitz*. Chapel Hill: The University of North Carolina Press: 2004, p. 243.

multiple layers of the escapes illustrate how these individuals were the exception to the experiences of many others in the camp.

The term "escapism" describes the mental and emotional withdrawal prisoners underwent to get away from the daily torture of the camp. It was "an activity or form of entertainment that allows people to forget about the real problems of life".[3] In a way, through music, art and song, some prisoners were able to resist authority and express their emotion in their personal ways. What many of the physical escapes provided the camp with was another way to forget life in the camp and provide a feeling of hope. For the German officials of Auschwitz a major threat to security within the camp was having a prisoner escape and interrupting camp operations. One of the main duties of the SS guards was to ensure the prisoners were kept in the dark about the operations of the camp.[4] The guards' duties started once the trains were unloaded on the ramp at Auschwitz from various ghettos and stations across Europe. They lied and deceived the passengers to ensure no violence or aggression erupted to make their jobs "easier".[5] Those who "survived" the selection process[6] would quickly figure out the operations of the camp. The officers of the camp understood

3 "Escapism," *Merriam-Webster's Collegiate Dictionary*, 11th ed., Springfield: Merriam-Webster, 2003.

4 Since Auschwitz had the most prisoners naturally it was the camp most prone to witness escape attempts based on its population. See: Krzysztof Wąsowicz, *Resistance in the Nazi Concentration Camps, 1933-1945*, Warszawa: PWN-Polish Scientific Publishers, 1982, p. 198.

5 [ED] This applies to the transports of the Jews from Western Europe. The SS guards treated political prisoners as well as Jews deported from occupied Poland in a brutal and aggressive way. See testimonies available in English by Halina Birenbaum, Władysław Bartoszewski, Kazimierz Albin, etc.

6 [ED] Only the Jewish people went through the selections. Political prisoners were registered in the camp immediately after arrival. It is important to remember that the Auschwitz camp served two duties: in the years 1940-1942: it was a concentration camp and the majority of the prisoners were political prisoners of Polish origin; and in the years 1942-1944 Auschwitz was primarily a death camp for Jews from all over Europe, but simultaneously it was also a concentration camp and the majority of the prisoners were Jews. This essay is about escapes and most of the escapes were carried out by political prisoners.

they needed to control the thought processes of the prisoners, which lead to harsh punishments and living standards. For the prisoners of the concentration camps every day became exactly the same, with extended roll calls, malnutrition, hard labor and limited sleep. These procedures were designed to emotionally and physically drain the prisoners and force them to put all their energy and effort towards working in the camp.

In terms of controlling and weakening large groups of people, the operations of Auschwitz were in large part successful. Still, some prisoners were able to maintain a certain amount of agency. In an interview with Auschwitz Survivor Tadeusz Smreczyński,[7] he explained that there were three elements that potentially helped people to survive in the concentration camp: good psychophysical health, incredible luck and the knowledge of the German language.[8] Smreczyński was able to escape from three separate German labor or concentration camps during the war. He added that having connections within the camp and the opportunity to have "better" working conditions than the majority of prisoners were also beneficial. His story is similar to many others who escaped who shared the belief that they would survive and see the end of the war. The thoughts of escape never left them; they all had a powerful motivation to leave the camp and make a better tomorrow.[9] For most of these prisoners, they worried "that the world would never learn about the crimes that were committed in Auschwitz, or that if any of these became known, [the outside world] would not believe it".[10]

---

7 [ED] Tadeusz Smreczyński was a Polish political prisoner. He was the former prisoner of Auschwitz and Mauthausen concentration camps and Linz III sub-camp of KL Mauthausen.

8 Tadeusz Smreczyński, *Meeting with UBC Go Global Witnessing Auschwitz: Conflicting Stories and Memories*. Krakow: 24 May 2014.

9 Henryk Świebocki, *London Has Been Informed: Reports by Auschwitz Escapees*, Oświęcim: Auschwitz-Birkenau State Museum, 1997, p. 8.

10 Langbein, *People in Auschwitz*, p. 3. [ED] Only a few of the escapees thought about informing the world about Auschwitz crimes. A lot of them were afraid for their families because they knew that in revenge for their escape SS-men would like to punish their fellow prisoners or their relatives, i.e., imprison members of their families. So the issue was complex.

For most escapes, the first step in organization involved a lot of barter, trade and bribery to obtain favors and supplies. This part was extremely risky because if your plan was compromised it usually resulted in severe punishment. Prisoners had to be aware of obstacles inside their own barracks such as spies that SS men paid off. Men such as Stanislaw Dorosiewicz were employees of the SS that built up their own network of spies inside the camp to uncover underground operations.[11] The escapees had to insure that their trading partners and allies could be trusted in this highly confined area. In some cases people would get desperate and attempt to pay off SS guards to help them out. In most cases the guards would simply double-cross the prisoners and inform the functionaries of Politische Abteilung (the camp Gestapo) or shoot them after receiving their payment, but there were always exceptions. One testimony recounts the experience of a Jewish prisoner, Siegfried Lederer, arranging with an SS guard Viktor Pestek to drive him to Prague disguised as a fellow German soldier.[12] In this rare case SS Pestek agreed and dropped him off safely across the border. Upon his arrival back to the camp Pestek was arrested and killed for his actions.[13] With this success other prisoners like Jerzy Tabeau tried the same feat but were unable to see it through. It still

---

11 Langbein, *People in Auschwitz*, p. 179.

12 Henryk Świebocki, *Auschwitz 1940 – 1945, IV*, Oświęcim: Auschwitz-Birkenau State Museum, 1999, p. 221.

13 [ED] According to a detailed article by Erich Kulka, "Pestek, who often visited the [Czech] Family Camp, fell in love with a beautiful Jewish Czech girl, Rene Neumann, and decided to smuggle her and her mother out of Auschwitz. He finally managed to elicit the confidence of a Jewish block elder, Siegfried Lederer, also a prisoner in the Family Camp. . . Pestek procured for the escape SS officer uniforms, and Lederer promised to arrange matters in Bohemia. When on April 5, 1944, after the morning roll-call, the sirens signalled the escape of Lederer, two disguised SS officers were already sitting in an express train to Prague. Pestek was on an official leave, and nobody in Auschwitz connected his absence with the escape of Lederer" (p. 406). In Erich Kulka, "Escapes of Jewish Prisoners from Auschwitz-Birkenau," *The Nazi Concentration Camps: Structure and Aims, the Image of the Prisoner, the Jews in the Camps: Proceedings of the Fourth Yad Vashem International Historical Conference, January 1980.* Jerusalem: Yad Vashem, 1984. [ED] In the camp Jerzy Tabeau was under the name Jerzy Wesołowski.

is unknown how, but word of the day of Tabeau's planned escape with his friend Roman Cieliczko got out. In fear that they would be compromised, Tabeau and Cieliczko gathered up their supplies and made a run for the Zigeunerlager camp in Birkenau. With their luck, equipped with wire cutters and rubber gloves, the two men were able to short the fuse of that particular camp section and escape through the electric barbed wire.[14] Tabeau survived the war and provided the allies with valuable information once he arrived back to Krakow.[15]

The escapes that had the highest success rate were those that were planned well in advance. There are cases like Tabeau who relied on spontaneity to survive, but in most cases that led to more problems. An escape from the point of view of Alfred Wetzler illustrates this idea of spontaneity versus organization. Alfred Wetzler was a Jewish man from Sered in Slovakia who was sent to Auschwitz in 1942. He worked in the camp morgue[16] moving corpses, and the work was exhausting both physically and mentally. After a few months in the camp, Wetzler attempted an escape through an unsupervised man hole.[17] Having never planned this escape he did not realize the other end was gated off, forcing him to return to the camp. He was lucky; this entire trip went unnoticed and he avoided severe punishment. This act of desperation shows the kind of emotional state prisoners were living through. If it was not for the help of his friend

---

14 Henryk Świebocki, *Five Escapees from Birkenau, Pro Memoria: Information Bulletin No. 5-6*, Oświęcim: State Museums Auschwitz-Birkenau Department Archive, 2014, p. 20. For more details see: Lachendro, "Selected Escapes of Auschwitz Prisoners, Auschwitz II-Birkenau."

15 [ED] Jerzy Tabeau wrote down his testimony during the war (between 1943-1944) in Kraków.

16 [ED] At the very beginning he had to collect corpses of dead prisoners all over the camp (only for few weeks). Then he worked as a Schreiber (writer/clerk) at Block 7 at Auschwitz I (later he worked as a Schreiber of Block 9 at Birkenau). Then he worked in the camp morgue (he had to write out death certificates of prisoners and register the number of golden teeth removed from the corpses). He also worked in many other places during his imprisonment.

17 Świebocki, *London Has Been Informed*, p. 24.

Rudolf Vrba, and Wetzler getting switched out of his job, the chances are Wetzler would not have lasted much longer. Finding any form of support inside the camp was the best way to cope with emotions; Vrba and Wetzler were hometown acquaintances before the war.[18]

After living in the camp for over a year Wetzler and Vrba worked their way through the ranks together and eventually became barrack clerks, keeping records of the prisoners.[19] Both men held the same post and quickly realized they were given an acceptable amount of freedom to move around and gain access to comparatively vast amounts of information.[20] It was not long before they came up with the idea of escaping. On April 7, 1944, Vrba and Wetzler went into "Mexico" (Birkenau III) to hide in a wood cavity[21] of a construction site, camouflaged with the scent of tobacco to evade the inevitable search teams. Having learned from past escapes, they knew that searches lasted for three days and three nights. After the third night they left their hide out and headed south for Slovakia and were fortunate to have the help of outsiders on their journey.[22]

---

18 [ED] Please see a fragment of Vrba's memoirs: "Fred Wetzler! He was from my hometown Trnava: and, though I had never spoken to him, for he was six years older than I was, I had always admired him, if only for his casual Bohemian manner and his easy way with girls" (p. 179). Rudolf Vrba, *I Escaped From Auschwitz*, London: Robson Books, 2006.

19 Rudolf Vrba and Alfred Wetzler, *The Auschwitz Protocol, The Vrba-Wetzler Report*, Oświęcim: State Museums Auschwitz-Birkenau Department Archive, 2014, p. 25. [ED] This was published in: Świebocki, *London Has Been Informed*, p. 169, and Vrba, *I Escaped From Auschwitz*, London: Robson Books, 2006, p. 327.

20 [ED] Prisoners, even kapos, did not have access to much information. Rudolf Vrba for some period of time was sorting belongings of those who became victims; thus he was able to see the selections as well as thousands of different belongings which constituted evidence of how many Jews were killed in the camp. He also heard that SS men were talking about deportations of Hungarian Jews.

21 [ED] It was a dugout. The entrance to it was covered by door frames and other building materials.

22 [ED] For more details see: "Alarm system after finding a prisoner missing" and "General characteristics of escapes" in Lachendro, "Escapes of Prisoners from Auschwitz," Auschwitz-Birkenau Memorial and Museum E-Learning, web, http://lekcja.auschwitz. org/en_15_ucieczki/.

In order to survive Vrba and Wetzler needed to have incredible luck and that is exactly what they had on their side. On numerous occasions they became lost or grew hungry, which forced them to take risks along the way. They were fortunate enough to run into the right people, Polish and Slovakian, to make it over the border into Slovakia. Once in Slovakia, the two men with their wealth of knowledge produced a sixty-page document that contained detailed lists of transports, the infrastructure of the camp and identifications of various Nazi supporters.[23] Vrba and Wetzler dedicated their lives to informing the world of the atrocities within the camp. Although their escape is one of the better known escapes,[24] they were not the first men to successfully escape; and most importantly they were not the first to be in contact with allied governments about what they had witnessed. That honor could go to men such as Captain Witold Pilecki, who is referred to as the volunteer of Auschwitz.

In 1940 a second lieutenant[25] of the Polish Army, Witold Pilecki, purposely got himself arrested and was sent to Auschwitz.[26] Ultimately for three years he was in the camp relaying information outside and building resistance cells within the camps. "Pilecki would write his reports by hand and then have them smuggled out of the camp to the Polish government-in-exile in London."[27] He was one of the first to pass on

23 Świebocki, *Five Escapees from Birkenau*, p. 21. **[ED]** The most important part of the report was the description of the mass extermination of Jewish people and statistics of how many, according to the countries, were killed in gas chambers in the years 1942-1944. The report also included a warning for Hungarian Jews.

24 Vrba and Wetzler, *The Auschwitz Protocol*.

25 On November 11, 1941, he was promoted to lieutenant, and two years later he became a cavalry captain (in Polish, rotmistrz; in German, Rittmeister). However, he was informed that he had been promoted captain only on February 23, 1944.

26 "Against the Odds: Pilecki Excerpt," *YouTube*, posted Oct. 26, 2008, https://www.youtube.com/watch?v=KzxBpQ6ILQw&feature=youtu.be. Also see Adam Cyra, *Polish Military Resistance Movement – On Exhibition*, Google Cultural Institute, https://www.google.com/culturalinstitute/beta/exhibit/gQhxPm00.

27 David de Sola, "The Man Who Volunteered for Auschwitz," *The Atlantic*, 2012, http://www.theatlantic.com/international/archive/2012/10/the-man-who-volunteered-for-auschwitz/263083/, accessed 15 July 2014.

information of the camps, building the resistance network inside that helped numerous prisoners survive.[28] His operation proved successful until 1943 when he feared that his operation was about to be exposed and he needed to escape. His official job in the camp was in the post office so getting word out to his contacts was made easier and sped up his estimated escape time. On April 26, 1943, he along with Jan Redzej and Edmund Ciesielski escaped from Auschwitz after organizing a night shift in the camp bakery located outside the camp.[29] The design of the bakery door was such that it locked from the outside, so once the door closed those inside would be locked in. On the night of the escape the door was kept ajar for the three men to escape and lock their supervisor inside. Jan Redzej was also able to cut the telephone lines in the process of escaping, giving them the essential extra time to evacuate. After arriving back in Warsaw, Pilecki assisted the Polish Home Army and took part in the Warsaw Uprising. He was captured in October, 1944 by German troops, became a POW and was liberated by US soldiers six months later. After the war he returned to Poland and was arrested in 1947, this time as a political threat to the new communist system. He was executed in 1948.[30] The ending of his life illustrates the isolation of information Poland dealt with for forty years after the war. If it was not for his reports during the war, his stories would have been lost forever, which is the case for many others who were silenced during the new occupation. It is estimated that over 800 prisoners attempted to escape from Auschwitz-Birkenau in its five years of operation.[31] Unfortunately with the available data that

28 "Captain Witold Pilecki and the Resistance in Auschwitz," Embassy of Poland in the U.S. YouTube Channel, web, https://www.youtube.com/watch?v=YVjoT5QBirs, accessed 14 July 2014.

29 Michał Gałek and Arkadiusz Klimek, *Witold's Report*, Auschwitz: K and L Press, 2009, p. 39.

30 For more information about Witold Pilecki see: *The Auschwitz Volunteer: Beyond Bravery, Captain Witold Pilecki [Auschwitz Prisoner No. 4859]*, translated by Jarek Garliński from Pilecki's original 1945 *Auschwitz Report*, Los Angeles: Aquila Polonica, 2012.

31 Świebocki, *Auschwitz 1940 – 1945, IV*, p. 232. [ED] According to the latest findings at least 928 prisoners attempted to escape from the Auschwitz camp complex (878 men and 50 women). For 196 prisoners the escape was successful. The escape was also successful

historians have, they can only account for 144 successful attempts and 327 arrests, leaving almost half of the estimated totals unknown. Either these prisoners never survived the journey or their stories have been silenced by other circumstances. Fortunately with the accounts that are available there is still enough information to learn about these people's struggles.

Generally the end goal of escapees was to save their own lives. Prisoners wanted to escape from the camp to stay alive. An additional very important goal was to keep the allies informed of the camps and of the mass murder of Jews, but this is only one aspect of the outcomes escapes provided. Another contributing factor was hope within the camp. The escape by Kazimierz Piechowski in 1942 embodies the concepts of making relationships within the camp, trading supplies and planning each situation.

In the documentary *Uciekinier, the Runaway*, Kazimierz Piechowski tells the story of how grand theft auto saved his life. In 1939 at the age of twenty when Piechowski attempted to get to France, where the Polish army was being formed, he was arrested and sent to Auschwitz. At the camp he worked in Block 11 loading up wagons with corpses that came from the death wall. Similar to Wetzler's experience in the camp morgue, Piechowski almost lost his faith within the camp from what he witnessed on a daily basis. Fortunately he was saved by "Kapo no. Two" who reassigned him to the Hauptwirtschaftslager storehouse located across the street from the main camp.[32] There he worked indoors, but soon after his

---

for 25 other prisoners, but after some time they were captured and incarcerated. The escape of 433 prisoners failed; they were captured and sent to the camp or shot during pursuit. In addition, two escapees from this group were killed by their mates and the other two drowned while crossing a river. For 254 people, no information concerning their fate after leaving the camp was found. Finally, no data was found for another 20 escaped prisoners. See: "Statistical characteristics of escapes" in Lachendro, "Escapes of Prisoners from Auschwitz."

32 Dir. Marek Pawłowski, *Uciekinier, The Runaway*, Telewizja: Zoyda Art Productions, 2007 (DVD). **[ED]** "Kapo no. Two" was Otto Küsel. On May 20, 1940, he was deported to Auschwitz from KL Sachsenhausen in a group of 30 German criminal prisoners. He obtained a camp number 2 and was appointed as Arbeitsdienst, a functionary prisoner responsible for assigning prisoners to jobs. As opposed to others he used his position to help prisoners by sending them, especially the older or the weaker, to so called 'good'

transfer his friend Eugeniusz Bendera learned he might be killed within the coming weeks. The two friends began to plan an escape from the camp. Bendera's privileged job working in the camp garage gave him access to a car, while Piechowski, working in the warehouse, had the potential to obtain uniforms and various supplies.

On Saturday, June 20, 1942, Piechowski, Bendera and two other prisoners,[33] in order to protect friends they left behind in the camp, formed a fake work group.[34] Saturdays were the best days for an escape because the warehouse closed at noon and at that time the SS guards left for the day. After tricking the guards at the gate and telling them that they needed to drop off supplies, the four men successfully reached the warehouse, taking four SS uniforms, ammunition and a car. They left the warehouse disguised as SS men, but their biggest obstacle was a barrier at one of the check posts of the so called "Large guard chain".[35] Fortunately Piechowski spoke German and happened to be wearing a high ranking German official uniform. He was able to trick the guards into opening up the gate, allowing the four

Kommandos where they performed relatively light labor. On December 29, 1942, he escaped from the camp together with three Polish political prisoners.

33 [ED] The two other prisoners were Stanisław Gustaw Jaster and Józef Lempart. Jaster took a report on Auschwitz provided by Witold Pilecki with orders to deliver it to the leaders of the Polish resistance.

34 When a prisoner would escape from a concentration camp the guards would question and torture known acquaintances to try and get information. This moral dilemma of escaping to save your life and endangering the ones you left behind limited various prisoners from escaping. [ED The SS men used cruel methods of repression, and these methods effectively discouraged many prisoners from escaping. In 1941, during roll calls the SS men would choose a group of ten or more prisoners from the work detail or the block to which the escapee belonged. Then the chosen ones were led to the cells in Block 11 where, without food and drink, they died of starvation after a few up to a dozen days. In the later period, Auschwitz authorities would bring to the camp the relatives of the escapees and find a place where the prisoners could see them well. Next to them, a board was installed informing readers about the reasons for bringing them to the camp. Then the arrested family members were sent to the camp, where they would become prisoners themselves; some of them perished in the camp. See more: "Repressions for escapes" in Lachendro, "Escapes of Prisoners from Auschwitz."

35 Lachendro, "Escapes of Prisoners from Auschwitz."

men to pass through and escape. Tadeusz Sobolewicz could remember the great psychological impact on the camp after Piechowski escaped.[36] What makes his escape unique is that Piechowski escaped through the front gate. It was common for escapees to steal civilian clothes or even SS uniforms, but taking a car and driving right past the camp authority is remarkable.

Like most instances when discussing the Holocaust, the overwhelming majority of cases ended in disappointment and death. As the findings of Henryk Świebocki illustrate, the majority of escapes were unsuccessful.[37] When luck is a major factor in the success of the plan, the outcomes usually do not turn out. Even if a prisoner planned a detailed escape, new obstacles would arise, forcing quick alterations. Essentially this would result in the death of those involved and cause a drop in morale amongst those that might become new escapees. An example of this is the story of Mala Zimetbaum and Edek Galiński.

Amongst the prisoners of the camp the story of Mala Zimetbaum, a Jewish messenger in Birkenau, and Edek Galiński, a Polish prisoner, became a source of both positive and negative responses. On the one hand these two prisoners were able to find love and forget about the place they lived.[38] Their fellow prisoners saw this couple as exceptional and grew to follow and respect them.[39] Their legend grew even more because in 1944 they were able to escape from the camp together. Wieslaw Kielar, who was a friend of Galiński, recalled people being overjoyed and constantly talking about the couple.[40] They became symbols of freedom in the camp, but all this would become undone on July 7, 1944, as Zimetbaum and

---

36 Pawłowski, *Uciekinier*.

37 Świebocki, *Auschwitz 1940 – 1945, IV*, p. 232. See also Lachendro, "Escapes of Prisoners from Auschwitz."

38 Adam Cyra, "Edward Galiński" and "Mala Zimetbaum," '*Traces of Them Remain...*' – *Inscriptions from the Block of Death On Exhibition*, Google Cultural Institute, https://www.google.com/culturalinstitute/beta/exhibit/5QLSTeQR2E--LA?hl=en.

39 "The Auschwitz Chronicles – Love," The State Museum Auschwitz- Birkenau Documentary Series, 2004.

40 Wiesław Kielar, *Anus Mundi, 1,500 Days in Auschwitz/Birkenau*, New York: Times Books, 1980, p. 241.

Galiński were arrested and then brought back to Auschwitz. Kielar could recall seeing the growing number of corpses lying in the mud from spontaneous escape attempts after their capture.[41] Zimetbaum and Galiński's story shows what power escapees held for their fellow prisoners. When some failed, the morale of the camp was hit hard and the best way to improve things was to accomplish successful escapes. Successful escapes created hope, and hope guided people to continue living and moving forward, despite the price prisoners had to pay for the escapes of others.

For the prisoners of Auschwitz, the idea of escaping was a complex concept to manage. Numerous components of an escape had to be extensively planned out to allow for the chance of success. This is what makes the stories of escapees from Auschwitz exceptional. Not only were some viewed as heroes within the camps, but some were also able to inform the outside world of the atrocities being performed inside the camp. These physical escapes are an important form of resistance against the concentration camp. These heroes arose in hope that their actions would outlive their lives.[42] For the historians of the Holocaust the task now is to continue telling their stories and spread their information to as many people as possible. These escapees risked their lives and often the lives of their families and their fellow prisoners to share their stories. In order to prevent this from happening again society needs to continue sharing their knowledge.

41 Kielar, *Anus Mundi*, p. 250.
42 Kielar, *Anus Mundi*, p. 240.

Vivian Tsang

Passive Resistance:
Keeping Humanity Alive in the Fences of Auschwitz

"I have more faith in Hitler than in anyone else. He alone has kept his promises, all his promises, to the Jewish people".[1] Elie Wiesel recalled a conversation he had with his neighbor while in the hospital block of KL Auschwitz. The words of his neighbor held true for many, as Auschwitz was a place where God's existence was questioned; where faith was put to the test; a place where individuality and personality were taken away; and a place designed to reduce people to nothing. Auschwitz was a place where Germans intended to dehumanize and kill the people imprisoned there. In attempts to preserve what was left of themselves (identity, personality, religion, culture), prisoners engaged in acts of passive resistance that could have placed them into even greater danger. What the Germans sought to destroy, some prisoners fought to maintain, even in the face of death. I will first examine the dehumanizing process of Auschwitz, and then forms of passive resistance, with particular focus on art, culture and religion.

The term "resistance" in the scope of Auschwitz falls under three categories: actions associated with saving prisoners in both a physical and moral sense, tasks which the prisoner community performed in attempts to document crimes against humanity at the camp (the Underground) and

---

1   Elie Wiesel, *The Night Trilogy*, New York: Hill and Wang, 2008, p. 99.

finally all actions aimed at undermining the German system.[2] I will focus on the first category, specifically on saving prisoners in a moral sense.

The Germans sought to dehumanize all of their prisoners. For many, this began when people were shipped in overpacked cattle cars from all over Europe to Auschwitz. In the case of the Jewish people, they were forced into cramped, dirty, and diseased ghettos, while having to wear distinguishing stars – the Star of David.[3] Upon arrival at Auschwitz, prisoners were pushed around and forced to hand over their belongings. Those deemed fit to work were then stripped down, shaved, given a striped uniform and had their names replaced with a number and a colored triangle. The colored triangles reduced people from professors, doctors, teachers, parents and so on into groups based on nationality, sexuality, or faith. Those deemed unfit to work were marched to the gas chambers and deceived even in their last minutes of life. It is important to reiterate that only those who passed the selection process were formally registered in camp records. People who were sent straight to the gas chambers were not accounted for; thus we do not have complete records as to the numbers of people who were imprisoned and murdered at Auschwitz-Birkenau.

Camp conditions also promoted the destruction of culture and humanity. The workday was extremely exhausting, as prisoners were given very little food and were forced to do extremely hard labor in all sorts of conditions, while being subject to beatings at any time. As Primo Levi described, "the discipline in both the Lager and Buna[4] is in no way relaxed:

2 Henryk Świebocki, *Auschwitz 1940-1945: Central Issues in the History of the Camp*, Vol. 4: The Resistance Movement, ed. Wacław Długoborski and Franciszek Piper, trans. William Brand. Oświęcim: The Auschwitz-Birkenau State Museum, 2000, p. 15.

3 [ED] In the General Government Jewish people were forced to wear armbands with the David's star. In other occupied Polish territories or other countries occupied by the Germans they usually wore patches in the shape of David's stars.

4 [ED] Buna was the name of the synthetic-rubber plant, which was being constructed by the German IG Farben chemical concern several kilometers east of Oświęcim. Prisoners of Auschwitz concentration camp began working at the construction site in April, 1941, marching there at first and later traveling by train. At the end of October, 1942, the separate Monowitz camp was established for prisoners. The living conditions were

the work, cold and hunger are sufficient to fill up every thinking moment".[5] The lethal combination of malnutrition and hard labor quickly led to catabolysis: when the body begins to break down fat and muscle in order to keep the person alive. Jewish prisoners who had a kosher diet could no longer maintain this – if one did not eat whatever was given to them, they would starve even quicker and die. This was an aspect of Jewish culture that could not have been maintained. After long and strenuous days of work, many prisoners were simply too exhausted to do anything except sleep in cramped wooden bunks. The camp also created a culture of fear with a type of morality that does not exist outside of the barbed wire fences. Prisoners would steal from their loved ones, prisoners would inform on one other for an extra crust of bread; in short, many would do anything for whatever they could get their hands on. While this was not the case for all of the prisoners, the conditions of the camp made it easy for one to do whatever one needed to survive another day.

Prisoners were forbidden from practicing religion, and religious leaders as well as members of religious groups were often persecuted and ridiculed. Nikodem Pieszczoch recalls seeing a group of Jews forced to sing the song "O Jerusalem" under the direction of a Catholic priest who was bloodied.[6] This was not a rare occurrence: Erwin Michalik stated that he had seen a Jewish prisoner and a priest, who was wearing a cassock, taken out of a line and forced to sing vulgar songs.[7] They were beaten unconscious because they refused to sing. Michalik added that he witnessed multiple incidents like the one described. It was not only religion that was forbidden: anything could be considered forbidden, and rules regarding what was forbidden or not were always changing. With that in mind, "anything could be resistance, since everything was forbidden.

better there than in Birkenau, but due to the hard labor many prisoners died or fell victim to selection. It was liquidated in January, 1945.

5   Primo Levi, *Survival in Auschwitz*. New York: Simon and Schuster, 1996, p. 126.

6   Nikodem Pieszczoch, *Auschwitz-Birkenau Museum Testimony*, APMA-B Statement Collection, vol. 72, p. 8.

7   Erwin Michalik, *Auschwitz-Birkenau Museum Testimony*, APMA-B Statement Collection, vol. 65, p. 127.

Any act qualified as resistance as long as it created the impression that the prisoners had retained something of their former personalities and individualities".[8] These acts that created impressions of former identities include artwork, craft, literature, religious activities, and simply things people did in their lives before Auschwitz. Primo Levi realized:

> The Lager was a great machine to reduce us to beasts, we must not become beasts; that even in this place one can survive, and therefore one must want to survive, to tell the story, to bear witness; and that to survive we must force ourselves to save at least the skeleton, the scaffolding, the form of civilization.[9]

Resistance was to save this "skeleton" of civilization, and to fight against the Nazi system to retain humanity in Auschwitz.

Abraham Maslow, a Jewish-American psychologist, proposed a hierarchy of human needs, published first in a 1943 paper,[10] but, in 1954, developed further in a book.[11] He theorized that humans have lower level needs that must be met before upper level needs could be fulfilled. Starting from the bottom, humans would first need their physiological needs met (hunger and thirst), followed by safety needs, and finally having their need to belong and be loved met. Once those three have been fulfilled, the person can them move up to higher level needs which are self-esteem and self-actualization needs. Practicing religion and engaging in risky behavior would be in the category of higher level needs. If we apply Maslow's hierarchy of needs to Auschwitz, we can clearly see that the lower level needs would not have been met, yet some prisoners managed to fulfill their upper level needs and engage in philosophical, artistic, and religious endeavors. The actions of these prisoners challenge Maslow's theory, but

---

8 Andrea Devoto qtd. in Świebocki, *Auschwitz 1940-1945*, p. 14.

9 Levi, *Survival in Auschwitz*, p. 41.

10 Abraham Maslow, "A Theory of Human Motivation," *Psychological Review*, 50(4), 1943, pp. 370-396.

11 Abraham Maslow, *Motivation and Personality*, New York: Harper Press, 1954.

also makes us question how these prisoners were able to behave this way, given the inhumane conditions they were in.

With the exhaustion of the extreme workday and lack of nutrition, many prisoners could not muster the strength and energy to engage in acts of passive resistance. Some forms of passive resistance required one to organize materials as well. This would be so in the case of creating artwork or looking for certain objects for religious purposes (for example: prayer books, cups, cloth). In an interview with Dr. Piotr Setkiewicz and Dr. Jacek Lachendro, I learned that prisoners who were able to somewhat carry on practicing their religion or create artwork were those who were more fortunate than others, which usually meant having a better job indoors. These jobs could come with extra benefits such as food and protection, and these prisoners had more time for themselves where they could create art, practice religion, or simply think.[12] Primo Levi described how being chosen to work indoors drastically changed one's chances of survival: "This means a strong probability of not falling seriously ill, of not being frozen, of overcoming the selections ... all this is a gift of fortune, to be enjoyed as intensely as possible and at once; for there is no certainty about tomorrow".[13] With this fortunate turn of events, Levi is not beaten and can "steal and sell soap and petrol without risk"[14] and also had the opportunity to "write what I would never dare tell anyone".[15] While it is true that those with better jobs could have more freedom and accessibility, it is not to say that the average prisoner could not manage to acquire materials needed to write, draw, or practice religion.

Zofia Stępień-Bator drew portraits of other prisoners, including that of Mala Zimetbaum.[16] She began creating her artwork while in the hospital block of Birkenau. Stępień-Bator's portraits were not simply of the

---

12 Dr. Piotr Setkiewicz and Dr. Jacek Lachendro, Personal interview, 14 May 2014.
13 Levi, *Survival in Auschwitz*, p. 140.
14 Ibid., p. 141.
15 Ibid., p. 142.
16 **[ED]** To learn more about Mala Zimetbaum please read Adam Cyra, "The Romeo and Juliet of our times", *Pro Memoria*, 5-6, pp. 25-28.

prisoners themselves, but it showed them with hair, civilian clothing, and even makeup. She strived to paint the prisoners in a brighter way. In her own words, "Everything was so ugly, grey, sad and dirty that I wanted to introduce a little beauty into my drawings".[17] Stępień-Bator's art is resistance because, as said earlier, creating art was forbidden, as well as attaining the materials for it. It is also important to note that her artwork not only served as an outlet of creativity and an expression of agency, but it also reminded prisoners of their individuality and humanity.

Peter Edel drew a self-portrait called Autoportret. His drawing shows two versions of himself: as a prisoner and how he was before internment. The art in itself is a form of resistance, but the content further adds to this, as he is trying to preserve what he was like before. Something else to take note of is what he wrote on the painting. It is a monologue. "Who is that?" "Yes, that's you!"[18] illustrates how different prisoners looked compared to before – that even they themselves could not recognize who they were. What he wrote is true for many prisoners – it was very difficult for prisoners to locate family members based on looks, as everyone looked different with a shaved head, but everyone looked the same in the same striped uniforms. Edel's drawing is a form of resistance, and shows how prisoners tried to introduce some aspect from the days of freedom into the camp, just like Zofia Stępień -Bator. Being an artist in Auschwitz could serve as a way of regaining one's agency.

In a post-war painting named *Kaddish* by David Olère, a member of the Sonderkommando, he shows Jewish prisoners with a prayer book, a talid, and a candle. They are reciting Kaddish, the Jewish mourner's prayer for the dead.[19] This painting sheds some light on the secret forms of resistance within the camps. Since all personal items, including Torahs,

17 Zofia Stępień-Bator in Jerzy Dałek et al., *Cierpienie i nadzieja*, trans. Jolanta Kosiec, Katowice: Krajowa Agencja Wydawnicza, 1989, p. 5.
18 Peter Edel in Dałek et al., *Cierpienie i nadzieja*, p. 3.
19 David Olère, *Kaddish*, oil on board, *Ghetto Fighters House Archives*, Ghetto Fighter's House, Israel, 1954.

talids, and candles were seized upon arrival, prisoners would have had to organize with other prisoners working in areas that had access to these items, particularly those in the Kanada[20] warehouses. These items could not simply be handed over and taken back to the barracks; they had to be smuggled, and often cost prisoners food or other items. It was not only extremely risky and dangerous to organize for these items, but also keeping them hidden from authorities in the camp was a challenge. The painting shows the great lengths that prisoners were willing to go to maintain their religious practices.

Zalmen Gradowski also recalls when "several dozen Jews gathered to recite the greeting to the Sabbath".[21] He comments on how the Jews "suppress all the protest that throws their hearts and souls into turmoil each day".[22] Finally, he mentions that a minyan (a group of ten male Jews who were necessary for all public services and reading of the Torah) was always present, which demonstrates how strongly this group of Jewish prisoners chose to abide by their culture and religion. There could have very well been an informer during these religious meetings, but the prisoners chose continue their religious activity, despite the risks that doing so carried.

Wacław Stacherski described a secret mass that was being held in Block 11. He states, "Yesterday, Sunday, I listened through the cellar windows to the mass that was being said in secret upstairs. Afterwards, I took a communion. I took communion. The wafer was lowered to me on a string".[23] This account again shows the lengths prisoners went through to be able to continue to practice religion. While we do not know how many

---

20 [ED] The colloquial name used within the camp for warehouses in which the property plundered from Jews who were victims of extermination was stored. In 1944 up to two thousand prisoners were employed at the Kanada warehouses unloading items and sorting them. They had access to luggage, where they found food, clothes, shoes, jewelry, cigarettes, etc. This surely explains the name of the warehouses and labor units there – Canada was then regarded as a land of prosperity.

21 Zalmen Gradowski in Świebocki, *Auschwitz 1940-1945*, p. 359.

22 Ibid., p. 360.

23 Wacław Stacherski in Świebocki, *Auschwitz 1940-1945*, p. 339.

people participated in this secret mass or any secret religious activity, we must also remember that there were informers all over the camps. There could have been an informer during the secret mass; something the prisoners risked during their activity.

We also learn in Jerzy Kijowski's account that even a confession had to be organized and done as unsuspectingly as possible.[24] Secret masses were also held in the basement of Block 15 so that the sound of the pumps would block out the singing during mass. Artur Karpik recalls how many Catholics concealed their religious feelings during the day and waited until they were in bed to pray.[25] Religion, like art, served as a way of regaining a sense of belonging. Religious groups could give a sense of community, while simply believing that God is omnipresent reminded prisoners that they were not alone.[26]

While some prisoners met with other prisoners in secret for confession or religious service, some prisoners questioned the existence of God. In *Night*, Wiesel hears a man ask, "Where is God?" while a child was being hung. Wiesel says, "And from within me, I heard a voice answer: 'Where He is? This is where – hanging here from this gallows . . .'".[27] It is interesting that Wiesel thought this way, yet he mentions that on the eve of Rosh Hashanah, he did not drink his soup until after the prayer was complete. At the same time that he was faithful, he was angry with his God. He questions God's actions, and says he no longer pleaded for anything. That said though, he still recited Kaddish for those who had died, and for himself as well. Wiesel's memoir is a great example showing how Judaism

24 Jerzy Kijowski, *Auschwitz-Birkenau Museum Testimony*, APMA-B Statement Collection, vol. 73, p. 17.

25 Artur Karpik, "Spostrzeżenia moje odnośnie praktyk religijnych w obozach koncentracyjnych," *Auschwitz-Birkenau Museum Testimony*, APMA-B Statement Collection, vol. 83, p. 35.

26 [ED] To read more about the religious life of the Christian prisoners see: Teresa Wontor-Cichy, "Christian clergy and the religious life at Auschwitz," Auschwitz-Birkenau Memorial and Museum E-Learning, web, http://lekcja.auschwitz.org/en_18_duchowienstwo/.

27 Wiesel, *The Night Trilogy*, p. 83.

dictated the way in which Jewish people lived. Even when their religion was taken away, their culture still existed. Within Auschwitz, practicing religion was strictly forbidden but some of the Jewish prisoners managed to still maintain some aspects of their culture, which could be considered a form of passive resistance.

Although the question of "where was God during the Holocaust?" is beyond the scope of this paper, Zbigniew Nosowski maintains that abandoning religion and God (in the context of the Holocaust) could be understood as giving victory to Hitler,[28] which is an idea that some tried to avoid. Some praised God during the good times, and cursed him during the bad. These arguments test faith in the existence of God, but if one is arguing with God, then in theory, one still believes in God. Arguing with God is an act of faith (thus, resistance) in itself, whether intentional or not.

Teaching and learning were also ways of retaining culture and regaining one's sense of agency and humanity inside Auschwitz. There were some 1,153 registered Polish schoolteachers at KL Auschwitz; however, the data is not conclusive as prisoners hid their true professions at registration to avoid selections, and potentially to get into better work commandos. Like religious priests, teachers and university professors were part of the Polish intelligentsia, and thus capable of organizing and managing resistance. To suppress any potential opposition from these people, the Germans imprisoned them in various camps. Because they had little to no experience with hard labor, many of them died fairly quickly when exposed to treacherous working days. Teachers also hid their profession from others because of the particularly cruel treatment that they faced. Czesław Ostańkowicz witnessed a teacher who was beaten to death with a stick after he had been caught teaching history.[29] But still, there are accounts of teachers who attempted to educate prisoners

28 Zbigniew Nosowski, *Where was God during the Shoah?* Oświęcim: The Auschwitz-Birkenau State Museum Reflection Room, [15 May 2014].

29 Czesław Ostańkowicz qtd. in Jacek Lachendro "Attempts to teach made by Polish teachers-prisoners of KL Auschwitz," *Clandestine Teaching Polish Female Prisoners in Ravensbrück Concentration Camp*, Sztutowo: Museum Stutthof, 2015. p. 87.

despite the danger and discrimination they faced from the Germans. "Lessons" were taught in various ways in the free time (in the evenings after roll calls or on Sundays): on walks around the camp, behind the barracks along what is known as "Birkenallee", or while lying on bunks, listening.[30] However, a key component of these lessons was trust. These prisoners faced violent punishment or even death if they were caught. One may wonder why a teacher would risk so much and put themselves in danger for the benefit of others. Survivor accounts show that often teachers felt responsible for younger prisoners. They did not want these younger prisoners to have an education gap, and thought beyond the camp – they wanted their students to be caught up for when they finally left the camp and went back to school. Teachers also feared that without some education in the camp, the younger prisoners would be demoralized.[31] Much like what art and religion did for other prisoners, education had a positive effect on both the teachers and their students. Engaging in literature, critical thinking, and various subjects ranging from Polish history to physics offered a temporary escape from the barbed wire confines the prisoners faced every day.

Adam Zych notes that "literary creation . . . [is] the manifestation of revolt against enslavement".[32] There were many poems written by prisoners inside Auschwitz. The subject matter ranged from personal reflections to describing life and death inside the camp. It is also worth noting that talks on Polish history and literature strengthened Polish prisoners' sense of national community and strengthened their belief that an independent Poland would be regained[33]. Mieczysława Chylińska recalls:

We were returning the elements of knowledge buried somewhere at the bottom of the memory of life, starting from the basic elements. It is hard

30 Lachendro "Attempts to teach," p. 87.
31 Lachendro "Attempts to teach," p. 88.
32 *The Auschwitz Poems: An Anthology*, ed. Adam Zych, Oświęcim: Auschwitz-Birkenau State Musem, 2011, p. 7.
33 Lachendro, "Attempts to teach," p. 88.

to describe how much we enjoyed that recalling, discussing. Reacting in defence of intellectual values led to recuperating dignity, despite all, what continued to happen in the camp.[34]

Thus, informal prisoner education in Auschwitz served as a way of regaining culture and agency for both the teachers and the students they taught. It also served as an escape from the realities of the camp, and restored dignity in the prisoners.

In a place where faiths were often broken, where connections with God were severed, where people transformed into beings with no will to live, and where acts of humanity seem like rare occurrences, some prisoners managed to resist the complete dehumanization forced upon them by the Germans. Though acts of passive resistance were often done within the confines of one's mind, bunk or a secret location and did not involve sabotage or armed action, they did preserve some of the morality, culture, and personality in the prisoners, which could have a large impact on survival in Auschwitz. This type of resistance is just as important as active resistance, as it served to take back and keep something that the Germans had tried so hard to pry away from the prisoners – their humanity and dignity. Furthermore, a single act of passive resistance resulted in positive effects for those involved. For instance, teachers fulfilled their passion to teach, while students had their thirst for learning quenched. Both parties regained a sense of agency. This was the same in the case of artwork and practicing religion as well. What we today classify as acts of passive resistance could have simply been a way for prisoners to regain a sense of identity or belonging. This meant that prisoners were no longer solely defined by their colored triangles. They were more than *just* a colored triangle and a number. The actions of these prisoners show that even in KL Auschwitz, humanity manages to shine through. We often forget that the prisoners were still people – people with emotions, people with bad and good days, people with purpose. Even though they were stripped

---

34 Mieczysława Chylińska qtd. in Lachendro, "Attempts to teach," p. 91.

of absolutely everything, they were still people, and they behaved how people would outside the fences of Auschwitz.

In conclusion, I would like to share what Elie Wiesel described as "the first human words" he heard upon arrival at KL Auschwitz:

> Comrades, you are now in the concentration camp Auschwitz. Ahead of you lies a long road paved with suffering. Don't lose hope. You have already eluded the worst danger: the selection. Therefore, you must muster your strength and keep your faith. We shall see the day of liberation. Have faith in life, a thousand times faith. By driving out despair, you will move away from death. Hell does not last forever ... And now, here is a prayer, or rather, a piece of advice: let there be camaraderie among you. We are all brothers and share the same fate. The same smoke hovers over all our heads. Help each other. That is the only way to survive.[35]

---

35 Wiesel, *The Night Trilogy*, p. 59.

Joanne Ng

Music in KL Auschwitz:
An Exploration of the Role and Meaning of Music at Auschwitz

Introduction

The existence of music within Konzentrationslager Auschwitz is paradoxical in essence. How was it possible that creation and destruction, beauty and atrocity, lived alongside one another? Music within the barbed wires served contradictory roles, for both pleasure and practicality. This paper will explore the perception of music at Auschwitz by oppressors and the oppressed in the camp, what music signified and what functions it served. An in-depth view of the orchestra[1] – the main provider of camp music

---

1 [ED] There were some orchestras consisting of prisoners which played in different parts of Auschwitz camp complex. The largest one, which comprised about 120 musicians, functioned in Auschwitz I from March, 1941, to January, 1945. In Auschwitz II-Birkenau a men's orchestra was established in August, 1942 and a women's orchestra in April of the following year (to read more on the women's orchestra see: Helena Dunicz-Niwińska, *One of the Girls in the Band: The Memoirs of a Violinist from Birkenau*, Oświęcim: Auschwitz-Birkenau State Museum, 2014). The two Birkenau orchestras remained in existence until the autumn of 1944 when the majority of the musicians were transferred to the camps in the depths of the Third Reich. The orchestra in Monowitz was founded in August, 1943 and played until the liquidation of the camp in January, 1945. The men's orchestras consisted of 30 to 40 musicians, and the women's of more than 40. The main task of musicians was playing marches near the gate when the prisoners went out to work and when they returned. The musicians also gave concerts on Sunday afternoons for the SS men and sometimes for their fellow prisoners. The repertoire of those concerts was mostly German and Austrian classical music, excerpts from operas

– followed by a case study of the women's orchestra and its conductor, Alma Rosé, will help explain that Bach and Beethoven enthusiasts did in fact thrive in conditions that authorized and cultivated daily acts of cruelty.

The Orchestra

Polish political prisoners were the first to suggest establishing a camp orchestra – "Lagerkapelle" – and by December, 1940, the SS granted them permission to request instruments from home. The purpose of the orchestra was to help fill the prisoners' spare time – and promptly, news spread that the recently organized orchestra was searching for musicians. Though the inspiration for and creation of the orchestra came from prisoner-musicians wanting to "play for themselves and their comrades",[2] for the SS, the most imperative function of the prisoner band was to have the musicians play during the departure and arrival of labor crews.[3] The rhythm of the music greatly facilitated the inmates in marching in step with one another, which made counting the prisoners much more efficient for the SS. Additional assignments included playing official concerts and during the holidays, all of which were for the Nazis' entertainment. [PICTURE 6]

and operettas, and popular melodies or songs. There were other, smaller ensembles in Birkenau (in the so called Zigeunerlager and the Theresienstadt family camp), and in some larger sub-camps. Joanne Ng focuses in this paper on the music played mainly by men's orchestra in Auschwitz I and the women's orchestra in Birkenau.

2 Jacek Lachendro, "The Orchestras in KL Auschwitz," *Auschwitz Studies*, 27, 2015, p. 12.

3 Guido Fackler, "Official Camp Orchestras in Auschwitz," *Music and the Holocaust*, web, http://holocaustmusic.ort.org/places/camps/death-camps/auschwitz/camp-orchestras/, accessed 16 December 2016.

Perception of Music at Auschwitz

Music also turned into a tool for the SS to exert their control over prisoners. They exploited talent and art to further propagate terror within the camp; music was thus utilized to humiliate and to harm the victims psychologically.[4] This was especially evident when the band played jubilant marches or prisoners were compelled to sing German patriotic or cheerful songs. Ultimately, twisting the intent of music as an outlet for beauty and creation was another way to demonstrate unlimited SS power and cruelty.

Music differed from other forms of art in the camp because each and every prisoner encountered music in Auschwitz during their incarceration. The melodies played by the orchestra were inescapable to all as they marched to and from work. It was a universal experience and perhaps the only unique commonality shared among all captives and oppressors alike. Primo Levi describes these "tunes", "marches and popular songs", as follows:

> They lie engraven on our minds and will be the last thing in Lager that we shall forget; they are the voice of the Lager, the perceptible expression of its geometrical madness, of the resolution of others to annihilate us first as men in order to kill us more slowly afterwards.[5]

Music, like any other art, is experienced subjectively and is a platform for various interpretations and meanings. While the SS used marches as a tool for intimidation, coordination and efficiency, they were most likely a reminder for the prisoners of the desolation and barrenness of their

---

4   Juliane Brauer, "How Can Music Be Torturous?: Music in Nazi Concentration and Extermination Camps," *Music & Politics*, 10(1), 2016, pp. 1-34.
5   Primo Levi, *Survival in Auschwitz: The Nazi Assault on Humanity*, New York: Simon and Schuster, 1996, p. 51.

lives. There was also a fundamental difference in the meaning of music for members of the orchestra and for other prisoners. For non-members of the orchestra, "the emotional impact of these scenes in contrast with the lively melodies played by the orchestra constituted a macabre dissonance", one that became particularly noticeable during the march back from work.[6] It is not a surprise then that the prisoners' view of music was one filled with contempt and that music morphed into an outlet through which to pour out their grievances.

Music was also irrevocably linked with life outside the camp; glimpses of a past life added to the suffering of many prisoners. Hate for the band members was also a reality, especially when they were perceived by non-members as lapdogs belonging to the SS, catering to their every whim even to the point of playing for their private parties.[7] In this instance, the distinction between prisoners and orchestra members was enough to further propagate unjust hierarchies, envy and misdirected hate. Musicians were wrongly accused of "living in 'silken' conditions and looking aloofly on the sufferings of their peers".[8]

6 Lachendro, "The Orchestras in KL Auschwitz," p. 37.
7 Richard Newman and Karen Kirtley, *Alma Rosé: Vienna to Auschwitz*, Portland: Amadeus Press, 2000, p. 267.
8 Lachendro, "The Orchestras in KL Auschwitz," p. 104. [ED] This information refers more to the women's orchestra than to men's ensembles. On the basis of the former prisoners' testimonies and memoirs "one might have the impression that the number of listeners having negative or ambivalent attitudes to the orchestra was greater in the women's sector than in the men's camp. The women prisoners took a more emotional attitude to music, and to a greater degree pointed out the dissonance between their grim situation and the sometimes merry music played by the orchestra ... One might also come away with the impression that some women prisoners noticed more frequently the contrast between their own appearance and living conditions, and those of the orchestra members ... It might ... be assumed that the contrast between living conditions of the women from the "Lagerkapelle" and the "ordinary" prisoners in the majority was so great that it evoked a range of negative emotions among the latter, and lodged deeply in their memory (more strongly than occurred among the prisoners in the men's camps)". See more: Lachendro, "The Orchestras in KL Auschwitz," pp. 98-99.

Role of Music for Prisoners

Playing in the orchestra provided opportunities for prisoners to improve their lives and it increased their chances of survival. "Membership in the Lagerkapelle did not indeed mean exemption from work, but it did offer an opportunity to be employed inside the camp",[9] and musicians received higher rations of food, both of which were clear privileges.[10] Many prisoners believed that being in the orchestra could save a life. Accordingly, they urged friends who could play an instrument to audition. Franciszek Stryj describes how being accepted to the orchestra was actually a question of "life and death". He recounts his audition for a position in the orchestra when, after having stopped playing, he asked himself: „Had I won my freedom, or the crematorium chimney?"[11] The urgency of the prisoners' situation would often also lead to a much higher tolerance towards some of the bandmasters' harsh behavior: "musicians [were able to] turn a blind eye to [bandmaster Nierychło's] behavior" and tolerate his temperament solely because the benefits of being in the orchestra made his strictness and outbursts bearable.[12]

Female prisoners likened the first conductor of the women's band, Zofia Czaykowska, to "an angel who had come to take [girls] by the hand"

---

9 [ED] This information refers to men's orchestras at Auschwitz camp complex. Musicians from the women's orchestra were exempted from work.

10 Ibid., pp. 26-27. [ED] However, it has to be emphasized, these "privileges" did not protect the musicians from sickness and death in the camp.

11 Ibid., p. 17.

12 Ibid., p. 14. [ED] Before the war Franciszek Nierychło played the oboe during recording sessions for the Polish Radio and in the orchestra at one of the theatres in Cracow. He was deported to Auschwitz on June 20, 1940, and received number 994 during the registration. In March, 1941, he was appointed the bandmaster and conductor of the orchestra. He imposed strict discipline on the musicians because he was trying to force them to play at the highest possible level. The prisoners themselves realized that playing in the orchestra increased their chances of surviving the camp, which inclined them to put up Nierychło's brutal treatment. See more: Lachendro, "The Orchestras in KL Auschwitz," pp. 14-15.

whenever she offered a position in the developing orchestra.[13] Entering the band provided an opportunity to live, usually in better conditions: a chance that could not be passed up. One member of the orchestra described her audition saying that she "did not realize that [her] life depended on the audition that day" and later added that she "still did not know that [she] had the best place in the concentration camp".[14]

Musical talent was an enviable commodity because such skill permitted prisoners to break away from experiencing themselves as "undifferentiated, passive, and powerless".[15] It was also something that individual prisoners tangibly benefited from. In Emilio Jani's case, his "connection with the orchestra grew looser, presumably because he performed more frequently for functionaries as a way of obtaining additional food".[16] Furthermore, the ability to play an instrument provided a mental escape from the physical confines of the camp. Thus, music became valuable and even gave prisoners such as Emilio the ability to bargain for better living conditions. Adam Kopyciński appropriately summed it up:

13 Newman and Kirtley, *Alma Rosé*, p. 233. [ED] Zofia Czaykowska was a teacher. She was deported to Auschwitz on April 27th, 1942, in the first transport of Polish women political prisoners (receiving number 6873). In April, 1943, she was appointed the director and a conductor of the orchestra in Birkenau. Czaykowska prepared the repertoire, led rehearsals, and conducted during playing of marches for the labor units. Because she had little experience at conducting, and most of women were amateurs, the level of playing was not high. Despite this, the orchestra started functioning and thanks to Czaykowska many young girls were saved. See more: Lachendro, "The Orchestras in KL Auschwitz," pp. 78-79.

14 Newman and Kirtley, *Alma Rosé*, p. 233.

15 Guido Fackler, "'We all feel this music is infernal . . .': Music on Command in Auschwitz," *The Last Expression: Art and Auschwitz*, ed. David Mickenberg, Corinne Granof, and Peter Hayes, Evanston: Northwestern University Press, 2003, p. 124.

16 Lachendro, "The Orchestras in KL Auschwitz," p. 22. [ED] Emilio Jani was a soloist from La Scala in Milan. He was deported in the transport of Jews from Italy on April 10, 1944. He sang for the prisoners registering new arrivals and made an impression on them. He was admitted to the orchestra in the main camp and sang during Sunday concerts in the summer of 1944.

Thanks to its power and suggestiveness, music strengthened in the camp listeners what was most important—their true nature. Perhaps that is why many certainly tried instinctively to make a certain cult of this most beautiful of the arts, which precisely there in camp condition could be, and certainly was, medicine for the sick soul of the prisoners.[17]

This type of medicine provided psychological strength and in time, became a form of resistance.

There were many instances of resistance that were of a musical nature, some of which included circus-like shows, impromptu birthday serenades and illegal celebrations. These occurrences offered comfort and peace – an escape "beyond the barbed wire to a far-away world of beauty that had vanished".[18] When the prisoners chose to appreciate the joys of music, humanity remained intact within the camp – an aspect that was precious to prisoners. Creating music became a way for musician-prisoners to help encourage their fellow inmates and even boost the mood. Kopyciński recalled that by 1944, the band would start playing American marches by John Phillip Sousa every time there was optimistic news from the world outside the barbed wires.[19]

Moreover, musical resistance came from regular inmates as well through the singing of their respective national anthems and folk songs. According to prisoner Marie Claude Vaillant-Couturier there was for example the case of a group of female prisoners that sang the French anthem on their way to the gas chambers.[20]

---

17 Newman and Kirtley, *Alma Rosé*, p. 267. [ED] Adam Kopyciński was a conductor of choirs and worked in the music department at the Polish Radio in Cracow before the war. He was deported to Auschwitz on January 8, 1942, and received the number 25294 during registration. After several weeks he was admitted to the orchestra in the main camp, playing the piano and from time to time conducting in the place of the bandmaster Franciszek Nierychło. In May, 1944, Adam Kopyciński became a conductor and bandmaster of the orchestra. He held these posts until the liquidation of the camp in January, 1945.
18 Newman and Kirtley, *Alma Rosé*, p. 265.
19 Lachendro, "The Orchestras in KL Auschwitz," p. 38.
20 Newman and Kirtley, *Alma Rosé*, p. 239.

Band member Anita Lasker-Wallfisch also confirms that membership in the orchestra gave her the possibility of gaining a professional identity.[21] She states that though she "may no longer have had a name," she was still identifiable and "could be referred to . . . [as] 'the cellist'".[22] Having an identity – something to claim as one's own and to which one can relate – was very important. Primo Levi attests to this: "Nothing belongs to them anymore . . . they will even take away our name; and if we want to keep it we will have to find in ourselves the strength to do so".[23] Following this rationale, Lasker-Wallfisch, and most likely the other band members as well, found their strength through their ability to make music and thus stay in the orchestra. In doing so, they managed to keep a part of themselves, be it their identities or dignity.

Music presented an outlet for prisoners – especially for the musicians – to use as an escape from their daily struggles and as a way to cope. Creating and playing music, as described by Lasker-Wallfisch, fostered powerful moments; it was a

> link with the outside, with beauty, with culture – a complete escape into an imaginary and unattainable world . . . in the truest sense . . . we lifted ourselves above the inferno of Birkenau into a sphere where we could not by touched by the degradation of concentration camp existence. On such occasion there was great closeness among us all.[24]

---

21 [ED] Anita Lasker (born 1925) studied cello before the war. On November 29, 1943, she was deported to Auschwitz (camp number 69388) where she played cello in the orchestra. On November 1, 1944, she was transferred to Bergen-Belsen where she stayed until the liberation. In 1946 she emigrated to England. She studied music there and married the pianist Peter Wallfisch. She was a co-founder of the English Chamber Orchestra. To learn more about Anita Lasker-Wallfisch read her memoir *Inherit the Truth 1939-1945: The Documented Experience of a Survivor of Auschwitz and Belsen*, London: Giles de la Mare, 1996.
22 Ibid., p. 256.
23 Ibid., p. 218.
24 Ibid., p. 262.

Camp artists Franciszek Targosz and Mieczysław Kościelniak both viewed the music block as a "certain kind of center that inspired artists to creativity".[25] They both frequented the music block to work on their pieces of art. This makes the notion of escape not solely applicable as a mental one for musicians who enjoyed playing but a physical one as well for artists such as Targosz and Kościelniak. Artists of all types and backgrounds were able to find a haven in music away from the realities of camp life, an escape that encouraged their creative processes.

Contradictions Found within Camp Music

It is difficult to reconcile the SS emotional response to and appreciation of music with their brutal actions in the camp. Szymon Laks,[26] an orchestra member asked: "Could people who love music to this extent, people who can cry when they hear it, be at the same time capable of committing so many atrocities on the rest of humanity?"[27]

Robert J. Lifton, a psychologist from Yale, attributes the concept of doubling to both prisoners and the SS personnel alike. It is a process by which one's self is removed from the profession; these are "people who have developed a 'professional self' that can override an earlier 'humane self' and even lend itself to inhumane causes".[28] This theoretical approach explains the prevalence of music and its appreciation among the SS. It is crucial to mention that the orchestra also gave concerts for the SS and

---

25 Lachendro, "The Orchestras in KL Auschwitz," p. 29.

26 [ED] Szymon Laks studied composing and conducting at conservatories in Warsaw and Paris before the war. He was deported to Auschwitz in a transport of Jews from France on July 19, 1942 (camp number 49543). After several weeks in the camp he was admitted to the orchestra, where he played the violin. Thanks to his musical education he quickly began preparing the repertoire and leading the rehearsals, and became an actual bandmaster. See more: Lachendro, "The Orchestras in KL Auschwitz," p. 60.

27 Newman and Kirtley, *Alma Rosé*, p. 228.

28 Ibid.

their families on Sundays right by Höss' villa just outside the camp. The dualities of the function of music at Auschwitz, for brutal practicality and simple pleasure, are thus highlighted through the roles of the orchestras. While the music is "used for abuse and humiliation", there is a "clear therapeutic value for both the prisoners and captor" at the same time.[29]

Alma Rosé and the Women's Orchestra

To complete this paper, we will analyze the woman's bandmaster Alma Rosé and the orchestra she conducted. It is an excellent case study to demonstrate the privileges of being in the orchestra, the use of music as a coping mechanism and the opportunities music provided for prisoners all around.

Rosé, an Austrian Jew, was born into music royalty with her father being the founder of the Rosé String Quartet and the long-time concertmaster of the Vienna Philharmonic, while her uncle was the renowned composer Gustav Mahler.[30] She continued the family tradition of being an accomplished and skilled violinist. She was transported to Auschwitz in July, 1943, after which she was placed in the women's medical experiments block. The Blockäteste Magda Hellinger eventually discovered Rosé's brilliance whereby her "talents presented Hellinger with an opportunity" to save a life in Block 10.[31] Through Hellinger's request, the SS granted Rosé permission to play a violin and it was through this that Rosé was released from the experimental block and named the new conductor of the women's orchestra. Rosé's life was saved because of her talent for music.

---

29 J. J. Moreno, "Orpheus in Hell," *Food Preferences and Taste: Continuity and Change*, ed. Helen M. Macbeth, Oxford: Berghahn Books, 2007, p. 265.
30 Kellie Dubel Brown, "Remembering Alma Rosé and the Women's Orchestra at Auschwitz," *American String Teacher* 59, 4, 2009, p. 50
31 Newman and Kirtley, *Alma Rosé*, p. 222.

Prior to Rosé's departure from Block 10, she would lead cabaret-like shows with fellow inmates. She would play while the others danced and during these short-lived moments, the reality of imprisonment and slavery was set aside.

It helped the women "realize they were alive in the Auschwitz dominion of death".[32] Their shows eventually got so popular that the SS would sometimes come and watch.[33] Hellinger recalled that "Alma had been the light at the center of one of those small glimpses of humanity" which made "life a little more bearable".[34]

To highlight the privileges that came with being in the orchestra, "it was said that in the name of music, Alma could get almost anything from the SS through the admiring and ambitious [chief overseer] Maria Mandel".[35] An iron stove was put into the music block, an unprecedented event, for the upkeep of instruments, and roll calls were held indoors for the orchestra so they did not have to waste time outdoors instead of practicing. All of these favorable conditions most certainly heightened each member's chance of survival, and further, they were given luxuries because of their relationship with music.

However, this did not mean the women in the orchestra did not have to fight for survival anymore. If anything, it made Rosé more strict and severe[36], as she knew the quality of their work determined their fate. As she bluntly put it, "If we don't play well, we'll go to the gas".[37] Yet at the same time, "whenever possible, she acted as if she were elsewhere" and that she "entered the music room from her plain cell as if making a stage entrance".[38] This was Rosé's way of escaping, through her art and passion.

32 Ibid., p. 224.
33 Ibid.
34 Ibid., p. 225.
35 Ibid., p. 250.
36 To learn more please read Megan Ferguson, "Impressions of Alma Rosé: Conflicting Perceptions of the Famous Conductor of the Birkenau Women's Orchestra in Other Prisoners' Accounts" in this volume.
37 Ibid., p. 254.
38 Ibid., p. 278.

This fantasy of hers and deep-rooted love for music is what helped her and other women from the orchestra cope through the darkest nights at Auschwitz.

Conclusion

The existence of music at KL Auschwitz by no means diminished the crimes and violations of human life in the camp. Instead this analysis suggests that despite prisoners' abhorrent circumstances, art and music were still a part of their lives. However, in an unprecedented environment such as Auschwitz, the presence of music assumed an assortment of roles, many of which were unconventional when compared to life outside of a concentration camp. The initial formation of a camp orchestra as a means to fill the prisoners' spare time soon morphed the orchestra into a method for the Nazis to display their authority and control. The ability to play music was then later commodified as this talent was able to improve living conditions and save lives. Conversely, music also afforded prisoners a mental escape from the harsh realities of camp life and now offers insight to scholars on the preservation of humanity and individual dignity at Auschwitz. Accordingly, the perception and meaning of music differed greatly between the oppressors and the oppressed, and within the latter category, between orchestra members and non-members.

Megan Ferguson[1]

Impressions of Alma Rosé:
Conflicting Perceptions of the Famous Conductor
of the Birkenau Women's Orchestra
in Other Prisoners' Accounts

When famous, well-known artists were brought to KL Auschwitz, they were usually treated not much differently than other prisoners, subjected to the same dehumanizing and humiliating procedures and exposed to the same cruelty and harsh living conditions. One prominent example of this is Alma Rosé, who would later become the conductor of the women's orchestra in Birkenau. Rosé was sent to Auschwitz in 1943 and upon her arrival, she, just like all the others, was treated as though she had become nothing more than another uniform and depersonalized prisoner. Undergoing the typical procedures upon arrival, Rosé's personal and professional identity was stripped from her and she became a subject of the medical experiments of the infamous SS doctor Carl Clauberg. Although at a later point Rosé was able to retain some of her artistic identity by becoming the conductor of the Birkenau women's orchestra, her initial subjugation to the depersonalizing procedures of transforming individuals into prisoner is a telling example of how the Nazi policies were indifferent to earlier social differentiation and appreciation. Still, although artists were no longer treated with the same sort of reverence as they had been in the past, music eventually became the savior of many prisoners, both by providing them with psychological comfort as well as allowing them a better chance of survival as members of the prisoner orchestras. As Jacek Lachendro writes in his article "The Orchestras of KL Auschwitz," orchestra members in

---

1   This text has been revised by the editors.

Auschwitz received special privileges. These included supplementary food rations, sleeping quarters in blocks with better living conditions, supplies of clean clothes and placement in the so-called "preferred" work kommandos.[2] From Jacek Lachendro, we learn that "the first prisoner orchestra was founded in March 1941".[3] It was a men's orchestra, and it mainly consisted of professional musicians who had belonged to orchestras before being interned in Auschwitz.[4] After seeing the prestige and power afforded to the creators of the Auschwitz men's orchestra, other members of SS organized their own prisoner orchestras. Similarly, in April, 1943, Maria Mandel, a high-ranking concentration camp overseer, instituted a women's orchestra, or Lagerkapelle, in Birkenau. These prisoner orchestras served multiple purposes: initially, the SS had used them to help keep order; they occasionally distracted newcomers from the harsh reality of the camp, and eased their cooperation with the camp administration.[5] This was probably based on the assumption that incoming prisoners would be more cooperative and docile if they believed that they were being welcomed to a place of

---

2 [ED] However these privileges did not protect the musicians from sickness and death in the camp.

3 [ED] The prisoners organized the orchestra and the camp authorities accepted the existence of the band in March, 1941.

4 Jacek Lachendro, "The Orchestras in KL Auschwitz," *Auschwitz Studies*, 27, 2015, pp. 7-148.

5 Shirli Gilbert, *Music in the Holocaust: Confronting Life in the Nazi Ghettos and Camps*, New York: Oxford University Press, 2005, p. 178. [ED] The SS established orchestras, first and foremost, to play marches near the gate to set the tempo for prisoner labor units and (although it was not the main aim) to entertain the members of the camp crew, especially during Sunday concerts. However, in fact, the SS used them on other occasions. S. Gilbert writes: "Numerous former inmates recalled that the presence of the orchestras had indeed restored a sense of calm, and led them to think that 'things could not be so bad'. The orchestras functioned to divert the newcomers from what was really happening to them and to mitigate their shock, making it easier to gain their cooperation". To clear a common misunderstanding, Gilbert's opinion refers only to a situation, when [from May 1944] "new transports were delivered directly onto the infamous ramp at Birkenau" (p. 177). At this time only the women's orchestra (not orchestras as Gilbert writes) could be heard by newcomers, and, it is needed to be emphasized, could be heard rather accidentally. To read more about it, see Lachendro, "The Orchestras in KL Auschwitz," pp. 99-101.

culture and civilization, a facade in which the orchestra was integral. For the prisoners, the orchestras could have both comforting and psychologically damaging effects; the music served as a temporary distraction from the reality of the camp,[6] but the orchestras were also experienced as tools of mockery and oppression. They played as the prisoners marched to their labor kommandos.[7] The SS forced the prisoners to march in time with the fast marches played by the orchestra, threatening them with brutal punishment or even death if their steps faltered.

The prisoner orchestras exemplified the formal aspect of music making in the Auschwitz I and Birkenau camps, but the expression and creation of music itself was not only limited to the Lagerkapellen. Music in Auschwitz also fulfilled informal purposes; according to Shirli Gilbert's *Music in the Holocaust*, clandestine songs created by the prisoners were useful, catchy methods of remembering information and experiences.[8] In rare cases, prisoners played music in their own bunks, but this was a relatively unusual occurrence due to the constant hunger and disease that plagued prisoners and forced them to focus all their available energy on endurance.[9] Music was important to the mental health of prisoners, but often the physical needs took priority. On the formal side of the spectrum, there were also official concerts held by the Lagerkapellen.[10] They, in addition to performing daily tasks, were forced to hold special concerts on Sundays for the Auschwitz guards.[11] As well, an ensemble of SS instrumentalists, the SS Battalion Orchestra, existed. It was created in Auschwitz in April, 1942, and existed to play only for the SS.[12]

---

6   Ibid., p. 149.
7   Lachendro, "The Orchestras in KL Auschwitz," p. 5.
8   Shirli Gilbert, *Music in the Holocaust: Confronting Life in the Nazi Ghettos and Camps*, New York: Oxford University Press, 2005, p. 151.
9   Gilbert, *Music in the Holocaust*, p. 178.
10 [ED] This applies not only to this orchestra, but also the men's and the women's orchestras in Birkenau, the men's orchestra in Monowitz, and some orchestras in several sub-camps gave concerts for the SS.
11 Lachendro, "The Orchestras of KL Auschwitz," p. 74.
12 Ibid., p. 4.

Likely due to the fact that some of the orchestras were not considered real labor kommandos,[13] the SS did not keep accurate records of the members of the prisoner orchestras. Also, most of the existing documents were destroyed by the SS when they evacuated the camp. Therefore, as is often the case in the context of Auschwitz, most of the information we possess comes from the testimonies of various prisoners. It is thus the accounts of the members of Alma Rosé's orchestra that we turn to in our attempt to come to a comprehensive portrayal of Alma Rosé during her time in the concentration camp.

Alma Rosé was born to a family of very accomplished musicians. Her uncle was the celebrated composer Gustav Mahler, and her father, Arnold Rosé, was the concertmaster of the Vienna Philharmonic. Rosé grew up in a world full of music, and she was a very talented violinist herself. In the 1930s, she toured with her all-female musical group, the Vienna Waltzing Girls.[14] Under the Nuremberg Laws, Rosé was classified as a Jew; after a few years of hiding, she was discovered trying to escape to Switzerland through the French border.[15] She was placed in the Drancy internment camp, and was eventually sent to Birkenau in the summer of 1943. Rosé was first selected for Block 10 of Auschwitz I, the "medical experiments block," where the SS imprisoned her with other women, mainly Jewish, leaving her to be one of the many victims of Carl Clauberg's sterilization experiments.[16] From the end of 1942 to January 1945 Clauberg carried out experiments[17] involving non-surgical injections to the cervix that

13 Ibid., p. 2.

14 Kellie Dubel Brown, "Remembering Alma Rosé and the Women's Orchestra at Auschwitz," *American String Teacher* 2009, 59, pp. 50-54.

15 [ED] As a Jew, Alma Rosé had to leave Austria. In March, 1939, she managed to emigrate to England. Her father joined her there several weeks later. In the spring of 1940 she was giving concerts in the Netherlands. It was the time of the German invasion of Western Europe, and she did not manage to return to her father. In December, 1942, she attempted to flee to Switzerland, but she was arrested in Dijon.

16 Richard Newman, "In the Shadow of Death," *Strad* 2000, 111, p. 964.

17 Irena Strzelecka, *Medical Crimes: Medical Experiments in Auschwitz*, Oswiecim: International Center for Education about Auschwitz and the Holocaust, 2008, p. 8.

rendered the victims infertile, but also oftentimes led to the prisoner's death.[18] The SS guards forced the women of the experimental block to stay inside at all times, restricting their contact to the rest of the camp. To cope with the situation of constant confinement, the women often resorted to performing small skits or plays to help pass the time, even "modeling" their nightdresses for each other.[19] Thinking she was going to her death, Alma Rosé asked to play the violin one last time.[20] After a guard supplied her with a violin, she played a concert for her fellow prisoners. When the SS guards learned of her outstanding musical skills, they transferred her to Birkenau to lead the women's orchestra.

As a professional musician before the war, Rosé was already quite well-known as a violinist, but she became a conductor in Auschwitz for the first time in her life. However, she accepted the post of orchestra kapo and quickly learned how to manage her own orchestra. Before Rosé's arrival in the camp, the orchestra had about 30 members, and it was struggling to play the same level of music as the men's orchestra did. Alma Rosé became the conductor of the Lagerkapelle in August, 1943, taking over the post from fellow prisoner Zofia Czaykowska, the original director and conductor of the orchestra. It was only under Rosé's direction that the orchestra truly flourished and after her death, the orchestra started to decline.

This article will examine the different perceptions, both positive and negative, that members of the Birkenau women's orchestra had of Alma Rosé, specifically taking into consideration the discrepancies between their testimonies. It is important for us to juxtapose all different

---

[ED] Clauberg carried out experiments, to learn how to sterilize "inferior races". When the Nazis embarked on the mass murder of the Jews in the gas chambers, they were planning to sterilize the Slavs and the small numbers of Germans mixed with Jewish blood, the so called "Mischlinge".

18 Ibid., p. 33.

19 Richard Newman, *Alma Rosé: Vienna to Auschwitz*, Cambridge: Amadeus Press, 2000, p. 224.

20 Newman, "In the Shadow of Death," p. 964.

sentiments and descriptions, as they reflect the difficulties of perceiving a person under circumstances as extreme as they were in the camp. As outsiders to the reality of the camp, we have to respect that each prisoner's experience was unique, and each is valid. We will critically engage with the texts, and will acknowledge obvious biases if necessary, but ultimately, it is not for us to choose right from wrong when it comes to the subjectivity of the prisoners. Still sometimes, as is the case with Rosé, we will encounter strong opposition in the portrayal of people and events. This can lead us to call into question certain depictions from within the survivors' discourse, not from a perspective imposed from the outside.

Under Alma Rosé's direction, the women's orchestra flourished. Rosé was the kapo of the orchestra, respected by both the prisoners and the SS. Although her death was a mystery at the time, most modern doctors who studied her symptoms believe that botulism was the cause of death.[21] Among prisoners however, there were allegations that she was poisoned at a party hosted by a fellow kapo, Elsa Schmidt.[22] In her 1977 memoir "Playing for Time," the French singer Fania Fénelon publicly showcased her negative perceptions of Alma Rosé. Up until that time, the Birkenau women's orchestra was practically an unknown subject; Fénelon's book was the first published prisoner testimony from a member of the women's orchestra.[23] Her testimony generated not only a vivid interest in the orchestra and its conductor, but also became the most prevalent source of information on the women's Lagerkapelle and, in turn, on Alma Rosé.

---

21 Ibid., p. 964.

22 Fania Fénelon, *Playing for Time*, trans. Judith Landry, New York: Atheneum Publishers, 1977, p. 209.

23 Fénelon's book caused a flood of interest in the orchestra, leading, for example, to the creation of the movie "Playing for Time," which was written by Arthur Miller and nominated for a Golden Globe in 1981. The movie starred a number of A-list actresses such as Vanessa Redgrave as Fania Fénelon and Jane Alexander as Alma Rosé. See also IMDb, "Playing for Time, 1980)," web, http://www.imdb.com/title/tt0081344/?ref_=fn_al_tt_1, accessed 12 September 2016.

Fénelon portrays herself as a close confidante of Alma Rosé's while they were imprisoned in the camp, and repeatedly mentions in her memoir that Rosé turned to her as a close companion and divulged intimate facts about herself. However, according to the testimonies of other orchestra members, it is likely that Fénelon's self-proclaimed close relationship with Alma Rosé was at least a slight misrepresentation. Zofia Cykowiak, a fellow orchestra member, for example stated: "Fania and Alma were not that close ... her driving ambition and schemes were often at odds with Alma".[24] So the distinct possibility that at least some of the quotations that Fénelon credits to Rosé are either exaggerated or inaccurate must be recognized.

Fénelon's memoir shows that she did not have a very generous view of Alma Rosé; in fact, one could say that she outright disliked her. She constantly reinforces in her book the idea that Alma Rosé was "unfeeling", and she even states that: "Instead of a heart she's got an empty violin case; it rings hollow ... Only music counts, for her".[25] Also, Fénelon accuses Rosé of not trying hard enough to earn better living conditions for her orchestra. She is under the impression that Alma Rosé could have asked Maria Mandel, an Oberaufseherin (Chief Supervisor) who supported the orchestra, for anything and she would have obliged, but that Rosé simply did not bother to ask, supposedly out of pure indifference towards her players and their suffering.[26]

When looking at Fénelon's portrayal of Alma Rosé, her recurring reference to Rosé's alleged "Germanness" seems particularly striking. At one point, Fénelon states that Alma told her: "I'm here to make music, not to indulge in sentimentality",[27] and there was "no sign of emotion in the conductor's expression". She concludes with the remark: "she was a German all right",[28] attributing Rosé's demeanor to her supposed "German"

24 Newman, *Alma Rosé*, p. 298.
25 Fénelon, *Playing for Time*, p. 38.
26 Ibid., p. 97.
27 Fénelon, *Playing for Time*, p. 116.
28 Ibid., p. 28.

heritage.[29] When Fénelon portrays Rosé as being cruel, harsh, or unfeeling, she calls her a German, or having "Germanic discipline".[30] Fénelon even states: "She was German, Himmler was one of the great leaders of her country. She was proud to play for him".[31] The chain of arguments creates a direct link between Germanness[32] and admiration for the Nazi leaders as nationalistic pride. Also the fact that Rosé was actually from Austria and not from Germany does not seem to matter to Fénelon.[33] In another particularly persuasive statement, Fénelon declares that "[Alma] couldn't be Jewish, she must belong wholly to the superior race".[34] This quotation again highlights how Fénelon's sentiments towards Rosé are translated into a racial matrix.[35] Correspondingly, when Fénelon refers to Rosé in a positive way, the conductor becomes Jewish again, and when

29 In the orchestra block, factions existed according to nationality; these factions included [ED] Poles, Russians, Ukrainians, and French, Greek, Polish, German, Belgian, Dutch, Hungarian, Czech, Austrian Jews) and were formed partially because of linguistic differences.

30 Newman, *Alma Rosé*, p. 279.

31 Ibid., p. 183.

32 Interestingly, Fénelon uses the word "German" in a very particular sense; to her, being "German" seems to be synonymous with being a devoted "Nazi". There is no room for differentiation.

33 In her eyes, being Austrian seems to equate to being German, an assumption called into question for example by Ruth Klüger in her novel *Still Alive,* published in 2001. Klüger writes: "were Austrians really Germans, as Hitler, himself an Austrian turned German, tried to persuade them?" Ruth Klüger, *Still Alive: A Holocaust Girlhood Remembered*, New York: Feminist Press, 2001, p. 24. This sentiment further complicates the issue of Austrian identity during the Nazi occupation, but it also helps to explain the attitude of the time, one which undoubtedly helped to foster Fénelon's thoughts about Alma Rosé.

34 Ibid., p. 184.

35 Fénelon suggests that Alma Rosé, a Jewish woman from Vienna, was somehow both a "real German" (p. 37) and a Jewess, repeatedly discussing Rosé's racial affiliation and alternating between both designations. Interestingly, she makes it sound as if both elements, character and racial affiliation, were stringently tied together. To Fénelon, the unfeeling Rosé "had to be" German, as if there was a causal connection between character and national/racial origin.

Fénelon speaks of Rosé's death and subsequent funeral, she refers to her body as "the corpse of a Jewess".[36] [37]

Finally, Fénelon's negative portrayal of Alma Rosé also includes the allegation that Rosé was abusive and constantly pandering to the SS. She claims that Rosé once slapped a player because of a mistake made during orchestra rehearsal[38] and states that on many other occasions, Rosé would smack the fingers of the other prisoners using her baton if she was displeased. However, after *Playing for Time* was published, many other members of the Lagerkapelle, such as Anita Lasker-Wallfisch[39] and Helena Dunicz Niwińska, came forward to dispute the claim that Alma Rosé was ever physically violent, casting some doubt on Fénelon's claim. In the memoir Helena Dunicz Niwińska wrote in 2014 partially as a way of responding to the accusations displayed by Fénelon,[40] the former member of the orchestra states: "[Alma] never stooped so low as strike an orchestra member, as Fania Fénelon falsely asserts in her memoirs".[41]

Fénelon's other accusation, that Rosé pandered to the SS, is most likely connected to her role as a prisoner functionary. Rosé's function in the camp was to be an effective conductor, but also as a kapo[42] of the orchestra she had to be subservient to the SS. Fénelon quotes Alma Rosé statement: "the officers must be satisfied. That's what we're here for, isn't it?"[43] It is

---

36 Fénelon, *Playing for Time*, p. 208.

37 This obvious juxtaposition between "German" and "Jewish" is also interesting when you consider it in the context of the camp: when Rosé acts in her role as kapo of the orchestra, she is identified as German, but the moment she has died, she is perceived as yet another murdered Jew.

38 Fénelon, *Playing for Time*, p. 90.

39 Newman, *Alma Rosé, Vienna to Auschwitz*, Amadeus Press: Cambridge, 2000, p. 11.

40 The two memoirs were written forty years apart, and while Fénelon wrote hers approximately 30 years after the liberation of Auschwitz, Niwińska wrote 70 years after the events she recalls.

41 Helena Dunicz Niwińska, *One of the Girls in the Band: The Memoirs of a Violinist from Birkenau*, Auschwitz-Birkenau State Museum: Oswiecim, 2014, p. 76.

42 Kapo was a functionary prisoner designated as a direct supervisor of other prisoners in the camp or a labor detail.

43 Fénelon, *Playing for Time*, p. 117.

not unlikely that Rosé assumed that any failure of the orchestra would lead to a loss of the members' privileges and maybe even to their deaths, and so presumably, she did everything in her power to keep the SS satisfied. Her role as a privileged prisoner-functionary put her in a position prone to moral ambiguities, and the different interpretations of her actions only show how precarious the situation was for everyone involved.

Most of the testimonies of former members of the Lagerkapelle, including Niwińska, Fénelon, Lasker-Wallfisch, Violette Silberstein,[44] and Hilde Zimche,[45] describe Alma Rosé as being very harsh. According to Niwińska, if anyone played a wrong note during a public concert, it was not unusual for Rosé to punish them with hard labor, such as scrubbing the floor of the barracks or carrying the kettle of food from the kitchen.[46] However, Fénelon and Helena Dunicz Niwińska, a Polish violinist, had different ideas about why Alma Rosé was so harsh towards her orchestra. Fénelon believed that Rosé only thought of the orchestra as a sort of "musical infantry, to be slapped and driven".[47] Niwińska, however, believed that Rosé as a professional musician was used to dealing with other professionals and her determination to correct every small mistake emerged from her professional career. It is also quite possible that being meticulous about every aspect of the orchestra's performance could have worked as a means of escape for Rosé, allowing her to use her professional identity to withdraw from the brutal reality of the camp. Anita Lasker-Wallfisch points to something similar when she writes: "what [Alma] did achieve, with the iron discipline she imposed on us, was that our attention was focused away from what was happening outside the block – away from the smoking chimney and the smell of burning flesh – to an F which should have been an F-sharp".[48] Thus Rosé's harsh demeanor could potentially

---

44 Newman, *Alma Rosé*, p. 273.
45 Ibid., p. 290.
46 Niwińska, *One of the Girls in the Band*, p. 75.
47 Fénelon, *Playing for Time*, p. 97.
48 Newman, *Alma Rosé*, p. 270.

be not a lack of compassion, but a mark of professionalism and a way to keep herself and the women-musicians focused only on the orchestra.[49] It is impossible for us to establish whether or not this distraction from the reality of the camp was deliberate, but she forced the women to be utterly engrossed in their work with the orchestra and this, in turn, might have helped them to survive.

Another opinion expressed by the members of the Lagerkapelle was that Alma Rosé was very highly respected in Birkenau; and not only by her orchestra, but also by some members of the SS, such as Maria Mandel, who even called her "Frau Alma".[50] Moreover, respecting Rosé as a musician and as the leader the members of the orchestra also cared about gaining her respect. Zofia Cykowiak remembers: "Alma's standards were higher than those of the SS. She therefore established herself as *the* authority. We did not respect SS praises, but we did respect Alma's".[51] Even Fania Fénelon described Rosé as someone who was to be respected, although she mentions this with a negative connotation, stating that Rosé seemed to feel like she deserved respect simply because she was the conductor.[52]

There are also a multitude of small scenes recollected by members of the orchestra which show a kind and caring side of Alma Rosé. Hilde Zimche, a percussionist and music copyist, admires what she perceives as Rosé's unbelievably resilient attitude. She writes "who but Alma could conceive of building something of beauty at Auschwitz-Birkenau?"[53] Helene Scheps, a violinist and concertmistress in the orchestra, stated that nothing was more important to Rosé than her music; according to Scheps, "music for her was the most beautiful and most important thing".[54] Helena Niwińska perceived Rosé as being understanding and sensitive. Writing about her recovery from typhus, Niwińska recollects: "I went to Alma and asked

---

49 Lachendro, "The Orchestras in KL Auschwitz," p. 74.
50 Newman, *Alma Rosé*, p. 287.
51 Ibid., p. 261.
52 Fénelon, *Playing for Time*, p. 97.
53 Newman, *Alma Rosé*, p. 245.
54 Ibid., p. 260.

her for time to regain my strength. She showed understanding. . . [which] testified to her concealed goodness and sympathy".[55] These positive memories show small acts of kindness or emotion that Rosé displayed, usually in private situations. They complement the picture of how Alma Rosé was seen by fellow prisoners. Although it is possible that these perceptions may be biased or distorted, the opinions that fellow orchestra members held about Alma Rosé are practically the only bits of information that we have about her life in the camp and, due to that fact, they are incredibly important to recognize. Also, as Zoe Vania Waxman puts it "survivors are seen as having a unique source of historical knowledge".[56]

It is clear that there are some biases affecting the descriptions of the former prisoners, and some of them may not in fact be truly representative of Alma Rosé. Moreover, they may distort readers' views of prisoners' experiences in Auschwitz. While we want to respect all such perceptions and opinions of the survivors as uniquely theirs, and valid, it is still necessary to analyze and evaluate them. This allows us to be just to victims who can no longer speak for themselves, and survivors who can be hurt by misrepresentations and biases. It is necessary to contest the various perceptions using comparison between the many different opinions held by survivors. We must critically engage with the survivors' texts and acknowledge obvious biases and distorted or exaggerated facts, such as those predominantly displayed in Fénelon's memoir.[57] However,

---

55 Niwińska, *One of the Girls in the Band*, p. 96.

56 Zoe Vania Waxman, *Writing the Holocaust*, New York: Oxford University Press, 2006, p. 154.

57 [ED] To emphasize the importance this clarification holds for other members of the orchestra, see Susan Eischeid: "For the few survivors living today, Fénelon's book still holds the power to wound. When asked what she would like the world to know, Helena Niwińska, in her 100th year and 40 years after the publication of *Playing for Time*, cited her concern that the new readers would accept unconditionally what Fania wrote. Niwińska stated firmly that Fania's book is unethical, hurtful, perpetuates outright slander against some of the women and violates the dignity of the other members of the orchestra. She reiterates her belief that it is time, finally, to put Fania's memoir to rest and to bring to a close the 'unthinkable career of Fania's falsified memories' and their

we still must recognize that different perceptions of Alma Rosé help us to construct a picture of who she was while imprisoned in Auschwitz. This is why the opinions of various prisoners and their perceptions of Alma Rosé are so important.[58] They show the many different sides of the conductor, thereby forcing us to acknowledge that there is not one true representation, but only a conglomerate of ambiguous facets, shaped by the extreme conditions of the camp environment.

international propagation through mass media". Susan Eischeid, *The Truth about Fania Fénelon and the Women's Orchestra of Auschwitz-Birkenau*, London: Palgrave Macmillan, 2016, p. 137. See also: Guido Fackler, "'We all feel this music is infernal...': Music on Command in Auschwitz," *The Last Expression: Art and Auschwitz*, ed. D. Mickenberg, C. Granoff, and P. Hayes, Evanston: Northwestern University Press, 2003, p. 121; Helena Dunicz-Niwińska, "Truth and Fantasy," *Pro Memoria*, Bulletin Number 3-4, January 1996, pp. 65-67, and many statements of former members of the orchestra in: Richard Newman with Karen Kirtley, *Alma Rosé, Vienna to Auschwitz*, Amadeus Press: Cambridge.

58 While Primo Levi asks us to strive to avoid judgment when talking about prisoners, his concept of the grey zone (described in this volume by Carlos Halaburda) does not apply to actions outside of the camp. Levi states specifically that our inability to judge what is right and what is wrong applies only to prisoners' behaviors and actions inside the camp. Other thinkers (for instance Emanuel Levinas) argue that the biggest victory of humanity over Nazis is that they did not succeed in changing ethical values of humans, and that the Holocaust did not change what people (in general) perceive as right and wrong. The memoirs and the intentions of their authors, because they are the result of activity outside of the camp, should be subjected to our evaluation and judgement.

Carlos Gustavo Halaburda

Afterword
Reading Lessons with Primo Levi:
The Survivor in the Grey Zone

Let me start with a story from a book by a Birkenau survivor.[59] In mid 1944, Auschwitz-Birkenau prisoner Edith Links had not seen her family for months. One day, she saw her parents, her sister with her baby and her grandmother, through the wires of Birkenau. They were about to be selected for the gas chambers. Edith shouted through the wires the name of her sister, Szarika. Edith knew that because of her sister's young age, Szarika could be the only one to survive if selected to work. However, as a mother of a baby she would be sent for immediate death, together with her child. Polish writer Seweryna Szmaglewska, who testified in the Nuremberg Trials, wrote Edith's story: "Not heeding the danger to which Edith expos[ed] herself, she shout[ed]: "Szari! Szari! Give the baby to grandma!" Not realizing that in obeying her sister she [was] sentencing her baby to death, Szari obediently turn[ed] to the old woman in black walking behind her and [gave] her the infant".[60] The SS sent the Links family to the gas chambers. Edith would have to endure the pain of feeling that she had sentenced her sister's baby to death to save Szarika's life.

In his philosophical testimony *The Drowned and The Saved* (1986),[61] Auschwitz survivor Primo Levi (1919-1987) formulated a well-known concept for approaching the experience of prisoners like Edith Links in Holocaust testimonial literature, which is called the grey zone. "It is a grey zone, poorly defined, where the two camps of masters and servants both diverge and converge. This grey zone possesses an incredibly complicated

---

59 Seweryna Szmaglewska, *Smoke over Birkenau*, trans. Jadwiga Rynas, Oswiecim: Auschwitz-Birkenau State Museum – Ksiazka i Wiedza, [1947] 2008, p. 256.
60 Szmaglewska, *Smoke over Birkenau*, p. 256
61 Primo Levi, *The Drowned and the Saved*, 1988, London: Abacus, 2014, p. 38.

internal structure and contains within itself enough to confuse our need to judge" writes Levi.[62] The grey zone was one of the multiple mechanisms of demoralization used by Nazi Germany to carry out mass extermination in their institutions of confinement. As they did with Edith Links, the Nazis turned countless of their victims into perpetrators of their own destruction. Levi calls this mechanism "National Socialism's most demonic crime".[63] There would be serious challenges for prisoners caught in this zone and who survived the Holocaust and later produced or became protagonists of the stories we read to bear witness to the Nazi genocides. What kind of readers do we need to be when we face these pages entrusted to us?

Primo Levi's grey zone offers a reading lesson to humanity. Lending our ears to those who were conscripts of their own tragedy entails avoiding all stigma, all moral judgment of the acts of those caught in the grey zone of Nazi crimes. Instead, Levi teaches us that reading survivor testimonies is a call to witness the fragility of the human condition when deprived of all choice in spaces of incommensurable suffering; it is a call to witness the extraordinary will to share stories of loss with us so that we can learn to regard the pain of others. A survivor's testimony is a remnant of human lives that Nazi Germany invested much effort in turning to ruins. Survivors' stories are pieces of human beauty as they tell us that, in spite of barbarism, in spite of all attempts to destroy the human in us, there is something that survives as a remnant: the capacity to love each other in the most strenuous of situations. And, above all, survivor testimonies are acts of faith in us, readers, as they express a collective desire for final redemption for the defeated of history. May this be the ultimate defiance of Levi's literature against oblivion. So I invite you, dear reader, to bear witness; with these lines I entrust to you Edith Link's tragedy, in tribute to her, to those who survived to share their story and to the millions that perished.

---

62 Levi, *The Drowned and the Saved*, p. 38.
63 Levi, *The Drowned and the Saved*, p. 52.

Carolina Franzen

Holocaust Survivors' Memoirs – Difficult Questions[64]

Today, hundreds of portraits of the prisoners of Auschwitz hang on the walls of a corridor in blocks number six and seven of the former concentration and extermination camp Auschwitz I. Despite the sheer number of photographs (which is of course little in contrast to the number of victims), despite their hanging (dense, in orderly rows with similar framing) and in contrast to what unites these portraits (the photographers' angle, the black and white, the uniforms and even the unifying effects of hunger and violence) – despite the many modes in which these portraits become unified – walking so closely along these rows as a beholder, looking at these people's faces, one after the other, even if hastily, looking from face to face, retrospectively re-individualizes these men, woman and children. The exhibition individualizes again those who were unified by the Nazi terror.

Certain demands seem to arise from engaging with the horrors of "Auschwitz",[65] one of them being that any attempt to learn about or from the Holocaust cannot or should not be abstracted from individual experience, on the one hand. Yet, on the other hand, it appears as a necessity

---

64 This text is based on a seminar held together with Anja Nowak at the Auschwitz-Birkenau State Memorial and Museum, and is influenced by the class discussion with Prof. Bożena Karwowska and the students of the *Witnessing Auschwitz* 2016 program. Special thanks goes to Jadwiga Pinderska-Lech and Gabriela Nikliborc for their instructive seminars on the publication of survivors' memoirs.

65 "Auschwitz" is intended to stand as a symbol in this text, in reference to Theodor W. Adorno who stated once very bluntly "And by Auschwitz I mean of course the entire system", found in Theodor W. Adorno, "Progress or Regression," *History and Freedom: Lectures 1964-1965*, Cambridge: Polity, 2006, pp. 3-9. Yet, in the following text Auschwitz means also very literally the three main camps and the many sub-camps it administratively consisted of under the authority of the SS.

likewise to listen to the many voices telling their stories, in their differentiating plenitude.

In contrast to these demands stand the realities of learning. Within and through memoirs, certain perspectives on history, perpetrators, victims and specific individuals are shaped. For a reader who does not know much about the Holocaust, it might often be one single memoir which will have to stand in for what is understood to be historical truth. It might therefore be one single memoir, one voice or one image only which represents the memory of the Holocaust.

The memoir *Playing for Time*[66] by Fania Fénelon might exemplify when this becomes a problem. Megan Ferguson's essay "Impressions of Alma Rosé" shows how the women's orchestra conductor, Alma Rosé, herself a prisoner, has been one-sidedly represented in Fénelon's memoir. Fénelon's representation stands in sharp contrast with how most survivors perceived Rosé in her position of a functionary prisoner with certain powers in the camp. Most survivors' memoirs present Rosé, and the complexity of the camp, differently. Yet, due to the publication's success, Fénelon's representation shaped public perception. It dominated the portrait of Rosé to such a degree that other survivors felt that their own stories, their own portraits and the portraits of the ones they knew, became generally misperceived. Some survivors felt wounded again, this time by a former co-prisoner and the public's acceptance of her interpretations.[67]

But also other circumstances fundamentally complicate any learning about the Holocaust. A major portion of victims' memories will always remain unknown. We will never hear the memories of the majority of victims, the ones who did not survive. We will also not be able to listen to the many who do not speak or write. Still, following the end of the war, many survivors have written memoirs to present their testimonies. Many of them are considered very accurate. Seweryna Szmaglewska's *Smoke*

---

66 Fania Fénelon, *Playing for Time*, New York: Atheneum, 1977.
67 See footnote 57 in Megan Ferguson's essay.

over Birkenau (original published in Polish as *Dymy nad Birkenau* in 1945), for example, has been used in the trials of perpetrators as evidence. Yet memory did not stop expanding. The increase of knowledge about and around the Holocaust has led many survivors in the recent past to collage together their memoirs. In most cases, what they experienced is now intertwined with what they themselves learned and envisioned about the Holocaust later on. Not all of it is true (and some representations may differ from the survivors' own, unique experiences). Also, writing has often become an attempt for the victims to confront trauma; and such an intent, as much as trauma itself, of course, changes the individual's narratives and their interpretation of their experiences.[68] For the ones who want to learn, this necessarily adds new layers and complicates their understanding of the past.

Primo Levi's claim that the camp made no one a better person (if anything, potentially the opposite) suggests that the perspective of a survivor might not necessarily represent an unbiased, non-unifying image of the past, or of people. Because memoirs are individuals' stories in all their complexity, these narratives are prone to biases, to misconstructions and all kinds of seeming distortions. Yet indeed the many stories which provide a background and (quietly) surround every single memoir compose together a complex and differentiated image of the past. The many voices can therefore sometimes contradict a single memoir's representation. If this contradiction does not become obvious to the readers of the memoir, then the many voices' memories are in fact in danger of disappearing. The plenitude of voices can become muted by a memoir's univocal voice because memoirs are rarely read in the way that the portraits at Auschwitz are perceived: in the midst of many others. Footnotes and introductions,

---

68 For an interesting analysis of how survivors like Ruth Klüger make themselves aware of the problems regarding memory and trauma within their texts, see Dagmar von Hoff and Herta Müller, "Erzählen, Erinnern und Moral: Ruth Klügers weiter leben: *Eine Jugend* (1992)," *Erinnerte Shoah: Die Literatur der Überlebenden/The Shoah Remembered: Literature of the Survivors*, ed. Walter Schmitz, Dresden: Thelen, 2003, pp. 223-238.

which may include information on obvious misrepresentations and personal biases, can therefore be an attempt to at least reference an individual memoir's missing counterparts. But in order to be able to oppose, explain and prevent unifying misconceptions, research performs almost a testing against the individual's memory.

Amir Wachtel

Lessons From the Prisoner Physicians of the Holocaust

Shortly after Hitler's rise to power as chancellor of Germany, the Nazi party began passing laws against Jews and other minorities. In fact, between April, 1933, and September, 1941, more than 250 legal measures were issued to segregate Jews from German society.[1] Groups and individuals deemed as unwanted included Jews, Roma/Sinti, communists, homosexuals, the feeble minded and the physically or mentally disabled, as well as a wide cross-section of "anti-socials", which meant alcoholics, sex workers, drug addicts, the homeless and other individuals.[2]

As Germany annexed or occupied other European countries their general policy regarding the Jews was to concentrate them into ghettos. The orders and policies of the German administration of the occupied territories transformed the ghetto from a Jewish neighborhood into an area of systematic mass murder through intense overcrowding, lack of food, disease and murder over the slightest infractions. The ghetto, however, was a temporary phase in the German policy towards the Jews. SS Obergruppenführer Reinhard Heydrich, in a correspondence with the commanders of the security police in occupied Poland on September 21, 1939, a mere three weeks after the invasion of Poland, wrote that the concentration of Jews in ghettos was the "first condition in realizing the final aim", and that achieving it "demanded more time", indicating the transitory nature

---

1   Robert N. Proctor, *Racial Hygiene: Medicine Under the Nazis*, Cambridge: Harvard University Press, 1988.
2   Ibid., p. 212.

of the ghetto.[3] Later came the deportation of the ghetto population to concentration and death camps, which in the case of the Warsaw ghetto was carried out by the SS and the Gestapo.[4] But even in the sealed off, chaotic spaces of the ghetto and concentration/death camp there existed medical personnel who were also prisoners and who attempted to provide care for their fellow inmates. Analyzing and discussing the ethical dilemmas they faced can help contemporary medical personnel reflect on several pertinent questions.[5] Is it possible to provide health care when one has no resources? Do the sanctity of life and the Hippocratic Oath render the taking of a life unacceptable under any circumstances? What exactly does it mean to be a health care professional?[6]

The German occupation of Poland rapidly changed the lives of Polish Jews. Among the many examples, they were burdened with economic sanctions, laws limiting their freedom of movement throughout their cities and country and laws forcing them to distinguish themselves via the wearing of armbands. Furthermore they were targeted for random acts of theft and violence and forced labor from 1939 onwards. The German authorities demanded that the Judenrat fund and organize the construction of walls around the Jewish district of Warsaw, which began on April 1, 1940, and ended in early June, 1940. As an excuse the Germans claimed that the area of Jewish residence was threatened by epidemics.[7] Ludwig Fischer, the head of the Warsaw District, officially established the creation of the Warsaw ghetto on October 2, 1940, by signing an

3 Yitzhak Arad, *Belzec, Sobibor, Treblinka: The Operation Reinhard Death Camps*, Bloomington: Indiana University Press, 1987, p. 2.
4 Barbara Engelking and Jacek Leociak, *The Warsaw Ghetto: A Guide to the Perished City*, New Haven and London: Yale University Press, 2009, p. 698.
5 My participation in the *Witnessing Auschwitz* seminar was possible thanks to the generous financial support of the UBC Faculty of Science. I am grateful to them for providing me with this opportunity and for helping me to conduct this research.
6 Evelyn Liberman, "Roles of Jewish Physicians and Allied Health Professionals in The Camps and Ghettos During the Holocaust," conference presentation, *American Public Health Association*, 800 I Street, NW Washington, DC, 20001-3710, 30 October 2012.
7 Engelking and Leociak, *The Warsaw Ghetto*, p. 58, p. 60.

official decree, although the exact borders of the ghetto would undergo continuous change for roughly another six weeks.[8] Following many changes and attempts at negotiating between the Judenrat and the German administration in Warsaw, the ghetto was sealed off on November 16, 1940. Leaving the ghetto boundaries through one of its twenty-two gateways was only permitted with a special pass. German gendarmerie, Polish police and Jewish police patrolled each entry.[9] At its most crowded the ghetto would imprison approximately 460,000 Jews. This was in March, 1941, although German data indicated that there could have been up to 490,000 people.[10]

The existence of the Warsaw ghetto can be divided into two periods: a time of indirect extermination and a time of direct extermination.[11] The first phase lasted from the creation of the ghetto until July 22, 1942, when the SS and Gestapo began deporting the ghetto population to the gas chambers of Treblinka. The second phase lasted from the beginning of the deportations until the destruction of the ghetto on May 16, 1943.[12] The first phase saw an average death rate of 2,535 people per month, which was predominantly the result of starvation, poverty, and disease.[13] The poor living conditions in the ghetto, which included intense overcrowding, abject poverty and a shortage of food were, at their root, the result of the policies of the German civil municipal administration in Warsaw. These policies resulted in intense overcrowding. For example, in November, 1940, when the ghetto was sealed, 400,000 Jewish people were packed into 1,483 houses.[14] The Supply Section, which was responsible for importing provisions, including foodstuffs into the ghetto, and the Judenrat, which

---

8   Ibid., p. 65.
9   Ibid., p. 72.
10 Ibid., p. 49.
11 Jacek Leociak, "Maps of Warsaw and the Warsaw Ghetto," *Witnessing Auschwitz* seminar, lecture, Warsaw: The Jewish Historical Institute, 30 May 2016.
12 Engelking and Leociak, *The Warsaw Ghetto*, p. 788.
13 Ibid., p. 49.
14 Ibid., p. 40.

distributed food amongst the ghetto population, were both Jewish and German organizations, specifically the Transferstelle, which determined the prices and profit margins of those foodstuffs. Engelking and Leociak wrote that the "Supply Section ... had little leeway for independent action, being almost entirely dependent on the policy of the occupiers toward the Jews".[15] Starvation had an especially detrimental effect in the ghetto. Jewish physicians in the Warsaw ghetto identified 18,320 deaths as due to starvation but were unable to identify the specific cause of death in 77,000 cases, and it is likely that a significant portion of these also died due to complications induced by starvation.[16] The intense overcrowding, lack of cleaning supplies and scarcity of bathing facilities meant that proper hygiene was impossible to maintain. This combined with the widespread malnutrition and general poor health allowed disease to develop and spread throughout the ghetto, with typhus and tuberculosis being especially problematic.[17]

Hospitals inside the ghetto were no strangers to the harsh conditions that prevailed. There were often two or three patients to a bed, and running water was scarce, meaning that toilets did not flush and washing patients and equipment was a struggle. Wards were lice-ridden, with little to no hospital garments for patients to wear nor a functioning heating system, and at times corpses were simply left in corridors.[18] Furthermore, there was too little food for the patients, the food that was available was of low quality, there were no linens, there were too few bandages and liniment, and the electricity was undependable, even in buildings where surgeries were being performed.[19] The medical institutions in the Warsaw ghetto were under immense strain; Charles Roland has estimated that Czyste hospital, the central medical institution of the Warsaw ghetto,

---

15 Ibid., p. 420.
16 Charles G. Roland, *Courage Under Siege: Starvation, Disease, and Death in the Warsaw Ghetto*, New York: Oxford University Press, 1992, p. 98.
17 Engelking and Leociak, *The Warsaw Ghetto*, p. 240.
18 Roland, *Courage Under Siege*, p. 86.
19 Engelking and Leociak, *The Warsaw Ghetto*, p. 263.

treated approximately 1,400 patients daily.[20] So how did the doctors working at these institutions treat patients when they had so little resources? And when the resources they had ran out and they were sure that their patients were going to die, could they still provide for them at all?

Firstly, in the face of dwindling resources and lack of medicine, physicians utilized their own ingenuity. Ghetto doctors attempted to do whatever they could to heal their patients. For example, dead tissue was cut away with ordinary scissors as opposed to surgical grade scalpels and burn victims were laid on sheets soaked in saline solution as opposed to treating them with cool water and the proper salves.[21] To treat starvation-induced anemia, doctors tried introducing raw animal blood in food, injecting intravenous iron, liver therapy, a combination of the two, and increasing vitamin B in the diet and small transfusions. These all produced little to no positive results or transient benefits, and in certain instances caused aggravated harm.[22] The ingenuity of the ghetto medical personnel took on one more form and that was the rescue of individuals awaiting deportation in the Umschlagplatz by getting them out dressed as doctors, removing them on carts loaded with corpses and taking them out in ambulance convoys.[23]

When there was no hope of curing the patient or properly treating them, consider the testimony of Dr. Adina Błady Szwajger. She was a pediatrician who worked in the tuberculosis ward with patients who had very poor prognoses in the Warsaw ghetto.[24] In her memoir she described the ward as, "a few small rooms on the third floor for children for whom

20 Roland, *Courage Under Siege*, p. 88.
21 Adina Blady Szwajger, *I Remember Nothing More*, London: Colins Harvill, 1990, p. 62.
22 Michal Szejnman, "Chapter 5: Changes in Peripheral Blood and Bone Marrow in Hunger Disease," *Hunger Disease: Studies By The Jewish Physicians In The Warsaw Ghetto*, ed. Myron Winick, New York: John Wiley and Sons, 1979, pp. 182-185.
23 Engelking and Leociak, *The Warsaw Ghetto*, pp. 264, p. 273.
24 Dr. Szwajger worked in various hospitals in the ghetto, including the Berson and Bauman children's hospital and in the pediatrics branch of Czyste hospital, which the Judenrat splintered into various buildings upon its moving within the ghetto limits.

there was no more hope. Children didn't recover from TB in those days".[25]
She wrote that while working with children whom she expected would
die in the coming weeks, she and her colleagues had the idea of creating
a "play room". They wanted to try "to put a smile on the faces of those
children deprived of everything".[26] They achieved this quite easily for the
toddlers who would willingly gather in a ward to listen to stories or play
make-pretend games like "house" where they would re-enact domestic
scenes as they were in pre-war times like the weekly Friday night din-
ner.[27] This was more difficult for the older children but the doctors were
eventually able to get them to sing songs and, with time, a very interesting dynamic developed between these child patients and their adult
physicians. Dr. Szwajger describes having conversations with the children
in which she spoke with the older children as though they were equals,
discussing their fears, their shared hunger and their shared struggles.[28]
The medical personnel in the hospital also organized a concert for Easter
where the children sang, danced, pretended to be rabbis and traditional
Jewish schoolboys, ate, laughed and played.[29]

The aforementioned example of Dr. Szwajger serves to illustrate another element of the responsibility of the health care professional that goes
beyond focusing on the physical condition of their patients. When there
is no hope for the patient, physicians should, according to the duties and
ethics of the healthcare profession, try their best to comfort their patients
and improve their mental well-being. Consider the following verse from
the modern version of the Hippocratic Oath, "I will remember that there
is art to medicine as well as science, and that warmth, sympathy, and
understanding may outweigh the surgeon's knife or the chemist's drug."
This insight was frequently crucial to practicing medicine in the ghetto
and camps, where the act of attempting to comfort and show affection

25 Szwajger, *I Remember Nothing More*, p. 28.
26 Ibid., p. 44.
27 Ibid.
28 Ibid., p. 45.
29 Ibid., p. 46.

and compassion was the only thing that doctors could do with the resources they had.

The ghetto was not the final destination for people living in them; Jews were transported en masse to death camps (Treblinka, Belzec, Sobibor, Chelmno/Kulmhof) as well as death and concentration camps such as Auschwitz and Majdanek. Upon arrival at death camps SS officers often violently herded the Jewish individuals out of the cattle cars within which they arrived and ordered them to drop their possessions or hand them to prisoners who worked to collect their belongings. In Auschwitz Jewish people then had to undergo a "medical examination", whereby, with merely a glance, an SS doctor would decide if they were fit to work or should be sent to the gas chambers. The vast majority of those Jews that arrived at the camps were immediately sent to their deaths in the gas chambers.

The conditions in these camps, for the minority of arrivals selected for work, were incredibly harsh. In describing the moment when she was tattooed with her number upon arriving at Birkenau, Dr. Hadassah Rosensaft, a survivor who worked as a prisoner doctor in the hospital in camp BIa of the women's section of Birkenau wrote, "At that moment, I lost my name, my identity, and became nothing more than a number. I was nobody".[30] The SS guards forced the prisoners to perform meaningless drills and exercises in the camp, especially in the initial quarantine period. Dr. Rosensaft reported being forced to carry empty beds back and forth between two destinations. Throughout their time at the camp, prisoners were confronted with the ill fate of those not selected for work upon arrival. Death permeated the entire premises, with survivors having reported

30 Hadassah Rosensaft, *Yesterday: My Story*, New York: Yad Vashem, 2004, p. 28. It is worth noting that the Polish prisoner doctors in Auschwitz hospitals worked under similar conditions and were confronted with similar moral dilemmas. There is much literature on the subject and a number of memoirs: Zdzisław Jan Ryn, ed., *Auschwitz survivors. Clinical – Psychiatric Studies*, Kraków: Wydawnictwo „Przegląd Lekarski", 2013; Władysław Fejkiel, "Głód w Oświęcimiu," in *Wspomnienia więźniów obozu oświęcimskiego*, Oświęcim: Państwowe Muzeum w Oświęcimiu, 1968; Ernst Klee, *Auschwitz, die NS-Medizin und ihre Opfer*, Frankfurt: Fischer, 2001; Miklos Nyiszli, *Auschwitz: A Doctor's Eyewitness* Account, New York: Arcade, 2011.

the nauseating scent of burning flesh and the sights of the crematoria chimneys spouting black smoke.[31] The SS harshly restricted food and used extreme forms of forced labor, where prisoners potentially worked 12-hour shifts, in the heart of winter and apex of summer. In addition, kapos and SS guards beat the prisoners.[32] Dr. Rosensaft described the year and three months she spent in Birkenau as "a time of humiliation, torture, starvation, disease, fear, hopelessness, and despair ... you can never comprehend what just one day in Auschwitz was like, for the truth was always worse than anything one could imagine".[33] The combination of the prisoner's disorientation, extreme slave labor, starvation and ill treatment all contributed to the high prisoner death rate at Auschwitz. These same conditions made it difficult for prisoner physicians to maintain the same standard of care that they administered prior to the ghetto and death/concentration camp.

Working in the hospital was a relatively valued position as it afforded work indoors that was not too strenuous, which increased one's chances of survival. But the camp hospital was a contradiction of a medical institution. On the one hand prisoner doctors attempted to treat and heal their patients to the best of their abilities, while on the other, SS doctors would carry out selections in the hospital. Furthermore, the SS radically limited medications, proper equipment, and other invaluable supplies. Dr. Louis Micheels, who survived Auschwitz by working as a prisoner doctor, described meeting a victim of an allied air raid on Auschwitz who lost both his legs. He was very scared because disabled prisoners were typically sent to the gas chamber. Dr. Micheels convinced the man that after saving his life and investing in him the resources required to rehabilitate

---

31 Lucie Adelsberger, *Auschwitz: A Doctor's Story*, Boston: Northeastern University Press, 1995, p. 62. Rosensaft, *Yesterday: My Story*, p. 29. Gisella Perl, *I Was A Doctor In Auschwitz*, New York: International Universities Press, 1948, p. 27.

32 Olga Lengyel, *Five Chimneys: A Woman Survivor's True Story of Auschwitz*, Chicago: Academy Chicago Publishers, 1995, pp. 48-49. Perl, *I Was A Doctor In Auschwitz*, p. 33.

33 Rosensaft, *Yesterday: My Story*, p. 39.

34 Louis J. Micheels, *Doctor #117641*, New Haven: Yale University Press, 1989, p. 124.

him the SS doctors would not send him to be gassed, yet soon after a selection did take place and this man was killed. Upon reflection of this event Dr. Micheels wrote, "Again the cruel contradiction that permeated every aspect of life in this world prevailed: to be healed was to be killed".[34]

The conditions in camp hospitals were utterly wretched. Dr. Lucie Adelsberger described the hospital block as being similar to the other barracks in that it did not have any electricity, no windows (there were only skylights along the roof instead), a leaky roof, and walls that had no insulation and let the cold and heat of the outside freely enter the structure.[35] She described it as housing hundreds of people on horrible quality straw mattresses and threadbare blankets:

> Emaciated, feverish individuals would lie crammed in their berths, next to, on top of, beneath each other, ten to a space that ordinarily would have sufficed for two or four people at the most ... Below [in the bottom bunks], where the seriously sick who no longer had the strength to sit up or crawl out of bed to attend their business were berthed, was a mire of feces- and urine-drenched blankets. The dying writhed among the dead, emitting a dull, extended moan that sounded like the cry of an animal perishing in the forest primeval.[36]

The SS also limited hospital supplies. Dr. Rosensaft described her hospital as having some mirrors, scissors, bandages that resembled toilet paper, a little ointment that she thought could have been Vaseline and approximately 100 pills for the entire camp; these were mostly aspirin.[37] The stories of several prisoner physicians indicate that even under these conditions they did the best they could to treat their patients. They relied on their ingenuity and perseverance, performing surgeries and other

---

35 Dr. Adelsberger survived nearly two years in Birkenau, from late May 1943 to mid January 1945, where she worked as a prisoner doctor in the Roma/Sinti camp.
36 Adelsberger, *Auschwitz: A Doctor's Story*, pp. 37-38.
37 Ibid., p. 33.

procedures with nearly no equipment. Several of the memoirs of prisoner physicians who survived Auschwitz imply that when there was nothing they could do they simply attempted to give their patients comfort and show them compassion and care. Recounting her time in Auschwitz, Dr. Gisella Perl wrote in her memoir about a patient who was poisoned and was slowly dying.[38] Without any instruments or drugs there was nothing she could do but "hold her in my arms at night and give her small comfort of love and tenderness".[39] Dr. Perl also recounted some of her patients with whom she had developed an especially strong bond, and she wrote, "I knew that even if I could not save them or cure them, my smiles, my tenderness, my promises of a better future helped them endure the last days of their lives".[40] She also wrote that their deep attachment to her also helped her to better cope with the difficulty of life in Auschwitz.

The resourcefulness of the prisoner doctors of Auschwitz also involved the crucial action of hiding sick patients from the SS doctors carrying out selections. Dr. Rosensaft recalled two occasions when she received warning of a selection and she and her colleagues dressed some of their sick patients in heavy coats and sent them to work in a labor unit for the day to spare them from being selected for death.[41] Dr. Micheels recalled hiding the records of especially sick patients and hiding some of the patients in the bathroom while the selection was taking place.[42] These efforts helped save ill prisoners from the gas chambers and helped buy more time for their recovery. These attempts were dangerous for the doctors because if they were caught they would have been killed.

These prisoner doctors, whether in the camp or in the ghetto, faced various ethical dilemmas, where in order to heal, protect or comfort their

---

38 Dr. Perl was a practicing Jewish gynecologist in Romania before she was deported to Auschwitz in early 1944, where she continued to work as a prisoner physician in the women's camp until it was evacuated in January, 1945.

39 Perl, *I Was A Doctor In Auschwitz*, p. 34.

40 Ibid., p. 139.

41 Rosensaft, *Yesterday: My Story*, pp. 36-37.

42 Micheels, *Doctor #117641*, p. 87.

patients they would have to kill or aid in the killing of some of their patients. In an article Tessa Chelouche referrs to this as the healing-killing paradox.[43] A reading of several of the memoirs and testimonies of prisoner physicians, and one account of a prisoner patient, revealed two recurring motives for the killing of patients by their prisoner doctors: to ease their patient's suffering and to protect other prisoners and patients. Two stories that exemplify these motives are that of Dr. Perl, who committed infanticide to protect the mothers of the infants she killed in Auschwitz, and that of Dr. Szwajger, who committed infanticide and euthanized elderly and youthful sick patients to prevent them from being killed during the liquidation of the Warsaw ghetto or suffering the transportation to Treblinka and likely being killed there. One important difference between ghetto and camp physicians was that camp doctors worked directly under SS supervision, while ghetto doctors did not. This meant that ghetto doctors had more freedom regarding the treatment of their patients.

Dr. Perl's actions, though controversial, saved the lives of numerous women. Upon arriving at Birkenau the SS guards ordered the pregnant transportees to step forward in order to move them to another camp with better living conditions and larger food rations. In her memoir Dr. Perl describes having seen one such group of pregnant women being murdered by SS personnel. She wrote of how the SS beat them with clubs and whips, kicked them in the stomachs, dragged them by their hair, unleashed guard dogs on them and finally threw the women into the crematorium alive.[44] After witnessing the brutal murders Dr. Perl felt a strong need to continue fighting for her own survival so that she could "save all the pregnant women in Camp [BII]C from this infernal fate".[45] She also wrote that "It was up to me to save the life of the mothers, if there was no other way than by destroying the life of their unborn children".[46] She went on to

---

43 Tessa Chelouche, "Some Ethical Dilemmas Faced by Jewish Doctors During the Holocaust," *Medicine and Law*, 24, 2005, p. 712.
44 Perl, *I Was A Doctor In Auschwitz*, p. 80.
45 Ibid., p. 81.
46 Ibid.

help deliver the babies of pregnant prisoners under the cover of night, surrounded by mud, dirt, and human excrement and without instruments, water, or the most elementary hygiene requirements.[47] Dr. Perl would then kill these infants; in the one example she discusses she strangles the baby, but she writes that, "I loved those newborn babies not as a doctor but as a mother and it was again and again my own child whom I killed to save the life of a woman ... And if I had not done it, both mother and child would have been cruelly murdered".[48]

A part of Dr. Szwajger's story which exemplifies the motive of providing mercy occurred in early September, 1942, when she was working at a hospital in the Warsaw ghetto on a day that the hospital was going to be liquidated. Dr. Szwajger wrote in her memoir that while performing her duties one of the nurses asked her to give her mother a lethal dose of morphine as the mother was too weak to escape the Germans liquidating the hospital and her daughter feared that she was going to be shot in her bed. Dr. Szwajger consented and then gave lethal doses of morphine to several other elderly patients in the room who were too weak to move. In her memoir she referred to these actions as having "helped them too".[49] She then went to the infant's ward with another colleague and gave all the sick babies lethal doses of morphine as well. At this point the liquidation had begun and Dr. Szwajer wrote that she could hear the mayhem downstairs as the Germans and Ukrainian Nazis were removing the sick. Finally, she went to the children's ward and gave all the children lethal doses of morphine, telling them the medicine was "going to make their pain disappear".[50] Dr. Szwajger's actions, while controversial, prevented her patients from suffering the transportation to a concentration or death camp, where they likely would have been immediately murdered as they were all ill and young or old, or from being killed by the Nazi's evacuating the hospital right then and there.

47 Ibid., p. 82.
48 Ibid.
49 Szwajger, *I Remember Nothing More*, p. 56.
50 Ibid., p. 57.

However, there were also cases of wrongdoing committed by prisoner physicians, such as in Czyste hospital in the Warsaw Ghetto, where friends of staff members allegedly received preferential treatment and where there were allegations of thievery and misappropriation.[51] The literature indicates, nevertheless, that this was not common practice.[52] The examples of Dr. Perl and Dr. Szwajger, while unique in their circumstance, are not isolated. There were other such events, for example when, in Auschwitz, a psychiatric patient endangered the lives of 600 other patients in the ward and Dr. Elie Cohen and a colleague gave him a lethal dose of insulin.[53] Or, in another case from Auschwitz, when Dr. Josef Mengele condemned the newborn baby of a prisoner named Ruth Elias to starve to death, and a prisoner doctor gave Ruth a syringe with which she could kill the baby as the doctor refused to directly break the Hippocratic Oath.[54]

In the case of having incredibly limited resources doctors attempted to conjure new procedures, techniques and solutions to the problems they faced on a daily basis in the treatment of their patients. When caring for patients who had no hope of recovery prisoner physicians attempted to provide them with compassion and care for their mental wellbeing. In their attempt to comfort their patients, doctors attempted to increase the standard of living of their patients right to the end of their lives. This was no easy task and Dr. Szwajger wrote that as she worked in the ghetto hospital and the conditions got worse and worse she "understood more and more clearly that you had to bring help right up to the very end but

---

51 Roland, *Courage Under Siege*, p. 87.
52 See Lucie Adelsberger *Auschwitz: A Doctor's Story.* Boston: Northeastern University Press, 1995; Lois J. Micheels, *Doctor #11764,* New Haven: Yale University Press, 1989, Gisella Perl, *I Was A Doctor In Auschwitz.* New York: International Universities Press, 1948; Hadasssah Rosensaft, *Yesterday: My Story.* New York: Yad Vashem, 2004 , Adina Blady Szwajger, *I Remember Nothing More.* London: Colins Harvill, 1990, and Ota Kraus and Erich Kulka, *The Death Factory in Auschwitz.* 1960. Oxford: Pergamon Press, 1966.
53 Chelouche, "Some Ethical Dilemmas Faced by Jewish Doctors During The Holocaust," p. 713.
54 Ibid.

first you had to be made of stone".[55] In some cases prisoner doctors were forced into scenarios where they felt that they had to take this idea to the extreme, and where the only comfort they could provide was a quick and painless death as in the case of Dr. Szwajger. In other cases they felt that they had to kill a patient to protect others, as was the case for Dr. Perl and Dr. Cohen. These doctors provide examples of when there may be some confusion as to whether death can actually be viewed as a sort of treatment. At the end of her memoir Dr. Szwajger wrote that, "For forty years after the war I was a doctor. I believe, I really believe, that one is a doctor in order to save life, anywhere and at any time".[56] In referencing her patients Dr. Perl wrote that, "I had to remain alive so as to save them from death ... I was their doctor".[57] However, the actions of prisoner physicians point to another dimension regarding the question of what it means to be a health care professional. Their actions imply that beyond saving a life, there is a duty to improve its quality, to attempt to ensure the wellbeing of patients. These ideas are all relevant in the health care systems of today where in parts of the world doctors have minimal resources at their disposal and where the debate over euthanasia is still raging.

55 Szwajger, *I Remember Nothing More*, p. 62.
56 Ibid., p. 166.
57 Perl, *I Was A Doctor In Auschwitz*, p. 65.

Jessica Passey

Who Liberated Whom from What?
The Soviet Liberation of Auschwitz

The word liberate is derived from the Latin word "liberare", which means to set free.[1] It refers to the freeing of a space, person or thing. In the context of the Soviet liberation of the Auschwitz camps and sub-camps in 1945, the word "liberation" can take on various meanings. In the context of World War II, the attitudes and views associated with the word liberation were, and still are, ambiguous. First, one has to ask: can the term liberation even be applied to the people who were prisoners of the Auschwitz camps? Can we as a contemporary audience apply this word to a place that did not adhere to any known model? Second, one has to register that the word liberation took on a different meaning depending on whom it was applied to, whether it was the prisoners of the camps, or the Polish people who were living in the so-called liberated country. Third, it is important to keep in mind that the writers of WWII history have had a major impact on the meaning and the use of the term "liberation"; the corresponding discourse is highly political and tied to national agendas of representation. The victors of WWII wrote their own stories of liberation. In the case of the Soviet Union for example, this meant strict censorship. The Soviet narrative had to project the image of Soviet forces as victorious heroes that liberated war-torn Eastern Europe.[2]

---

1 *Oxford Dictionary of Current English*, Oxford: Oxford University Press, 2001.
2 [ED] The Russian narrative is well portrayed by the Russian national exhibition in the Auschwitz-Birkenau Museum.
   See http://auschwitz.org/en/visiting/national-exhibitions/russia/.

In general, the meaning of the word liberation lies in the hands and minds of who behold it as well as the context in which it exists. A drastic example: behind the barbed wires of the Auschwitz camps, the German Nazis also used the word "liberation". The sign on the gate of the Auschwitz I camp that said "Arbeit macht frei" illustrated the German Nazi idea of "liberation". This Nazi view of liberation propagated throughout the Auschwitz camps, illustrates the different connotations that can be associated with "liberation" and how this word took on very different meanings. This can also be seen in the bathrooms with depictions contrasting the "bad" and the "proper" ways to wash oneself, and inside the barracks in commandment-like scriptures on how to be a (German-like-) civilized person. All this was to create (false) hope for the prisoners, implying that with correct behavior liberation was actually possible. However, for most prisoners, the only way to leave the camp lay in fact in their death.[3] Within the camps, many of the prisoners told each other that the only way out was through the chimney. They even made ironic couplets about it, such as "Arbeit macht frei durch Krematorium Nummer drei" (work will set you free through crematorium number three) or "Arbeit macht frei durch den Schornstein" (work will set you free through the chimney).

From a military perspective, the Soviet liberation of Auschwitz has to be framed as follows: "liberation is a term which in the context of war is usually employed selectively and subjectively, i.e. for military operations that are approved".[4] The Soviets portrayed themselves as liberators, creating an image of a stupendous victory for Eastern Europe. However, in Poland the reality of the Soviet liberation was that of another unwanted occupation.[5] It marked the moment when Poland did not transition back

3   Primo Levi, "The Grey Zone," *The Drowned and the Saved*, New York: Vintage International, 1989, pp. 3-4.
4   Norman Davies, "Liberation," *The Oxford Companion to World War II*, Oxford: Oxford University Press, 2001, pp. 688-689.
5   John Erickson, "Liberation, Soviet Style 1944-1945," *History Today*, 34, 1984, p. 36.

into an autonomous nation. Instead Poland "endured half a century of Communist rule that made a mockery of the promises of the liberation".[6] In his book *The Bitter Road to Freedom: A New History of the Liberation of Europe,* William Hitchcock showed how the Soviet liberation of Poland affected the populace. Many patriotic Polish people were in fact persecuted by the Soviets and the Polish communists.

After evacuation in Auschwitz (Stammlager I), Birkenau, Monowitz and the Auschwitz sub-camps there were approximately 9,000 prisoners left, mainly Jews and Slavic people (Polish people, Russians, Ukrainians and Yugoslavians).[7] These prisoners had either been too weak or too ill to evacuate the camps. What was to happen to them was uncertain, but the SS ran out of time to liquidate the camps completely before the Soviets arrived, so they were simply left behind. Before the moment of liberation there was a six to seven-day loophole as a consequence of withdrawing the permanent SS sentry posts. The camp was guarded only by SS patrols. Some prisoners left the camp, but the majority stayed. A number of them then died or were murdered by the German patrols. A doctor in Auschwitz's camp hospital and former camp prisoner, Dr Irena Konieczna, recalled that at the time of liberation: "[t]otal anarchy reigned in the camp. No one obeyed anyone, or showed any respect to the previous prisoner functionaries. No one carried corpses out of the block and no one cleaned up the filth".[8]

The Soviet soldiers of the 60th Army of the First Ukrainian Front reached Buna-Monowitz (Auschwitz III) from the eastern part of the

---

6   William I. Hitchcock, *The Bitter Road to Freedom: A New History of the Liberation of Europe*, New York and London: Free Press, 2008, pp. 3-4.

7   Andrzej Strzelecki, *The Evacuation, Dismantling and Liberation of KL Auschwitz*, Oświęcim: Auschwitz-Birkenau State Museum, 2001, p. 221. See also Jacek Lachendro, *Auschwitz after Liberation*, Oświęcim: Auschwitz-Birkenau State Museum, 2015, pp. 31, 35-45, 49-51, 58-65, 70-78, 85-108 [ED].

8   Irena Konieczna, *Voices of Memory 1: The Evacuation, Liquidation, and Liberation of Auschwitz*, ed. Andrzej Strzelecki, Oswięcim: Auschwitz-Birkenau State Museum, 2008, p. 30. To read more about the "interregnum", see also: Strzelecki, *The Evacuation*, pp. 207-216; Lachendro, *Auschwitz after Liberation*, pp. 11-25.

region in the morning on January 27, 1945. From there, they liberated Auschwitz I and Birkenau on that same day in the afternoon. It took around four days to organize medical staff for the remaining prisoners (who were mostly Jewish).[9] The Soviets set up field hospitals, and with the aid of the Polish Red Cross and other Polish people who volunteered, treated the prisoners and documented what happened. The prisoners' situation was described as follows:

> According to statements by the physicians at the hospital, these patients are suffering from tuberculosis, pleuritis, exsudativa, phurunculosis, cardiac insufficiency and defects, frostbite, eczema due to vitamin deficiency, alimentary dystrophy, and other diseases brought about and caused by the conditions of life in the camp.[10]

The average weight of an adult was around thirty-two kilograms; however it was documented that some prisoners weighed around twenty kilograms.

In Birkenau and the main camp the liberators found around six hundred corpses. They were the bodies of prisoners who had been shot by the SS or had died of starvation.[11] The corpses were buried in mass graves near the main camp on February 28, 1945. There were also special Soviet and Polish commissions established.[12] Their task was to preserve evidence of

9   [ED] The Soviet and Polish medical personnel took care of around 4,500 former prisoners.
10 Jan Sehn, "Protocol of the Main Commission for the Investigation of the German Crimes in Poland," *Voices of Memory 1*, p. 80.
11 Strzelecki, *The Evacuation*, p. 220.
12 [ED] The two commissions were not established simultaneously. In February and March 1945, the Procuracy of the First Ukrainian Front, acting under the supervision of the Extraordinary Soviet State Commission for the Investigation of the Crimes of the German-Fascist Aggressors, worked to secure and examine evidence of the crimes that the Germans committed in Auschwitz Concentration Camp. The Polish commission called the Commission for the Investigation of German-Nazi Crimes in Oświęcim (and later the District Commission for the Investigation of German Crimes in Cracow), carried out similar work from April.

the crimes that happened in the camps of Auschwitz. The Soviet commission autopsied 536 corpses from the camp. According to the commission 474 of these people had died from exhaustion. These commissions also gathered materials and belongings from the camp storage houses and classified these items as evidence.

Alexander Voronstov was the cameraman for the Soviet troops who liberated Auschwitz, and in this function he recorded the prisoners and the camp after the liberation. He believes

> that not even the commanders of our army had any idea of the dimensions of the crime committed in this largest camps ... Time has no sway over these recollections. It has not squeezed all the horrible things I saw and filmed out of my mind.[13]

Soviet journalists gave the first reports on the atrocities of Auschwitz in February, 1945. For example there was: Boris Polevoy, "Kombinat smjerti w Oswiencymie" [the Factory of Death in Auschwitz] (*Pravda*, Feb. 2). On May 7 the official communiqué of the Extraordinary State Commission of the Soviet Union for the Investigation of the Crimes of the German-Fascist Aggressors was published in *Pravda* and titled "On the German Government's Monstrous Crimes in Auschwitz". From the prisoner testimonies and on the basis of calculations of the "throughput" of the crematoria, it was estimated that there were around four million victims.[14] Due to the lack of knowledge and evidence, because the SS destroyed the overwhelming majority of documents of KL Auschwitz during the evacuation and liquidation of the camp, the exact number of those who perished in the German Nazi death and work camps is still uncertain. According to estimations of the Auschwitz Research Centre[15] between 1940-1945 around 1.3 million people (Jewish people 1.09 million,

13 Voronstov, "Voices of Memory 1," p. 32.
14 Lachendro, *Auschwitz after Liberation*, p. 165.
15 Franciszek Piper, *Auschwitz: How Many Perished Jews, Poles, Gypsies...*, Kraków: Poligrafia ITS, 1992, pp. 51-52. See also http://auschwitz.org/en/history/the-number-of-victims/.

Polish people 147,000, Roma-Sinti people 23,000, Soviet POWs 15,000, and other nationalities 25,000) were deported to the Auschwitz camps, of which 1.1 million people were murdered (Jewish people 960,000, Polish people 74,000, Roma-Sinti people 21,000, Soviet POWs 15,000, and other nationalities 12,000). Liberation thus only reached the smallest fraction of the victims, and for those who lived to see it, it did not necessarily bring immediate relief.

To the remaining prisoners in the Auschwitz camps, the liberation was nevertheless a sign of hope.[16] They "welcomed the Soviet soldiers as true liberators, but the "paradox [was] that soldiers who were the formal representatives of Stalinist totalitarianism were bringing freedom to the prisoners of Nazi totalitarianism".[17] They were free, but it was difficult for them to adapt to the post-war reality. Many Polish people saw the Soviets mostly as oppressors who merely brought another occupation. In many parts of the Soviet-liberated Poland and other areas in Central and Eastern Europe, the Soviet army troops were greeted with both friendly and hostile attitudes from the local populations, as well as with fear and anxiety. According to William I. Hitchcock, drunkenness, vandalism, sexual harassment and assault, and over all belligerent agression were common characteristics of the liberating soldiers. He writes:

> For all the elation that oppressed Europeans felt at the demise of the Nazi regime, they often found it difficult to comprehend the destructiveness and rapacious acquisitiveness of their liberators.[18]

This, coupled with the communist socialist politics that unfolded in the Soviet-liberated areas, started to cause contention between the other Allied Forces and the Soviets: "Soviet actions in Eastern Europe helped

---

16 Jerry Adler and Andrew Nagorski, "The Last Day of Auschwitz (Cover Story)," *Newsweek*, 125(3), 1995, p. 46.
17 Strzelecki, *Voices of Memory 1*, p. 10.
18 William I. Hitchcock, *The Bitter Road to Freedom: A New History of the Liberation of Europe*, New York and London: Free Press, 2008, p. 27.

produce Western hostility toward their former ally".[19] Soviet liberation propaganda was a stark contrast to the internal crimes that happened within the borders of the Soviet Union during this time period. Poland endured fifty years of communist rule after the Soviet liberation. Hitchcock concludes that for Poland, there was actually no liberation: "that woeful nation saw its borders redrawn by Stalin's imperious demands, and millions of Poles were incorporated into Soviet Belorussia and Ukraine".[20]

To further add to the controversy of applying the term liberation to prisoners of Auschwitz, one must look at the events that unfolded in the post-war years.[21] After the liberation of the camps, many prisoners were able to return home to their families. But the Jewish prisoners who were freed from the camps, no matter where their home was before the war, had no family and no home to return to. In Europe in 1933 there were over 9.5 million Jews;[22] in Poland, there were over three million. Poland had the largest Jewish population in Europe prior to the war. In 1945, the European Jewish population had shrunk to 3.8 million.[23] According to estimates, about six million European Jews died due to the Nazi persecutions and genocide during the war.[24] When Jewish former prisoners left Auschwitz they were usually the only, or one of a few, survivors in their families.[25]

19 Raymond E. Zickel, ed., *Soviet Union: A Case Study*, Michigan: Michigan University Press, 1991, p. 79.

20 Hitchcock, *The Bitter Road to Freedom*, p. 27.

21 Piotr Setkiewicz, Personal interview, 22 May 2015.

22 United States Holocaust Memorial Museum, "Jewish Population of Europe in 1933: Population Data by Country," *Holocaust Encyclopedia*, https://www.ushmm.org/wlc/en/article.php?ModuleId=10005161, accessed 20 November 2016.

23 Michael Lipka, "The Continuing Decline of Europe's Jewish Population," *Pew Research Centre* (February 2015), http://www.pewresearch.org/fact-tank/2015/02/09/europes-jewish-population/, accessed 20 November 2016.

24 Lipka, "The Continuing Decline of Europe's Jewish Population."

25 Jacek Lachendro, "The German Occupation in Poland: Political and Racist Principles of Nazi Extermination Policy," lecture, *Witnessing Auschwitz* seminar, 2015, Oswięcim: Auschwitz-Birkenau State Museum, 12 May 2015, lecture.

Also, in many cases there was already another family living in their home. German occupiers confiscated the properties from the Jewish population and either gave them to German settlers, or Polish people moved into the vacant houses. Those who survived the war wanted to reclaim their homes. But those who lived in them did not want give up their housing.

Also, anti-Semitism existed in Poland even during the post-war years,[26] and at times resulted in pogroms.[27] An important aspect that reinforced post-war anti-Semitism was political racism.[28] In Poland, there

> was a fierce ongoing battle between passionate pro- and anti-government forces, in which Jews assumed a highly visible and remarkably uniform pro-government position, in sharp distinction to the antigovernment attitudes of what was evidently a sizeable majority of Polish society.[29]

At the same time when prominent members of the Polish Home Army were persecuted, there were Jews among those who were bringing "the new order" to the liberated country. Moreover, some of them were very prominent, especially on executive positions in the Ministry of Public Security. This change in societal agency between the two groups further fuelled tensions after the liberation.

Many liberated Jews feared to go home because of the trauma and anti-Semitism that they faced. This caused many Jewish survivors, and

---

26 The anti-Semitism that still existed in postwar Poland was based on religious, economical, and political factors. According to Jan T. Gross' *Fear- Anti-Semitism in Poland after Auschwitz*, there were three aspects of post-war anti-Semitism: economical (housing and personal possessions), blood libels and religious prejudice, and political racism.

27 [ED] The most important pogroms took place in Kraków (1945) and Kielce (1946) and there were also so called "train actions". It is estimated that approx. 1000 Jews were killed in post-war Poland.

28 [ED] Other important factors that should be added to the list are Nazi German propaganda and the brutalization of society during WWII.

29 David Engel, "Patterns of Anti-Jewish Violence in Poland 1944-1946," *Yad Vashem Shoah Resource Center*, 26, 1998, pp. 1, 43-85.

other refugees, to move westwards to other territories in Europe.[30] In the allied zones of Germany, France, Britain, Belgium, and Greece[31] survivors were placed in displaced persons camps (DP camps) or in refugee centers organized by Western Allied Forces,[32] the Red Cross and the United Nations Relief and Rehabilitation Administration. For some, liberation led to a situation of instability and insecurity.

All this illustrates the amount of hardship survivors faced after the liberation. They had to rediscover who they were, and also had to recreate their homes and families. A heavy emotional burden for Polish people was that they encountered solitary graves and mass graves in camps, forests, meadows, and other areas. For Jewish victims, the emotional burdens were tremendous. A prevailing feeling was that of loneliness and abandonment. Survivors sought out their families, but for many the search was to no avail. Even to this day, many Jewish survivors are still searching for their loved ones. Many of them did not understand why they had survived, and why their families and loved ones perished. Not only did they feel fear and guilt, many suffered from Post-Traumatic Stress Disorder and social alienation. The general populaces did not necessarily understand what happened to them or what these survivors felt after the liberation. Thus most people did not know how to reach out to them or what care to give them. The sense of guilt and acute loss they felt made it difficult to leave their experiences behind. For most survivors, the events of the Holocaust did not come to an end with the moment of liberation. So with

30 United States Holocaust Memorial Museum, *The Aftermath of the Holocaust, United States Holocaust Memorial Museum Holocaust Encyclopedia*, 2 July 2016, https://www.ushmm.org/wlc/en/article.php?ModuleId=10005129, accessed 2 October 2016.

31 Bernard Wasserstein, "European Refugee Movements after World War II," *BBC History*, 17 February 2011, http://www.bbc.co.uk/history/worldwars/wwtwo/refugees_01.shtml, accessed 2 October 2016.

32 "Allied Powers: International Alliance," *Encyclopaedia Britannica*, https://www.britannica.com/topic/Allied-Powers-international-alliance#ref754272, accessed 29 August 2016.

the trauma,[33] destruction and feelings of guilt that followed the liberation in mind, how can the question "who liberated whom and from what?" be applied to the liberation of Auschwitz? It can be applied in that the general idea of a liberation denied. In this author's opinion, due to the nature of the events and the various sentiments expressed in survivors' testimonies, the word "liberation" is simply not adequate in the case of the Auschwitz camps. It is true that the survivors were freed from the physical barriers of the camps, but due to the political developments that ensued in Poland after 1945, and considering that most survivors were not able to leave their camp experiences behind, the term "liberation" is not applicable in the context and zones of Auschwitz' camps and sub camps.

33 [ED] See Shoshana Felman and Dori Laub, *Testimony: Crises of Witnessing in Literature, Psychoanalysis, and History*, New York: Routledge, 1992; and Marianne Hirsch, *The Generation of Postmemory: Writing and Visual Culture After the Holocaust*, New York: Columbia University Press, 2012.

Meredith Shaw

Commemorative Efforts Outside of Those at Former Camp Complexes: Northeast Poland's "Non-Lieux" and "Lieux de Mémoire"[1]

Between August 26-27, 1941, 1,400 Jews from Tykocin were shot in a nearby forest by occupying German forces.[2] On July 12, 1941, 3,000 Jewish men were killed by the occupying German forces at Białystok's "Pietrasze, a field outside the town".[3] Two days before that, Jewish residents of the town of Jedwabne had been burned to death in a local barn as part of a pogrom.[4] Those killings, and the series of mass graves that they left

1 My thanks to Dr. Roma Sendyka for introducing me to the discussion of sites of Holocaust mass graves as sites, and non-sites, of memory, as well as for her suggestions for, and footnotes to, this text. To Dr. Ewa Wampuszyc I am grateful for her comments on an earlier version of the chapter.

2 "Tykocin," *The YIVO Encyclopedia of Jews in Eastern Europe*, web, http://www.yivoencyclopedia.org/article.aspx/Tykocin, accessed 26 June 2015.

3 "We Remember Jewish Białystok," last modified August 17, 2014, web, http://www.zchor.org/bialystok/bialystok.htm, accessed 26 June 2015.

4 Shevach Weiss, "The Speech of Proff Shevach Weiss, the Ambassador of Israel to Poland," *The Sixtieth Anniversary of the Massacre in Jedwabne: Two Speeches Delivered in Jedwabne, 10 July 2001,–Polin, Studies in Polish Jewry* 14, ed. Antony Polonsky, Oxford: Littman Library of Jewish Civilization, 2001, p. xxi. Weiss declines in his address to give a number for those murdered in the 10 July pogrom in Jedwabne. In the context of the broader controversy around the Jedwabne pogrom ignited by Jan T. Gross's *Neighbors*, the number of Jewish people killed on the 10 July, 1941 is particularly controversial. Estimates range from 300 or 400 people (the number of bodies found in the IPN's "partial exhumation of 2001") to the 1,600 people indicated in the "account of the Jedwabne massacre … deposited by Szmul Wasersztein with the Białystok Voivodeship

behind, are examples of what the activist for Holocaust commemoration in Eastern Europe Patrick Desbois has termed the "Holocaust by bullets".[5] The term refers to a feature of the Holocaust that was particularly pervasive in Eastern Europe (including Poland's easternmost provinces): the mass executions of Jews outside of the confines of concentration and death camps.[6] Many Jewish residents from the Białystok area[7] were deported to concentration camps and death camps during the period of German occupation. It remains the case, though, that smaller, decentralized sites of execution were particularly prevalent in this northeastern area of Poland.[8] Commemoration of these sites faces challenges shaped

   Jewish Historical Commission in April 1945" and used by Gross in *Neighbors*. See Anna Cienciała, "The Jedwabne Massacre: Update and Review," *The Polish Review*, 48(1), 2003, p. 53.

5 Patrick Desbois, *The Holocaust by Bullets: A Priest's Journey to Uncover the Truth Behind the Murder of 1.5 Million Jews*, New York: St. Martin's Griffin, 2009.

6 Patrick Desbois, "Yahad – In Unum's Research of Mass Grave Sites of Holocaust Victims," *Killing Sites Research and Remembrance*, vol. 1 of International Holocaust Remembrance Alliance series, ed. Dr. Thomas Lutz, et al., Berlin: Metropol, 2015, p. 87.

7 The Białystok voivodeship was, in 1975, split into the Białystok and Łomża voivodeships. In 1999, the two were recombined as the Podlaskie voivodeship. A "voivodeship" or "województwo" (in Polish) is a regional administrative unit. In this article, I refer to the area in question as the "Podlaskie region" to call attention to the general geographic space under discussion, rather than to the official administrative unit.

8 "Execution Sites of Jewish Victims investigated by Yahad-In Unum," Yahad-In Unum, 2012, web, http://yahadmap.org/#map/, accessed 3 June 2015. Although now marked by sites of mass graves, the region is one that had a history of flourishing multiculturalism. There has been a great deal of debate, in respect to the regions affected by the "Holocaust by bullets", as well as in regard to Poland as a whole, over the correct balance between commemorating the gravesites while also keeping alive the memory of Jewish life. For approaches to the question that range from advocating the active commemoration of the sites of mass graves as imperative for the sake of those buried there, to advocating for active commemoration for the sake of its educational purposes, to decrials of the degree to which the history of Jewish life in Poland has been forgotten, see Meilech Bindinger, "Cemeteries and Mass Graves Are at Risk," and Michael Schudrich, "Jewish Law and Exhumation," *Killing Sites Research and Remembrance*, vol. 1 of International Holocaust Remembrance Alliance series, ed. Dr. Thomas Lutz, et al., Berlin: Metropol, 2015, and Katrin Steffen, "Disputed Memory - Jewish Past, Polish Remembrance,"

both by the history of the Holocaust in the region and by the nature of the physical spaces where these mass graves are located. The issue of the decentralized series of mass graves of the "Holocaust by bullets" is one that has not been thoroughly researched. In fact, it was only in 2014 that there was the first major European conference to discuss research on the killing sites where the "Holocaust by bullets" was held. Convened by the International Holocaust Remembrance Alliance, the conference brought together people and organizations dedicated to marking, commemorating and protecting sites of mass graves on the basis of reasons ranging from the anthropological, to the educational, to the religious.[9] Whether speaking from education-based impulses to recognize the life and loss of former Jewish communities in the area, or religious-based missions to ensure respect for places of the dead, delegates made clear the importance of mass graves being well-treated and recognized as places of commemoration.[10] Whether commemorative efforts take the form of "aesthetic [or] cognitive commemoration",[11] those efforts may stand as proof against

Osteuropa, 2008, 8(10), pp. 199-218. For the debate in the broader Polish context, see the discussions surrounding the balance between speaking to the centuries of Jewish life in Poland and to the experience of the Holocaust that arose with the creation of the Museum of the History of Polish Jews: David G. Roskies, "Polin: A Light Unto the Nations," *Jewish Review of Books*, Winter 2015, http://jewishreviewofbooks.com/articles/1435/polin-a-light-unto-the-nations/. In this chapter, I focus on commemoration of the sites of mass graves in the Podlaskie region in large part because there remains a great deal of research to be done on this topic.

9   International Holocaust Remembrance Alliance, ed., *Killing Sites: Research and Remembrance*, IHRA series, Vol. 1, Berlin: Metropol Verlag 2015, p. 13..

10 Although motivations for wishing to see sites commemorated often overlap, see the conference papers of Dieter Pohl and Andrej Angrick, *Killing Sites Research and Remembrance*. Vol. 1 of IHRA series, pp. 31-46 and pp. 47 – 60, for a more education-inspired approach, and that of Chief Rabbi of Poland Michael Schudrich's for an approach that stems from religious concerns, *Killing Sites Research and Remembrance*. Vol. 1 of IHRA series, pp. 79 - 84.

11 Historians Christhard Hoffmann and Matt Erlin draw a distinction between such forms of commemoration as memorials and educative programs. See "The Dilemmas of Commemoration," *German Politics and Society*, 17(352), 1999, p. 5.

the memory of the sites of mass graves eroding. For, as this paper will discuss, the sites of mass graves are particularly prone to slipping from communal memory.

Scholars debate over whether sites of mass graves are, in fact, always places of "non-memory" or, to employ the term stemming from the work of Pierre Nora, "non-lieux de mémoire".[12] In the present examination of the commemoration of sites of mass graves, "non-lieux de mémoire" refers to those places that will not figure in the memory or consciousness of the towns that border them.[13] Nora, a historian and theoretician of memory, differentiates between spontaneous "environments of memory"(milieu de mémoire) and those places in which memory has lost that spontaneous aspect and has to be consciously reconstructed (lieux de mémoire).[14] He contends that even those places where memory has

12 A term employed by Claude Lanzmann, the director of the film *Shoah*, and referenced in a talk by Roma Sendyka (*Witnessing Auschwitz* seminar, lecture for the University of British Columbia, Krakow, Poland, 25 May 2015). See Roma Sendyka, "Prism: Understanding Non-Sites of Memory," *EuTropes: The Paradox of European Empire*, trans. Jennifer Croft, ed. J. W. Boyer and B. Bolden, Paris: University of Chicago Center in Paris, 2014, pp. 183-201, and Roma Sendyka, "Sites That Haunt: Affects and Non-Sites of Memory," trans. J. Croft, *East European Politics and Societies*, 20.10 2016, pp. 1-16 for discussion of Lanzmann's terms as examined in: Michel Deguy, ed., *Au sujet de Shoah: Le Film de Claude Lanzmann*, Paris: Éditions Berlin, 1990, and François Gantheret, "L'Entretien de Claude Lanzmann, Les non-lieux de mémoire," *Nouvelle Revue de Psychanalyse*, 33, 1985, pp. 293-305. My thanks, also, to Dr. Sendyka for calling my attention to Daniel Libeskind's language of "voids" and Aleida Assman's "phantom sites" that have been applied to the sites of mass graves, as well as Georges Didi-Huberman's language, which expresses the opposite, i.e., "site[s], despite everything"; see *Claude Lanzmann's Shoah: Key Essays*, Stuart Liebman, ed., Oxford: Oxford University Press, 2007, as referenced in Sendyka, "Prism," pp. 183-201.

13 Used in a broader context, "non-lieux de mémoire" could refer to those spaces that are not held in a more widely-defined collective memory to be sites for commemoration. The focus of this article is, however, the extent to which the physical spaces left behind by the "Holocaust by bullets" are treated as sites for commemoration. It is in that context that the status of the sites in the memories of the towns that border them becomes particularly important.

14 Pierre Nora, "Between Memory and History: Les Lieux de Mémoire," trans. Marc Roudebush, *Representations*, 26, 1989, p. 7.

been *reconstructed* may nevertheless remain places of memory. In the debate over how to commemorate the sites of mass graves, Nora's terms help in examining the challenges facing commemoration of those sites and serve as a framework for the goals of commemorative efforts in the region. Nora makes the point that "milieux de mémoire" are all but lost.[15] It seems possible, though, to see elements of "milieux de mémoire" in the commemorative function of the Auschwitz site. There, a community of survivors for whom memory of the camp is not a reconstruction have led commemorative efforts at the site and still visit it. In that place, the spontaneity of memory seems to connect, in a limited sense, with the idea of an environment of memory. The point is relevant because those characteristics are much less tenable when it comes to the commemoration of northeastern Poland's mass graves. Not only were there few Jewish survivors from the region but, of the survivors, few remained in the region. The result is that commemorative efforts often fall to the non-Jewish populations of the areas close to the sites. In that context, whether a site of a mass grave becomes an active part of a town's series of commemorative activities (thus moving into the realm of a "lieu de mémoire"), or remains a "non-lieu de mémoire", depends to a great degree on decisions made within the town. As other articles in this volume have highlighted, narratives (based on an authors' own sense of a site) can function to create "sites of memory" for their readers or audience; these articles have illuminated how the existence of those "sites of memory" in texts about a region or site can highlight the frequent absence of active commemoration at a local level that would create "lieux de mémoire" of the physical sites.[16] In the remainder of this article, I will examine the forces that pull sites of mass graves towards remaining "non-lieux de

15 Ibid.
16 I am particularly grateful to Dr. Bożena Karwowska for sharing with me her thoughts on the interplay between spaces created by narratives and those of the physical site. To learn more please read Bożena Karwowska, "Places of Muted Speech," in *Geograficzne przestrzenie utekstowione*, B. Karwowska, et.al (eds), Białystok: Wydawnictwo Uniwersytetu w Białymstoku, 2017.

mémoire" and analyze how those forces intersect with narratives that draw their readers' attention to the once present Jewish communities and the processes of their disappearance. I will do so in the context of the Podlaskie region, a region with a history of the Holocaust that makes it particularly prone to such narrative and commemorative absences.

While commemoration from within local communities is key to the status of a site as either a "lieu de mémoire" or a "non-lieu de mémoire", ground-up commemoration also faces particular challenges that are informed by prewar Christian-Jewish relations, the region's wartime history of Soviet and German occupation and the borderless nature of the killing sites that those periods left behind.[17] The task left for individuals and organizations at work in this area is to create a "pull" toward commemoration and constructing sites of memory, something that will counteract forces that encourage the sites of mass graves to remain "non-lieux de mémoire".

The decimation of the Podlaskie Jewish population has left little opportunity for the region's sites of mass graves to become a part of anything approaching the spontaneous and unreconstructed memory of a "milieu de mémoire". Over 90 percent of the region's Jewish citizens were killed in the Holocaust. Accounts from the time suggest that those Jews who escaped executions carried out in their towns, and who could have acted as carriers of memory, were often able to escape only as far as Białystok. There, they lived a precarious existence as "illegals" in the Białystok ghetto,

---

17 The importance of recognizing the region's history of occupation by both the Soviet and German forces for understanding the history of the Holocaust in the region has been brought to the foreground by Timothy Snyder's *Bloodlands*. Published in 2010, *Bloodlands* emphasizes the violence seen in the areas caught between Soviet and German forces and has served to highlight the region on the broader map of the Holocaust. See also Jeffrey S. Kopstein and Jason Wittenberg's article, "Deadly Communities: Local Political Milieus and the Persecution of Jews in Occupied Poland," *Comparative Political Studies*, 44(3,) 2011, pp. 259-283, for analysis of, and original research on, the relationship of prewar levels of Jewish-Christian integration, and of the occupation of areas east of the Molotov-Ribbentrop Line by both Soviet and German forces, with the pogroms carried out following German occupation of the region in 1941.

vulnerable (as were the ghetto's other residents) to shootings or deportations.[18] Of the approximately 350,000 Jewish people in the Białystok region before the war,[19] only about 760 survivors remained in Białystok by the summer of 1945.[20]

The number of Jewish residents of the region continued to drop after the war. In his book *Bialystok to Birkenau*, Michel Mielnicki, a Holocaust survivor and former resident of Wasilków (a town about eight kilometers from Białystok), writes of trying to return to his hometown in the hope of finding his brother and sister, only to be "advised that a returning Jew ventured into Wasilkow at his peril".[21] Mielnicki speaks too, of the lack of a desire or pull to return to the region, in addition to an active push away from it as experienced by his sister. He writes: "far quicker than I, [Lenka] heard about the renewal of anti-Semitic violence in Poland. She knew our mother and father were dead. . . . So, what was there for her to go back to?"[22] The decision of Jewish survivors to leave the area was not limited to those whose experiences or memories were shaped by extremely negative relations with non-Jews in the region. Unlike Michel Mielnicki, who makes a point of dedicating his book to those "murdered by fascist Poles" along with those murdered by "German Nazis", Holocaust survivor and memoirist Felicja Nowak dedicates her memoir, in part, to the Polish Christian family who saved her life. In the course of her memoir, *My Star*, Nowak points to many non-Jewish Poles who took on the risk of facilitating her concealment outside of the Białystok ghetto. She also points, however, to a postwar climate in which some of her rescuers did

18 Felicja Nowak, *My Star – Memoirs of a Holocaust Survivor*, trans. Andrzej Bursa, Toronto: Polish Canadian Publishing Fund, 1996, p. 82.
19 "We Remember Jewish Białystok," last modified 17 August 2014, web, http://www.zchor.org/bialystok/bialystok.htm.
20 Lucjan Dobroszycki, *Survivors of the Holocaust in Poland – A Portrait Based on Jewish Community Records*, New York: M. E. Sharpe, 1994, p. 68.
21 Michel Mielnicki and John Munro, *Bialystok to Birkenau – The Holocaust Journey of Michel Mielnicki as told to John Munro*, Vancouver: Ronsdale Press, 2000, p. 220.
22 Mielnicki, *Bialystok to Birkenau*, p. 216.

not want their deeds to be publicly commemorated for fear of reprisals.[23] This fear suggests the presence, after the war, of attitudes that would not have encouraged Jewish survivors to remain in the area.[24] Indicative of another pull away from the region for Jewish survivors facing a decimated Jewish community, Nowak's own reason for leaving the Białystok area in 1944 was to join her uncle's family, who had survived the war, in Moscow.[25]

Mielnicki and Nowak are only two examples of people who chose not to remain in their former homes; nonetheless, they point to a phenomenon visible on a wider scale in the postwar population statistics for the region. Collected Jewish Community Records for the years 1944-1947 indicate that while in the summer of 1945 there were approximately 760 Jews living in the Białystok region, by the end of 1945, that number had fallen to 661 people.[26] The significant barriers faced by Jews in the region and the continually decreasing numbers of Jews in the region after the war substantiates the point that, in many cases, it would be the descendants of non-Jewish people living in the region, not the descendants of former

23 Nowak, *My Star*, p. 6.
24 As brought to my attention by Dr. Bożena Karwowska, it is worth considering here that the proportionately large number of Jewish to non-Jewish Poles in this region could have posed a challenge for those asked to provide shelter and hide multiple neighbors. Felicja Nowak, for instance, discusses friends of her family who wished to hide her, but did not feel that they had the resources to do so. Such people's actions remain separate from those of people who after the war chose to target those who had hidden Jews. One can also argue that their actions (or lack thereof), do not pose the same challenges to commemoration.
25 Nowak, *My Star*, p. 153.
26 Dobroszycki, *Survivors of the Holocaust in Poland*, p. 76. Population numbers for the period are difficult to ascertain with certainty given the large numbers of people relocating in the direct aftermath of the Holocaust and of the war. Furthermore, many Jews would likely have been wary of identifying themselves as such in the postwar years. That said, there seems to be a general consensus amongst records and scholars that the population statistics listed are in the correct order of magnitude. See also *The YIVO Encyclopedia of Jews in Eastern Europe* ("Białystok," *The YIVO Encyclopedia of Jews in Eastern Europe*, web, http://www.yivoencyclopedia.org/article.aspx/Białystok).

Jewish residents, who live in the territory where the mass graves are located and who may be familiar with the sites of mass graves.

As a result of the near-total destruction of the region's Jewish communities, the few who could actively portray the sites of mass graves as "sites of memory" did not remain in the region to foster such a sense of the space. The case of Felicja Nowak, for example, is telling. In describing her visit to Białystok's Pietrasze and relating how she "bowed" and "laid down [her] bouquet of flowers" in the place where her father had been shot, she reminds her readers that the site is a place for commemoration. Specifically, she reminds her readers that it is a place for the commemoration of those who were killed there "only because they were Jews".[27] Although her text emphasizes for her audience (both residents of the region and others) that sites of mass graves are sites for commemoration, it also points to the broader challenges of commemoration in the region: Nowak's visit to Pietrasze was made as she prepared for her emigration from Poland in 1971. As a result of the decimation of the region's Jewish population, no extensive community remained for which the sites of mass graves were automatically sites[28] of commemoration. Instead, the role of determining which sites would become sites of commemoration was left to the local non-Jewish communities.[29]

27 Nowak, *My Star*, p. 169.
28 [ED] There were many after-war exhumations, also led by Jewish institutions. So the feeling was that at least some of the sites were not fit to become places of commemoration. See Alina Skibinska, "Exhumation protocols: An unknown and moving source for the study of wartime and postwar crimes" (paper presented at the International Conference to mark the Opening of the Core Exhibition of POLIN Museum of the History of Polish Jews, in *Warsaw: From Ibrahim ibn Yakub to 6 Anielewicz Street*, Warsaw, Poland, 11-14 May 2015).
29 As other contributions to this volume attest, a narrative such as Felicja Nowak's can serve to create a "lieu de mémoire" of its own in the minds of its readers even where one is not as firmly engrained in the treatment of the site itself. Although not memoirs, Władysław Pasikowski's film *Aftermath* and Tadeusz Słobodzianek's play "Our Class", like the memoir of Felicja Nowak, simultaneously create "lieux de mémoire" in the minds of their audiences and point to the challenges to the formation of "lieux de mémoire" at the sites of mass graves themselves. As artistic representations of pogroms and of the

The discussion of sites of mass graves brought to light in widely-popular works about the region[30] raises the question of whether locally-based commemorative efforts remain important in the context of those sites that remain somewhat or widely known today. The answer may be found in attitudes toward avoiding highly visible commemorative efforts without signs of local support among individuals and organizations planning to memorialize sites in the Podlaskie region. While the concerns of those individuals and organizations vary, the point remains. Karen Kaplan, an individual sponsor of a monument outside of the town of Rajgród,[31] addressed the reluctance of much of her family to erect a memorial there in a speech given in May, 2015. Kaplan explained her family's reluctance as stemming from a fear that such a visible assertion of the Jewish heritage of the town and of its loss could provoke antisemitism among the now entirely non-Jewish population.[32] Similarly, while the organization Yahad-In Unum is "dedicated to systematically identifying and documenting the sites of Jewish mass executions", recommendations made by the organization's founder reflect a similar reluctance to engage in anything but "discreet" commemoration without signs of local dedication to commemoration. In a presentation on "Yahad – In Unum's Research of Mass Grave Sites of Holocaust Victims" founder Patrick Desbois explained, "We also recommend that the work of protecting and commemorating be done

---

spaces they leave behind, both works highlight their authors' sense that those spaces are ones for commemoration while, at the same time, pointing to the forces that would exert a pull against active commemoration of those sites. It is on that latter issue of the forces that would encourage sites to remain "non-lieux de mémoire" that the subsequent paragraphs will focus.

30 See analysis of two such examples: Jan T. Gross's *Neighbors: The Destruction of the Jewish Community in Jedwabne, Poland*, Princeton: Princeton University Press, 2001, and Władysław Pasikowski's film *Aftermath*, (Poland, 2012), to follow.

31 The monument was intended to commemorate the murder of around one hundred members of the town's Jewish community, including that of Kaplan's father's family. Karen Kaplan, "Descendants of Rajgród – Presentation," presented to the *Witnessing Auschwitz* seminar, Michałowo, Poland, 28 May 2015.)

32 Ibid.

as discreetly as possible. If there were to be a public announcement of the protection of thousands of mass graves of the Holocaust in Eastern Europe, the remains of victims that are lying in various private and public places may be desacralized, so that the territory's owner would avoid any perceived trouble".[33] Regardless of whether those concerns about the results of vocal commemorative efforts are justified in every case, one can certainly find examples from the region to suggest that a site becoming known to be a site of mass graves does not preclude it from remaining a "non-lieux de mémoire"[34] locally. First published in 2000, Jan T. Gross's *Neighbors: The Destruction of the Jewish Community in Jedwabne, Poland*[35] argues that it had been people who lived in the town, rather than the German occupying forces, who carried out the murder of the town's Jewish citizens in the July 1941 pogrom.[36] In the series of disputes that followed the publication of the book, the mass grave of the town's Jews became a center of attention. However, Marta Kurkowska, Fellow of the United States Holocaust Memorial Museum's Center for Advanced Holocaust Studies, reports that despite (or perhaps because of) that additional focus on the site, the years following the publication of *Neighbors* saw little ongoing support from local officials for memorial services on the site.[37] The memorial erected on the site has also been subjected to vandalism. The example of Jedwabne suggests that the mere awareness of a mass grave site, whether locally or internationally, does not guarantee the creation of a secure or consistently recognized site of memory.

It is important also to acknowledge that just because a site of mass graves may be known only to locals, does not render those sites

33 Desbois, "Yahad – In Unum's Research of Mass Grave Sites of Holocaust Victims," p. 95.
34 As discussed previously, I use "non-lieu de mémoire" in the sense of a site that has not been incorporated into a town's broader commemoration of the war years.
35 Gross, *Neighbors*; published in Polish in 2000, and in English in 2001.
36 Ibid., p. 16.
37 Marta Kurkowska, "Jedwabne and Wizna – Monuments and Memory in the Łomza Region," *Polin*, 20, 2008, p. 256.

automatically (or permanently) "non-lieux de mémoire". What it does mean, however, is that the local community determines how clearly the sites are marked as gravesites and to what extent those memorials become a part of war commemorations. According to Katrin Steffen, however, "the non-Jewish members of Polish society failed to take on this role".[38] She underscores that there were too few Jewish people remaining after the Holocaust to act as "bearers of collective memory . . . and thus compensate for the passing of the generation that experienced the events first hand". On the other hand, Agnieszka Nieradko of the Rabbinical Commission in Poland holds that "local communities have kept the memory alive for seventy years about the fate of their Jewish neighbors". Referring to the Rabbinical Commission's work to find and preserve Holocaust graves, Nieradko suggests that those "local communities . . . should be the starting point for . . . [the Rabbinical Commission's] work".[39] Taking Steffen's and Nieradko's statements together could suggest that, even in the case of those gravesites that have been left as "non-lieux de mémoire", memory of the communities killed there remains, even when it is not expressed through spatial commemoration. More broadly, though, the disconnect between Steffen's and Nieradko's interpretations of the state of memory of Jews in Poland points to the fact that levels of commemoration vary from one community to the next. That acknowledgement sheds a different light on how the term "non-lieux de mémoire" is applied. Roma Sendyka, for example, includes in her explanation of "non-lieux de mémoire" a description of these places as sites with "past[s] known only to locals",[40] reflecting the fact that, generally, those sites that are actively commemorated are those known to a wider group. It seems worth noting, however,

---

38 Steffen, "Disputed Memory," p. 206.

39 Agnieszka Nieradko, "Rabbinical Commission for Jewish Cemeteries in Poland," *Killing Sites Research and Remembrance*, vol. 1 of International Holocaust Remembrance Alliance series, ed. Dr. Thomas Lutz, et al., Berlin: Metropol, 2015, p. 176.

40 Roma Sendyka, "Prism: Understanding a Non-Memory Place," abstract for paper presented at the University of Chicago Center in Paris, web, https://centerinparis.uchicago.edu/page/panel-2-abstracts.

that the difference between a site of mass graves remaining a "non-lieu de mémoire" or becoming a "lieu de mémoire" is not dependent on partici-pants in commemorative efforts beyond those people from the communi-ty by which the gravesite is situated. Considering a "lieu de mémoire" to be a site where active (though not spontaneous) commemoration occurs, one could use the concepts of "non-lieux de mémoire" and "lieux de mémoire" to differentiate between those sites that are not a central part of a town's consciousness[41] and those that are.

By way of example, we can look at one of Podlaskie's small towns where the memorial to that town's murdered Jewish population had re-mained peripheral to the town's memorial services until recently. At the urging of a local school principal, its care was taken up by her students and since that time, it has become a more integrated part of the town's memorial services, moving the site from the terrain of a "non-lieu de mémoire" to something approximating a "lieu de mémoire" in the town's consciousness.[42]

Although commemoration from within local communities is key, ground-up commemoration faces particular challenges, or what can be thought of as forces that would dissuade local populations from working to commemorate more actively the graves of their former Jewish neigh-bors. Scholars of Polish history and memory posit that the outbreak of the Second World War and the results of the Yalta Agreement robbed Poland

41 "Central" in the sense of being commemorated at least to the degree of other memori-alized, non-Holocaust related events in the town.
42 Marta Kurkowska, "Jedwabne and Wizna," p. 257. The town referenced here is Jedwabne. Note here the contrast between the earlier attempts at commemoration through offi-cial channels that had garnered little support (examined in the preceding paragraphs of this article), and the recent success of a local principal, who has sought to make commemoration of the former Jewish residents of the town a more integrated part of the collective memory of future Jedwabne generations. A second series of contrasts is equally important in order to render more nuanced observations that, even when made on the level of specific localities, are by nature, general. [ED] In Poland, vandalism takes place also in Catholic cemeteries. Commemoration: this cannot be done without the consent of local authorities.

of its national independence and led to an emphasis in Polish national memory of the war as a "national catastrophe".[43] Such an emphasis has left little room for memory of the Holocaust as a Jewish catastrophe. Furthermore, during the communist period, propaganda dedicated to portraying those killed during the war as anti-fascist martyrs also served to ignore the anti-Jewish, rather than solely anti-Polish, efforts of the Nazi German occupiers, leading to a common perception of the camps as first and foremost a "Polish tragedy". There are examples throughout Poland of memorials to Polish citizens killed during the Holocaust which ignore the religious identity of the victims, i.e., memorials that make no mention of the victims' Jewishness and which speak of the victims as "political and war prisoners".[44] With the fall of Communism came a return to a more open acknowledgment of the religious affiliations and identities of Nazi victims.[45]

While such an opening holds the potential for the pluralization of memory, the taking up of the memory of Jewish losses by the non-Jewish Polish community as part of their history remains complicated in many areas, including the Podlaskie region. The relationship between the region's Jewish and Christian communities had been a historically complex one. Even before the Holocaust, when members of Jewish communities had figured prominently in the region, they had been regarded by many as

---

43 Kai Struve, "Rites of Violence? The Pogroms of Summer 1941," *Polin*, 24, 2012, p. 264. See also Marta Kurkowska, "Jedwabne and Wizna" and Deidre Berger, "Protecting Memory: Preserving and Memorializing the Holocaust Mass Graves of Eastern Europe," *Killing Sites Research and Remembrance*, vol. 1 of International Holocaust Remembrance Alliance series, ed. Dr. Thomas Lutz, et al., Berlin: Metropol, 2015.

44 Wording taken from a plaque erected during the communist period to commemorate the victims of Auschwitz-III Monowitz, the significant majority of whom were Jewish ("Memorial Sites for the Buna/Monowitz Concentration Camp," Wolheim Memorial, accessed 8 July 2015, http://www.wollheim-memorial.de/en/gedenkorte_fuer_das_kz_bunamonowitz). See also Felicja Nowak's discussion of the memorial standing in Białystok's Pietrasze in 1971 that bore "no indication that . . . [those who were murdered there] were killed only because they were Jews" (Nowak, *My Star*, p. 169).

45 Steffen, "Disputed Memory," p. 199.

separate from the Christian-Polish communities. Despite shared participation in some cultural endeavours, economic competition and language barriers between those members of the Jewish community who spoke predominantly Yiddish and Russian, and Polish-speaking Christians, exacerbated the separation between the communities and their memories.[46]

The particular history of the Holocaust in the Podlaskie region also appears to encourage the suppression of both the story of a distinct, Jewish tragedy, and its commemoration. A national survey conducted in 1998 showed that adults (then described as "young Poles") worried "that Polish suffering during the Second World war might not be sufficiently acknowledged if Jewish suffering is highlighted".[47] The emphasis on the war as an attack on the Polish nation may be all the stronger, and the pull to commemorate the particular fate of the Jews commensurately weaker, in the area of eastern Poland that was attacked and occupied by both the Soviets and the Germans. The Podlaskie region falls within the area of "double occupation", the area of Poland east of the Molotov-Ribbentrop Line.[48] In that region, non-Jewish Poles, though not targeted for extermination to the same extent as Jewish Poles, were still subject to the violence perpetrated by both the Soviet and the German occupiers. Memory of the hardships of the two occupations can encourage a regional memory in which "Polish Jews . . . and their suffering would hold only a marginal significance in the tales of wartime martyrdom", as Marta Kurkowska describes "official memory" in the context of the Podlaskie region.[49] Such regional memory can, as a result, leave little room for active commemoration of the hardships faced by a community seen by many as the "Other".

---

46 "The Processes of Collective Memory in Białystok," lecture to the UBC *Witnessing Auschwitz* seminar, Białystok, Poland, 27 May 2015. See also Kopstein and Wittenberg, "Deadly Communities," p. 4.

47 Jolanta Ambrosewicz-Jacobs, "The Development of Holocaust Education in Post-Communist Poland," *Polin* 20, 2008, p. 277.

48 Snyder, *Bloodlands*, p. 190.

49 Kurkowska, "Jedwabne and Wizna," p. 249.

Even beyond the issue of a limited pull to recognize the losses of the Jewish communities in the region, the period of double occupation also encouraged outbreaks of local violence against Jewish populations that have, in some instances, created a push against speaking about former fellow townspeople who were Jewish. In the context of double occupation, some members of the non-Jewish Polish community developed the belief (a belief encouraged by the German occupiers[50]) that the Jewish population of the region had collaborated with the Soviet occupiers. The issue of the alleged Jewish-Soviet collaboration is a particularly fraught one. Certainly, there were individuals, Jews included, who collaborated with the Soviets. Michel Mielnicki provides one such example in his memoir (discussed earlier in this article) when he speaks of his father's work with the NKVD.[51] Speaking more broadly, political scientists Jeffrey Kopstein and Jason Wittenberg acknowledge "the initially warm welcome that some Jews gave to the Soviets" in 1939.[52] Yet what Kopstein and Wittenberg also emphasize is that the degree to which perceptions of Jewish-Soviet collaboration were tied to pre-existing antisemitic tropes of "Judeo-Bolshevism" renders generalizations problematic.[53][54] Collaboration and the

50 Timothy Snyder, *Bloodlands*, London: The Bodley Head, 2010, p. 194.
51 Mielnicki, *Bialystok to Birkenau*, p. 84.
52 Kopstein and Wittenberg, "Deadly Communities," p. 7.
53 Ibid.
54 A "warm welcome" to the Soviets on the part of members of any ethnic group in Poland shocked those Poles who already feared Soviet influence and Soviet occupation. My thanks to Dr. Setkiewicz for bringing that point, and the broader debate that surrounds such issues, to my attention. The last several years have seen serious debate within Poland over the depth and reach of sympathy for, and cooperation with, the Soviet occupiers amongst Poland's Jewish communities in this period. Scholars, including Marek Wierzbicki, have brought to light instances in which Jewish communists participated in denunciations of, and attacks on, "Polish soldiers, officers, and policemen" (Marek Wierzbicki, "Western Belarus in September 1939: Polish-Jewish Relations in the kresy," in *Shared History - Divided Memory*, eds. Elazar Barkan, Elizabeth A. Cole, Kai Struve, Leipzig: Leipziger Universitätsverlag GmbH, 2007, p. 140). Debate over the context in which such events should be placed is contentious and subject to politicization. Wierzbicki places what he defines as the "enthusiastic welcome of the Soviets" in the context

allegations of collaboration are relevant to our discussion for the role that they played in facilitating the scapegoating of Jews for the Soviet invasion and for Soviet violence against local populations. Enmity for Jewish residents of the region grew as a result of jealousy relating to the improved position of some Jews under the Soviets (relative only, Kopstein

of a "borderlands" region in which, he argues, expectations of, and loyalties to, the Polish state may well have differed between Jewish and non-Jewish Poles: in the "inter-war period," Wierzbicki argues, "prospects for a decent life" were few and "anti-Jewish discrimination" was present (Wierzbicki, "Western Belarus in September 1939," p. 138). Within the discipline of sociology, scholar Tadeusz Piotrowski puts forward a similar argument for the inter-war period as marked by a distancing between Jewish and non-Jewish communities as some members of Jewish communities entered communist circles in prewar years (*Poland's Holocaust: Ethnic Strife, Collaboration with Occupying Forces and Genocide in the Second Republic, 1918-1947*, Jefferson, N.C.: McFarland, 1998). Writing for the *Sarmation Review*, Piotr Wrobel cautions against explanations that overlook the divergent appeal of communism and divergent reactions to Soviet occupation within diverse Jewish communities ("Marek Jan Chodakiewicz's *The Massacre in Jedwabne, July 10, 1941: Before, During, and After* - (Review)," *The Sarmation Review*, 26(3), 2006. Joanna Michlic raises a similar critique in her contribution to the volume *Shared History – Divided Memory. Jews and others in Soviet-Occupied Poland, 1939 – 1941*: Michlic's work, in particular, points to as yet unresolved questions regarding the degree to which discussion of collaboration with the Soviet occupiers amongst Jews in Poland is colored by pre-existing beliefs in Judeo-communism and by the distinct perspectives of sources that vary between those collected by members of the NKVD and those compiled and preserved in the Ringelblum archives by members of the Oneg Shabbat group operating out of the Warsaw ghetto (Andrzej Żbikowski, "*Polacy i Żydzi w zaborze sowieckim. Stosunki polsko-żydowskie na ziemiach północno-wschodnich II Rzeczypospolitej pod okupacją sowiecką (1939-1941)*, Marek Wierzbicki, Warszawa 2001: [recenzja] – [Poles and Jews in the Soviet annexation. Polish-Jewish relations in the lands of the north-east of the Second Republic under Soviet occupation (1939-1941): A Review], *Pamięć i Sprawiedliwość*, 2002, p. 305). Further commentary on the debates outlined here is available to an English-speaking audience in texts including: *Jews in eastern Poland and the USSR, 1939-46*, eds. Norman Davies and Antony Polonsky, Hampshire: Macmillan in association with the School of Slavonic and East European Studies, University of London, 1991; Antony Polonsky and Joanna Michlic eds., *The Neighbours Respond: The Controversy over the Jedwabne Massacre in Poland*, Princeton: Princeton University Press, 2009; and Elazar Barkan, Elizabeth A. Cole, Kai Struve eds., *Shared History – Divided Memory*, Leipzig: Leipziger Universitätsverlag GmbH, 2007.

and Wittenberg remind us, to "the earlier inferior status" of Jews[55]) and a reinforced sense of Jews as the "Other" (stemming from the perception of Jews as part of a Jewish-Bolshevik alliance).

In some areas, what resulted were pogroms encouraged by the German occupying forces and carried out by locals against their Jewish neighbors.[56] Writing about the children of Jedwabne, Kurkowska suggests that "the trauma of individual and private memory of those who knew what really happened" would not "reach them", meaning the future non-Jewish generations in Jedwabne.[57] Tadeusz Słobodzianek's play *Our Class* brings those issues to the fore through his imaginings of postwar conversations in which those involved in the pogroms "decided on . . . what was [to be] secret and what was sacred".[58] Similarly Władysław Pasikowski's film *Aftermath* unmasks local violence (rather than the violence of an external aggressor) against a Jewish community as a force that leads to the silencing of commemorative efforts.[59]

While the history of the "Holocaust by bullets" poses challenges to commemorative efforts, so too do the spaces it has left behind.[60] Memory, Pierre Nora writes, "takes root in the concrete, in spaces, . . . images, and

55 Kopstein and Wittenberg, "Deadly Communities," p. 7.
56 Those areas included the examples of Jedwabne and Radziłów discussed by Jan T. Gross in *Neighbors*. See also Jeffrey Kopstein and Jason Wittenberg's "Deadly Communities: Local Political Milieus and the Persecution of Jews in Occupied Poland" for a discussion of why pogroms occurred in some communities and not in others. While Kopstein and Wittenberg suggest that, statistically speaking, the degree of political integration of Jewish and non-Jewish communities may have been the deciding factor for the occurrence, or not, of pogroms, they emphasize the prominent role played by allegations of collaboration in the scapegoating of the Jews, as well as in the works of subsequent nationalist historians who wrote on the region (Kopstein and Wittenberg, "Deadly Communities," p. 7).
57 Kurkowska, "Jedwabne and Wizna," p. 249.
58 Tadeusz Słobodzianek, *Our Class*, version by Ryan Craig, trans. Catherine Grosvenor, London: Oberon Books, 2012, p. 150.
59 *Aftermath*, dir. Władysław Pasikowski (Poland, 2012). Pasikowski's film, like Słobodzianek's *Our Class*, is based on the issues raised by Gross's *Neighbors*.
60 Desbois, "Yahad – In Unum's Research of Mass Grave Sites of Holocaust Victims," p. 87.

objects".[61] Though "lieux de mémoire" only fill in for real memory,[62] even the process of sites that are "non-lieux de mémoire" becoming "lieux de mémoire" would likely be assisted by the existence of concrete and readily demarcated sites for memorials or for memorial services. Instead, what the "Holocaust by bullets" has left behind are mass graves with borders that can be difficult to distinguish. Writing about obstacles to protection and memorialization, Deidre Berger, Director of the American Jewish Committee in Berlin, writes of the challenges associated with establishing the borders of sites years or even decades after the fact: "determining the perimeters of sites and establishing boundaries proved to be a considerable challenge after so many years of neglect".[63] Similarly, Roma Sendyka recognizes the challenge of knowing that you are in a site for commemoration when the borders of that space are unclear. In particular, she uses the example of the territory of the concentration camp Płaszów, which is now being used as a park, and extends this example to similar spaces across Eastern Europe.[64] If one cannot see the borders of the commemorative site, it is perhaps harder to feel oneself to be in such a site. The same issue applies to the mass graves of the Podlaskie region, contributing to the likelihood of them remaining "non-lieux de mémoire".[65]

It is not only the undefined borders of mass gravesites that render the sites less likely to create a pull to more active commemoration. The porousness of those boundaries also creates the potential for concerns over land use. Those concerns can translate into active pushes against seeing the sites more firmly established in the communal mindset as graves

---

61 Nora, "Between Memory and History," p. 9.

62 Ibid., p. 12.

63 Deidre Berger, "Protecting Memory," p. 101. [ED] See also the work of Caroline Sturdy Colls, *Forensis: The Architecture of Public Truth*, ed. Forensic Arrchitecture, Berlin: Sternberg Press, 2014, and Colls, *Holocaust Archaeologies: Approaches and Future Directions*, New York: Springer, 2015, on the development of research techniques allowing for the determination of the borders of killing sites.

64 Sendyka, *Witnessing Auschwitz* seminar.

65 Ibid.

and, therefore, as sacred sites of commemoration. As regards some of the barriers to active commemoration of the sites of mass graves, I have already mentioned Patrick Desbois, who speaks of what he sees as a widespread preference among owners of land where mass graves are located to "desacralize" the land and, thus, "avoid any perceived trouble".[66] Similarly, Chief Rabbi of Poland, Michael Schudrich, references the potential and perceived "inconvenien[ce]" of a mass grave found in "someone's field" currently used, for instance, for agricultural purposes. Many have expressed fear that to emphasize the nature of the land as a graveyard would be to undermine its current uses.[67]

In the context of historical and spatial forces that encourage people to keep the sites of mass graves on the periphery of commemorative efforts, the task of organizations and individuals at work in the region rest in an attempt to construct a meaningful pull to remember those mass graves and the communities of people buried within them. The unreconstructed memory "borne by [a] living societ[y]" that one would associate with a "milieu de mémoire" is unattainable in the context of the region's decimated Jewish population.[68] There is no form of commemoration to fill the void left behind by a lost population. The goal, rather, would be to see those sites that have been marked, but not actively commemorated, become a more central part of a town's consciousness. In discussing "lieux de mémoire", Nora makes the point that they require a certain "commemorative vigilance" and that, particularly in the case of the memory of minorities, "history would [otherwise] soon sweep them away".[69] The range of work done by organizations in the region points to the different ways in which one might seek to create a greater pull towards commemoration and "commemorative vigilance" at a local level. In the very first years after the end of the war, Noe Grüss, one of the founders of the Central Jewish

---

66 Desbois, "Yahad – In Unum's Research of Mass Grave Sites of Holocaust Victims," p. 95.
67 Schudrich, "Jewish Law and Exhumation," p. 80.
68 Nora, "Between Memory and History," p. 8.
69 Ibid., p. 12.

Historical Commission (CŻKH), expressed a desire for what Christhard Hoffmann and Matt Erlin termed "cognitive commemoration"[70] that was to be attained through the erection of a memorial "not . . . made of marble or stone, but . . . one in people's hearts and memory".[71] Groups currently at work in the region, such as Michałowo's Multicultural Center, and those such as Yahad-In Unum and the Lo-Tishkach European Jewish Cemeteries Initiative that are primarily concerned with finding and marking gravesites, include education in their mandates. A recent study on Holocaust education in Poland by the director of Holocaust Studies at the Jagiellonian University[72] also points to the way in which aesthetic and "cognitive commemoration" can function together. The author of the study writes: "Informal education, frequently conducted by NGOs, reaches a larger audience particularly in towns where Holocaust memorials are located".[73] In those instances, the work of memorial-based and education-based commemorative efforts come together to try to create a pull towards greater "commemorative vigilance".[74]

To the extent that there is still some spontaneity to the commemorative aspect at Auschwitz, there too it will likely pass along with the survivors. At the site of the Auschwitz Camp Complex, though, the educational and research aspects of the Museum are already acting to ensure that the site remains a place of memory and to foster long-term "commemorative vigilance". However, in Podlaskie (the region under discussion in this article), the creation of "commemorative vigilance" faces distinct challenges. Religious miscorrelation between the murdered Jewish population

---

70 Christhard Hoffmann and Matt Erlin, "The Dilemmas of Commemoration," p. 5.

71 Noe Grüss qtd. in Natalia Aleksiun, "The Central Jewish Historical Commission in Poland 1944 – 1947," *Polin*, 20, 2008, p. 77.

72 Jolanta Ambrosewicz-Jacobs, "The Development of Holocaust Education in Post-Communist Poland," *Polin* 20, 2008, pp. 271-304.

73 Ibid., p. 301.

74 See also the film *A Town Called Brzostek*, dir. Simon Target (Poland, 2014) on the work of Professor Jonathan Webber to rebuild the cemetery in his family's town of Brzostek. My thanks to Dr. Roma Sendyka for bringing this example to my attention.

and those who remain to remember them highlights the scale of the decimation of Jewish communities and points to the importance of commemoration from within local, non-Jewish communities;[75] at the same time, the history of the double occupation and the borderless nature of the sites of mass graves function to lessen the pull to commemorate no-longer existing Jewish communities within the local communities of today. These challenges are only partly mediated by narratives and artistic representations that work to assert their vision of the region as one marked by sites for commemoration. It is in this light that the efforts of individuals and organizations (both local and not) who work toward commemoration in the region can be viewed. Importantly, such individual and institutional efforts form a part of a broader effort to reconstruct a pull toward commemoration. In creating a pull to remember, they encourage the "commemorative vigilance" required to prevent the erosion of memory of the sites, and of the individuals and communities whose loss they mark.

75 Sendyka, *Witnessing Auschwitz* seminar.

Emily Winckler

A Language Lost:
The Holocaust's Impact on Yiddish
Language and Literature

Yiddish, the language of Eastern European Jews, likely emerged approximately one thousand years ago.[1] Jews spoke Yiddish for centuries in Poland, during the First Republic (Polish-Lithuanian Commonwealth). It is fair to say that the language was in a time of genesis and growth up until the 20th century, at which time it hit a violent period of attrition. Because of the several changes made to European borders during the nineteenth and twentieth centuries, most of the world's Jews lived in Eastern and Central Europe during this time. Due to their lack of stable land ownership or rights to citizenship, Jews forged a strong *Jewish* culture rather than *national* identities, and the area became the centre of the world's Jewish population and cultural hub pre-1939. This Jewish, or Yiddish, culture flourished in Eastern and Central Europe and gave birth to a rich Yiddish literary history. Before 1939, Yiddish was the language that gave a voice to and defined Ashkenazi Jewish life and culture not only in this area, but (because of emigrations) also abroad, permeating outwards through literature and correspondence between Jews around the world. Regrettably, the language, and with it its literary tradition, is nearly wiped out of common memory and usage today. In this paper, I will argue that this degradation is a direct result of the Holocaust. This is due not only to the death of Yiddish speakers, but also to post-Holocaust emigration waves,

1   I am grateful beyond words to Dr. Karolina Szymaniak (Jewish Historical Institute) for her continued support and academic guidance.

assimilation and attitudes towards the language and Judaism. I will pay special attention to Auschwitz[2] and its impact on this degradation.

The Yiddish language was thriving before the Holocaust, not only in terms of culture and its being spoken, but also in terms of its literary tradition and predominance. Functioning as the center of the language's world, Poland, and specifically Warsaw, was home to many celebrated writers publishing primarily in Yiddish. In the 1930s, there were a total of 16,147,000[3] Jews living throughout the world. Of those Jews, a total of 9,372,000 people were living in Europe, a staggering 58%.[4] With roughly 350,000 Jews in Warsaw alone, Poland was undoubtedly the center of Jewish life at the time. These Jews, being Ashkenazi, spoke Yiddish. Their influence on European Jews and those abroad was significant, resulting in Yiddish being "either the first or the second language of about two-thirds of the Jewish people"[5] in the world at the time. The interwar period was a particularly fruitful time for Yiddish literature, coinciding with Poland's independence. When Poland's borders were re-drawn out at Versailles, a large part of the area known as the "Pale of settlement", (an area in which Russia had required Jews to live) became Polish.[6] This brought many Jews and Yiddish-speakers into Polish borders and deepened the

2 Auschwitz has commonly been considered the epicenter of the Holocaust. Although it is inaccurate to equate a single place or experience with the Holocaust entirely, Auschwitz acts as an important case study for Holocaust historians not only because of the sheer number of victims murdered and detained there, but because of the myriad of experiences they had: Auschwitz allows the individual to learn that every victim experienced the Holocaust differently; one may even argue, as Roskies and Diamant said in their publication, "Holocaust Literature: a History and Guide", that "the 'postmodern' world began in Auschwitz." David Roskies, *Holocaust Literature: A History and Guide,* New England: Brandeis University Press, 2012, p. 5.

3 Evyatar Friesel, *Atlas of Modern Jewish History*, New York: Oxford University Press, 1990, p.64.

4 Ibid., p. 64.

5 Ibid., p. 64.

6 Dr. Karolina Szymaniak, "Jewish Warsaw: Yiddish Literature and Culture 1918-39," *Witnessing Auschwitz* seminar, lecture for the University of British Columbia, Jewish Historical Institute, Warsaw, Poland, 9 May 2014.

Yiddish influence on the state. Just before this interwar period, a writer by the name of Yitskhok Leyb Peretz had brought the significance of Yiddish writing into the heart of Warsaw's culture.[7] In fact, the Nobel Prize Winner Isaac Singer began writing in Warsaw's Yiddish literature circle. With this legacy, The Association of Jewish Writers and Journalists was set up in Warsaw, existing from 1916 until Poland fell to Germany in 1939.[8] Even at this time when there were nearly 300,000 Yiddish speakers in the heart of Warsaw, Yiddish literature was met with criticism, especially from Polish writers who saw it as secondary or rudimentary.[9] Unlike other minority groups, Jews did not have a natione-state at this time, and Yiddish gave them a voice despite this. This cultural factor brought Jews together, another important impact Yiddish had on Europe and Yiddish speakers.

Yiddish, as a language, has a long and interesting history. Even before the Holocaust, there was a push-back against its gaining predominance amongst Jews from other Jews. The issue of Hebrewists versus Yiddishists is deeply engrained in Jewish history and intertwined with political movements. Yiddish was commonly associated with the BUND and other pro-Communist movements concerned with local interests,[10] while Hebrew was connected to Zionist interests. A heated debate erupted between the two groups regarding whether Yiddish or Hebrew should be the national language of the Jews, an argument that came to a head at the Chernowitz conference in 1908. The conference lasted five days, was visited by celebrated authors and activists such as Peretz and the famous BUND member Esther, and it was ultimately decided that "Yiddish [was] a national language of the Jewish people, and [thus called] for its political, social and cultural equal rights".[11] This official turning point, in

---

7 Ibid.
8 Ibid.
9 Ibid.
10 Dovid Katz, *Words on Fire: The Unfinished Story of Yiddish*, New York: Basic Books, 2004, p. 5.
11 Ibid., p. 268.

conjunction with the wealth of literature being published and the growing interest of non-Yiddish speakers in Yiddish literature beginning in the 1890s, sparked an exciting period for Yiddish authors everywhere. Directly preceding the Holocaust, Yiddish was in a "golden period" in which authors were producing Yiddish works spanning a spectrum from "very religious to outspokenly atheist", giving a voice to every Jew, as well as contributing to scholarship outside of the Jewish world.[12] Not only was Yiddish literature flourishing in Europe, but also in America: in the 1890s emigrant settlers began setting up Yiddish presses, followed quickly by intellectual Yiddish authors in the early 1900s.[13] Despite the Zionist "war on Yiddish", a term coined by Mates Mizesh, the language continued to grow and inspired many intellectual publications, including Borokhov's "Aims," which aimed to "give Yiddish everything that national languages have" by universalizing the pronunciation and spelling of the language.[14] In fact, as late as the 1920s, before Yiddish met its biggest opponent yet, it was the preferred language by Soviet officials for Jews in the pale of settlement; they even "paid Yiddish writers and paid for the publications of their books".[15]

With the Holocaust, however, came a stark shift in the history of Yiddish. By targeting European Jewry, the Nazis indirectly targeted the Yiddish language. The goal of the Holocaust was to rid Europe of Jews and Jewish culture, of which Yiddish was, ultimately, a main component. We may wish to say that the Nazis were not successful in their attempt; however, the impact that the Holocaust had on the Yiddish language suggests otherwise. The largest impact on Yiddish can be seen by examining statistics from before and after the Holocaust, but degradation of the language, literature and culture began the moment Nazi Germany started its program of mass murder and extermination in Europe.

12 Ibid., p. 284.
13 Ibid., pp. 326-331.
14 Ibid., p. 277.
15 Ibid., p. 302.

Although speaking Yiddish was allowed in concentration camps such as Auschwitz[16] and was often an asset to prisoners due to its close relation to German, allowing them to better understand orders, the language was nonetheless subjugated in areas of occupation and throughout Europe. For example, in the 1930s Soviets began shutting down Yiddish institutions and arresting and executing Yiddish writers.[17] Not only would Yiddish give one away as being Jewish, but speaking and or writing in Yiddish may have been considered second-rate or dangerous, even an act of resistance, to Nazi Germany as well as the Soviets during a time that communication was being tightly censured and regulated. This contributed not to only a loss of the language through external circumstances but also to an even more dangerous phenomenon of inward degradation. This self-inflicted ridding of language and literature due to its cultural implications marked the beginning of a dangerous trend for the Yiddish language. After the war, negative attitudes towards Yiddish began to spring up in Israel: a common saying was "Idish – adishut" (Yiddish brings indifference, or Yiddish = Apathy).[18] In Israel, Hebrew became the national language, and Yiddish was eradicated by the very Jews who escaped Europe perhaps once speaking it.

Undoubtedly, however, the largest and most direct impact that the Holocaust had on Yiddish was, of course, the sheer extermination of its speakers. Of the six million Jews murdered at the hands of the Nazis, the vast majority were Central and Eastern European Ashkenazi Jews who spoke Yiddish. With their deaths came the death of their mother tongue, culture, and literary tradition. Because of the large influence Yiddish had gained over the Jewish world before the Holocaust, it was not only Jews from this region that were speaking Yiddish. For example, Gryka Israel Mayer, transported to KL Auschwitz from Paris, France, was registered

16 Dr. Piotr Setkiewicz, Director of the Centre for Research, Auschwitz-Birkenau State Museum, Personal interview, 15 May 2014.
17 Katz, *Words on Fire*, p. 305.
18 Ibid., p. 309.

as speaking "Jidisch" in 1942[19] along with other members of the same transport. The Nazis were massacring Yiddish speakers from all areas of Europe. This created a linguistic drought that spanned much further than the borders of Poland. In fact, the entire Pan-European influence of Yiddish culture was impacted in every region by the Holocaust. By wiping out the current Yiddish speakers of Europe, Nazi Germany also effectively disabled the chances of the Jewish generations that would come next to properly experience and learn Yiddish language and tradition. By European Jewry extant at the time, the National Socialists managed to impact Jewish culture into present day and, arguably, forever.

It is impossible to write in reference to the Holocaust without directly acknowledging the tragedies and crimes committed to the Jews and other victims such as Poles, political prisoners, the physically handicapped and others. In Auschwitz alone, 1.1 million people were killed, predominantly Jews.[20] Of the 11 million people murdered at the hands of the government-organized mass-killings, six million were killed for no other reason than being religiously, or "ethnically" Jewish. The vast majority of the people herded into Nazi death and concentration camps did not survive, and thus what it was like to be a prisoner of Auschwitz, Treblinka, Majdanek, Ravensbruck, Dachau, and so on, is largely incomprehensible. Auschwitz, a joint concentration-death camp, was the largest of all the camps.[21] Because of the unique nature of Auschwitz as both a labor and death camp, it is from here that many authors and survivors have penned their works: including those of Primo Levi, Elie Wiesel, and other celebrated authors. The Holocaust represents the utter degradation of humanity and the undeniable existence of evil. The implications of the Holocaust on our world have been vast and it is the job of all who know about it to remember.

The wealth of literature that was flowing out of Poland into the Yiddish cultural world pre-Holocaust helped bring the language to these

---

19 Gryka Isreal Mayer registration form KL Auschwitz supplied by Dr. Płosa, Auschwitz Birkenau State Museum Archives.
20 *Auschwitz-Birkenau State Museum*, web, www.auschwitz.org, accessed 19 January 2017.
21 Ibid.

far-reaching areas of Europe, but was ultimately silenced by these exterminations. Literature written in Yiddish was still being produced during the Holocaust, but mostly in secret or protest. For example, much of the Yiddish literature and correspondence of the time was heavily coded in order to protect the safety of the writers.[22] The voice of the author was restricted in his own language, the language which once gave him absolute freedom, thus limiting what could be produced. Yiddish literature still existed in many forms, however, including songs, poems, diaries and perhaps most famously, reportage. Emanuel Ringelblum's Oyneg Shabes Archive (itself a code name) documented the lives of Jews in the Warsaw Ghetto,[23] their subsequent deportations, and the fate of Polish Jews as a whole. The archive continued to print cultural and academic literature in secret until the deportation of writers and the liquidation of the Warsaw Ghetto in 1943. In Vilna, another Jewish ghetto of Eastern Europe, Abraham Sutzkever penned the six-line poem "A bliml" (a flower) using Yiddish to commemorate the Jewish spirit and will to rebel against their fate, despite its being so very inescapable: "for wanting to smuggle a flower through the gates / My neighbour paid the price of seven lashes / . . . / My neighbour bears his scars with no regrets: / Spring breathes through his flesh, with so much yearning".[24] Notes and diaries from within the camps were also produced in Yiddish, such as those written by Lejb Langfus, Zalman Gradowski and Zalman Lewenthal.[25] They documented the prisoners' lives inside KL Auschwitz and provided contact with the outside world.[26] From inside Auschwitz also came Avraham Levite's anthology of Jewish writers in the camp. In a Yiddish-focused publication, Levite set out to write a "plea from the 'other planet' that was Auschwitz to postwar generations, calling upon them to appreciate a fully Jewish and critical

22 Roskies, *Holocaust Literature: A History and Guide*, p. 24.
23 Havi Ben-Sasson, "Oneg-Shabbat-Overview," *Yad Vashem*, web, http://www.yadvashem. org/yv/en/exhibitions/ringelblum/overview.asp, accessed 19 January 2017.
24 Roskies, *Holocaust Literature: A History and Guide*, p. 60.
25 Letters provided by Dr. Płosa, Auschwitz-Birkenau State Museum Archives.
26 [ED] They were hidden, buried near the crematoria.

historical voice that was forged within its bounds".[27] Levite's choice to use Yiddish as his primary language, along with memories of suffering as the primary focus of his anthology, speaks volumes in terms of how directly the Holocaust, and Auschwitz, affected the language as a whole. In his own words, Levite's anthology was to record not only the writers' deaths in Auschwitz, but their lives: "We alone must tell our own story. The account we give in our writing is meant to record our tragedy, give an impression of it and represent it. We want to tell the story as we're able, in our own language".[28] This introduction, written on January 3rd, 1945, is all that remains from the anthology; the voices of Levite's comrades were lost. We see that the works produced by the writers of the Oyneg Shabes Archive, Sutzkever and his peers, and prisoners of Auschwitz, were functioning in a very different way and for a far more solemn purpose than that of Yiddish literature pre-Holocaust. Earlier expressions of Yiddish literature celebrated Jewish life, culture and scholarship, a vibrant community that was growing and developing. The examples of Yiddish literature being produced during the Holocaust exhibit the exact opposite, as they function to *preserve* the dying culture, language, and peoples as they perished in the millions across Europe. Similarly, in the years following the horror, the Holocaust remained the focus of Yiddish press around the world: "what with Nazi killers on the loose, honor courts settling the score . . . and the scandal of reparations".[29] Out of this flourished "khurbn-literatur", Yiddish for "Holocaust literature": the autobiographies, memoirs and diaries of survivors taking the spotlight in Yiddish literary publications.[30] In fact, "Yiddish - the language of the meek, the passive, and the pious - became in the wake of the Holocaust the repository of uncensored, unyielding, politically incorrect Jewish rage".[31]

27 David Suchoff, "A Yiddish Text from Auschwitz: Critical History and the Anthological Imagination," *Prooftexts*, 19(1), 1999, pp. 59-69.
28 Ibid., p. 65.
29 Roskies, *Holocaust Literature: A History and Guide*, p. 104.
30 Ibid., p. 105.
31 Ibid., p. 9.

Peace did not come for Yiddish speakers after the end of the Second World War and the Eastern European German occupation. In fact, in the years after the Holocaust, the Yiddish language and its literature continued to be destroyed at a similar pace as Jews began to emigrate out of the region. Elias Schulman was extremely correct when he suggested that "the Holocaust . . . shook Yiddish [culture] to its foundations".[32] In the wake of the Holocaust, European Jewry were not only left to rebuild their homes, but every aspect of their lives down to their language and culture. For many, this task was impossible: "life among the debris of the Yiddish civilization had too little to offer".[33] Thus three distinct waves of emigration from Poland and other Eastern European states followed the Holocaust. To forget the claustrophobic memory of the Holocaust, "most Yiddish emigrants chose to leave Europe behind . . . and set sail for new and more promising worlds . . . the vast majority for the United States"[34] and Israel. After the Second World War, Polish borders were moved west, leaving many Poles in newly allocated land, specifically that of the USSR. The first major wave of emigration out of Soviet territory came about in the years directly following the Holocaust, simply for to be free of the territory. The second wave of emigration was known as the "Zionist emigration".[35] Taking place in the 1970s, this movement of peoples was almost entirely towards Israel and was spurred by Zionist motives. However, not all of these emigration waves were motivated by choice. Jews in the USSR and occupied Soviet territories such as Poland faced conditions that were not unlike those of the wartime. The third wave of mass-emigration for Jews from the USSR took place in the 1990s and, unlike the two previous

---

32 Elias Schulman, *The Holocaust in Yiddish Literature*, New York: Education Department of the Workmen's Circle, 1983, p. 5.

33 Paul Kriwaczek, *Yiddish Civilisation: The Rise and Fall of a Forgotten Nation*, New York: Vintage Books, 2006, p. 295.

34 Ibid., p. 295.

35 Noah Lewin-Epstein, Yaacov Ro'i, and Paul Ritterband, *Russian Jews on Three Continents Migration and Resettlement*, Hoboken: Taylor and Francis, 2013, p. 29.

emigration waves, was caused by a "'push' rather than a 'pull'" force due to the "emergence of a public, virulent, grass-roots Anti-Semitism".[36]

In addition to the obvious cultural effects these emigrations had on Jews and the countries they left behind, it also heavily impacted the usage of Yiddish in everyday life. Acculturation to new countries such as America or areas of Western Europe led to the loss of Yiddish for many, including those who moved to Israel. As previously discussed, in Israel, a new Hebrew, attached to Hebrewists and Zionism, became the cultural norm for common usage, largely eliminating the need for Yiddish. As generations aged, Yiddish was ultimately lost in familial and cultural memory due to the assimilation of second and third generation sons and daughters who aligned with their places of birth and the languages that accompanied them. For example, despite the large Jewish community in Vancouver today, there are very few Yiddish speakers. According to Raffi Freedman, a young Jew from Vancouver, "Yiddish will probably die in forty years. Only [people's] grandparents speak it, it no longer has relevance in young Jews' lives".[37] If it were not for the Holocaust, many of these people would have remained in eastern Europe, continuing with Yiddish literary and linguistic culture, and our world demography would be largely different in terms of the Jewish diaspora, culture and, of course, language.

According to Dr. Adara Goldberg at the Vancouver Holocaust Education Centre, today the Yiddish language is only spoken in extremely secluded areas of the world where Yiddish culture continues to be observed. The semantics of the language describe a particular time and culture: the Yiddish/Jewish culture that existed before the Holocaust. There are not words in the Yiddish language to describe many things that exist today; therefore a truly *Yiddish* speaking community has to abide by these cultural standards and rules. It is for this reason that so few Yiddish communities continue to exist in today's world. In terms of literature, writers producing in Yiddish post-Holocaust are few and far between. Almost

---

36 Ibid., p. 30.
37 Raffi Freedman, Vancouver, Personal interview, 2 July 2014.

all of these writers produce their work simultaneously, or primarily, in other languages, but provide a Yiddish edition. Furthermore, most of the writing done in Yiddish is dedicated to the subject of the Holocaust, as discussed previously. While this use of the language protects the authenticity of the material, it also suggests that perhaps this is all that there is left to say in Yiddish. Perhaps the language can only truly describe the Yiddish culture that existed before the Holocaust and Auschwitz, and now it serves to chronicle its death, as with the publications of the Oyneg Shabes Archive and letters from within the camps. According to Dr. Goldberg, there has been a recent resurgence of desire to learn Yiddish around the world, but it is difficult to say whether this revival will be authentic or far-reaching. The question of authenticity asks this: will Yiddish ever be used in daily activities as the speaker's first language? Or will it simply be revived for revival's sake? In Warsaw the young Jews of Moishe House Warsaw spoke about their task of re-creating an authentic Jewish culture, one that of course includes Yiddish. When asked, they expressed concerns about their own authenticity and the justice they will be doing their Jewish ancestors, and how practical this revival is in present day.[38] Yiddish will not be lost entirely if this trend continues.

The loss of the Yiddish language is important for many reasons. Not only does it mark a change in Jewish culture, but it also severs epochs of history, and their peoples, from one another. The myriad of Yiddish literature that once defined Jewish culture no longer has meaning to the descendants of the communities to which those authors belonged. Those who do not dedicate their lives to studying Jewish history and Yiddish language will no longer read life stories of important eastern and central European Jews in their un-translated states. Within half a century, the entire face of a culture has changed. Specifically in terms of the Holocaust and the narrative of Auschwitz, the loss of Yiddish is fearsome. Like the testimonies and letters written by Auschwitz victims such as Lejb Langfus, Zalman Gradowski and Zalman Lewenthal, many of the primary

38 Aleksander Dobrzynski at Moishe House, Warsaw, Personal interview, 28 May 2014.

sources from the Holocaust were produced in Yiddish. If in the future these texts can only be read by academics who have spent years learning the language and are no longer accessible to any sort of public, thousands of Jewish voices will be silenced for their descendants. The importance of reading testimonies in their original form is worthy of a debate, but due to connotations expressed within different languages and also due to words that simply cannot be translated between languages without losing meaning, I argue that reading primary versions is an experience that cannot be accurately captured by translations. The loss of the Yiddish language in Jewish culture makes the experiences of the Jews of the Holocaust not only inaccessible, but makes the already incomprehensible material even less relatable to those who do not read the language of the testimonies. In addition to this, in the words of Mates Mizesh from the Chernowitz conference, with the loss of Yiddish, the Jewish "people will lose its unique content, its soul, it will lose its living spiritual world".[39]

As Paul Kriwaczek explains in his brilliant publication *Yiddish Civilization: The Rise and Fall of a Forgotten Nation,* "the old Poland is gone forever . . . in the distant future, Polish people will recount to each other stories about the time, long, long ago, when Jews lived among [them]".[40] The aftermath of the Holocaust followed by Soviet domination in Poland and anti- Yiddish sentiments in Israel and abroad, led to the destruction of much of Yiddish civilization and language. Yiddish language is coming dangerously close to extinction. Although there is interest in rehabilitation of Yiddish language and culture present today, the language that once flourished worldwide and boasted a rich literary and intellectual history still hovers on the edge of disappearance due to the loss of memory caused by the Holocaust. During the Holocaust, six million Jews were massacred, and with them, an entire language, semantic system, and cultural background. Being the first or second language of two thirds of the Jewish population during the 1930s, it is reasonable to

39 Katz, *Words on Fire*, p. 272.
40 Kriwaczek, *Yiddish Civilization*, p. 2.

believe that many of the Holocaust testimonies available are written in Yiddish. Although versions may exist in other languages, if Yiddish is lost, who will read these testimonies? Will these survivors', or victims', voices be lost entirely? Not only this, but the thousands of texts produced by Jews before the Holocaust, the memories and contributions to the literary and intellectual worlds they made while living, may be entirely forgotten. This is a terrifying possibility that explains why Yiddish is not only important to today's Jewish population's in terms of connection to their past, but also for the commemoration and remembrance of the Holocaust. Approximately 600,000 people can speak Yiddish today, as opposed to the roughly seven million of the pre-Holocaust world. Due to the death of speakers, post-Holocaust emigration waves and cultural and linguistic assimilations, the Holocaust led to the brutal degradation of the Yiddish language, literature and ultimately, culture. We are left to ponder: can Yiddish exist in a world after Auschwitz?

Ellyn Hill

A Borrowed Belonging: Hair at Auschwitz

Introductory Remarks: Anja Nowak

Part of the main exhibition at the Auschwitz-Birkenau State Museum is a room in which visitors find a large quantity of human hair on display. During the extermination process, the hair had been cut off the victims' heads and later been sent to Germany to be industrially processed. The hair in the spacious display case in Block 4 is but a tiny fraction of that which has been left behind by the Nazis when vacating the camp.[1] By now, it has deteriorated severely and lost most of its distinctive color and structure. There is certainly no need to describe the effect of the sight of this pile of hair has on the visitor. It might nevertheless be worthwhile to reflect a bit further on the status of this particular exhibit, because to a certain degree it encapsulates crucial dimensions of the museum site itself. Just as in the gas chamber building and the cellars of Block 11,

---

1 There were approximately 7,000 kilograms of hair left behind in warehouses that belonged to the Auschwitz *Lederfabrik* (the former tannery). See Andrzej Strzelecki, "Utilization of the Victims Corpses," *Auschwitz 1940-1945 I-V: Central Issues in the History of the Camp*, Vol. 2, ed. Waclaw Dlugoborski and Franciszek Piper, Oświęcim: Auschwitz-Birkenau State Museum, 2000, pp. 399-418, p. 409. According to Dr. Jacek Lachendro, the hair that is on display in the case today was found on the premises of the carpet factory *G. Schoeffler* in Kietrz (Katscher). It was transported to the Museum in 1947. See also Strzelecki, *Auschwitz 1940-1945 I-V*, p. 410 and Andrzej Strzelecki, "The Plunder of Victims and Their Corpses," *Anatomy of the Auschwitz Death Camp*, ed. Michael Berenbaum and Yisrael Gutman, Bloomington: United States Holocaust Memorial Museum and Indiana University Press, 1998, pp. 246-266, p. 261.

visitors are asked not to take pictures in the room where the hair is exhibited.[2] It seems as if this restraint indicates the points where the site touches most closely on its character of being a memorial. The fact that the Museum will always be first of all an extensive graveyard becomes most evident where we as visitors are confronted with the very little that is physically left of the victims and with the precise sites of their torture and murder. What is formalized in the ban on taking photos is a demand for piety and respect. It answers to the fact that with the hair, we encounter the last remnants of the victim's bodies. And this creates a dilemma.

From a certain standpoint, the hair as the last bodily residue might very well ask for the dignity of a funeral. But because it is undoubtedly one of the most powerful exhibits and probably seldom fails to convey the horrors of the crimes committed, it is also a crucial element in the educational process. Its exhibition therefore has to maintain a fragile balance: that of exposing human remains to the eyes of the public while protecting them as much as possible from the transgression that is implied.

Another fact points to the same conflict: the hair is not preserved in any way. Unlike other exhibits, it has not been subjected to any chemical treatment to slow down its deterioration. It is not treated as an object, but allowed to slowly sink into its own disintegration. The exhibit shows a precarious balance between the demands of piety, commemoration, historical evidence and education, displaying a complexity that pervades the whole compound of the museum site.

Hair at Auschwitz

The approximately 1,950 kilograms of human hair on display at The Auschwitz Birkenau State Museum comprises only a small amount of

---

2 For rules for Visiting the Auschwitz-Birkenau Memorial and Museum, see: http://en.auschwitz.org/z/index.php?option=com_content&task=view&id=66&Itemid=31.
3 Strzelecki, "The Plunder of Victims and Their Corpses," p. 260.

the hair shaved off of Jewish people's heads during the camp operations. Yet a far greater amount of hair had already been sent to industrial firms such as Teppichfabrik G. Schoffler AG in nearby Kietrz (Katscher) and to factories such as the Alex Zink Company in Bavaria.[3] Workers at these enterprises utilized the hair as raw material for the production of consumer products such as hair nets, fabric, socks and ropes. Soviet experts estimated that the 7,000 kilograms that the Soviet Army found came from 140,000 prisoners,[4] while approximately 1.3 million people, upwards of 90% of them Jewish, had been deported to Auschwitz by German-Nazi officials. These numbers help us gain a sense of how much more hair had actually been shaved from the heads of those sent to the camp.

The display of hair at the Auschwitz State Museum contains very little information, which might already reflect the fact that the hair and its display is a very contested matter; as human remains the hair asks for our piety; at the same time, as irrefutable evidence of the crimes committed, such remains are important educational tokens. As such, the display of these kinds of remains raises urgent questions, which this paper will try to negotiate: How can we cope with the contested status of the hair? Should we classify it as human remains and treat it accordingly, or can we justify treating it like other belongings, such as the shoes or glasses of those sent to Auschwitz? To open the discussion, I will depict the hair removal process as told through memoirs, bearing in mind how age and gender played a role in the retelling and remembrance of such events. Further, the religious symbolism of hair, particularly in the context of Judaism, and particularly for Jewish women, will be addressed. Doing so holds a unique sense of importance in that it permits us a vantage-point spanning Jewish communities. Broadly, this area of inquiry thereby includes all Jews of the WWII era irrespective of whether they found themselves inside or outside Auschwitz, including the dead, the survivors and the

---

4 Władysław Niessner, "Preservation and Ethical Dilemmas Associated with Conserving Auschwitz-Birkenau Victims' Hair," *Preserving for the Future: Material from an International Preservation Conference*, 23-25 June 2003, trans. William Brand, Oświęcim: Auschwitz-Birkenau State Museum, p. 63.

subsequent generations born after Auschwitz; as such, religious views on hair broadens the Jewish voice to include members of Jewish communities who did not survive Auschwitz or who were never imprisoned at Auschwitz but were/are yet affected by the happenings at Auschwitz as a camp turned museum and memorial.

As Niessner notes in his article "Preservation and Ethical Dilemmas Associated with Conserving Auschwitz-Birkenau Victims' Hair", German SS officials at Auschwitz ordered hair removal in the camp for the functional purpose of limiting the spread of lice amongst prisoners, thereby maintaining more sanitary and hygienic conditions.[5] However, at the time of camp operations, hair also had a value on two tiers: symbolic (for the prisoners) and monetary (for the SS). On the symbolic plane, the shaved head of a prisoner functioned to assert the prisoner-body spatially, not as a person confined to Auschwitz, but as an object temporarily designated for work and later to be converted into a number of raw products: hair, but also gold dental fillings, bone and ash. All processed prisoners ultimately awaiting the same fate. Temporally, the removal of hair thus represents the moment when the prisoner crossed the threshold into the dehumanized, stripped-down existence Italian philosopher Georgio Agamben called "bare life" (vita nuda), when the prisoner-body was ultimately severed from its cultural meanings that would otherwise designate its prescribed termination as murder. The conscription of a prisoner-body to the camp by means of a shaved head also meant that attempts at escaping Auschwitz were thereby complicated: blending in with non-prisoners was nigh impossible and in German-Nazi occupied Poland, the consequence was often death for anyone caught trying to help escapees.[6]

---

5 Strzelecki, "The Plunder of Victims and Their Corpses," p. 259. Niessner, "Preservation and Ethical Dilemmas," p. 65.
    [ED] This was also a way to prevent prisoners from escaping. For example, at the very beginning female prisoners were not shaved during the registration procedure. After the first woman had managed to escape from Auschwitz (her name was Janina Nowak), the camp authorities also decided to remove the hair of female prisoners.
6 Niessner, "Preservation and Ethical Dilemmas," p. 65. Strzelecki, "The Plunder of Victims and Their Corpses," p. 259.

On a monetary plane, SS administration sent out orders in 1942 to collect all hair longer than two centimetres cut off from deportees. Re-purposing the hair as raw material for goods manufactured in the industrial sector, one kilogram of hair had a value of 0.5 RM by 1943. In the determination to extract all value from prisoner-bodies, that is, in the sense of labor output as well as physical materials, all for the benefit of the Third Reich, German Nazis collected hair from both those deportees selected for labor and those selected for death. Unlike in other death camps such as Treblinka, Sobibor and Belzec, where women selected for the gas-chambers were shaved by barber kommandos called Friseure prior to death, at Auschwitz, Friseure shaved only the heads of those selected for labor while the Sonderkommando shaved the women selected for death after taking their bodies out of the gas-chambers. This difference illustrates the distinction between dehumanization achieved by the SS in the aforementioned death-camps through shaving the heads of those sent to death and the objectification by the SS officials of Auschwitz where the victims were shaved post-mortem. This distinction is drawn with a very fine line, however, as all bodies of deportees, dead and living, were relegated to an objectified status under the Third Reich, ultimately to become actual objects; in other words, products and, most relevant for our purposes here, thus belongings. The hair we see on display at the Museum today is different from the objects which this material was intended to be manufactured into, such as fabric and stockings. It is different only in that it was discovered shortly after the war while still at the raw material stage. The fact persists that this hair was stolen.

Belongings created from human hair, such as rope and thread, and whose origin is located at the very nexus of German-Nazi genocide and enterprise, have a physical form and useful function that jars a traditional understanding of remains and in this way posits a question mark between the entitlements and needs of the living versus a solemn respect for the dead. Even at the stage of raw material, however, the hair already had an important history, undeniably classifying it as a by-product of genocide, for the procedures of acquisition and readying of the hair for production cannot be described without the acknowledgement of the degradation and death of the human bodies that grew the hair.

The process of shaving each head took about one minute and no more than two minutes, quick, ragged work that saved time at the furthered expense of human sensibility.[7] Once the hair was cut off, another kommando of prisoners called the "Reinkommando" ("the Cleaners"), described by Filip Müller as "fifteen Jewish prisoners [who] were permanently employed in the crematorium to deal with the raw material",[8] collected and "dipped [the hair] into a dilute salmiac (Sal ammoniac) solution to remove dirt and contaminants".[9] The Reinkommando then dried the hair either by placing it on the warm brick floors of the lofts above the crematoria furnaces (fueled primarily by human fat) and chimneys, or by hanging it on strings stretched across these lofts.[10] Once the hair had dried, the Reinkommando combed it out and put it into paper sacks.[11] This process is confirmed through the description in the memoir of the Sonderkommando prisoner Filip Müller:

> Spread all over the brick floor warmed from the crematorium ovens below, was women's hair of every colour and hue . . . Washing lines were strung across the room. Pegged on these lines like wet washing were further batches of hair which had first been washed . . . When the hair was nearly dry, it was spread on the warm floor to finish off. Finally it was combed out by prisoners and put into paper bags.[12]

The history recounted above was in part obtained from testimonies in survivor memoirs. Before examining Holocaust survivor accounts on any

---

7 Niessner, "Preservation and Ethical Dilemmas," p. 65.
8 Filip Müller, *Auschwitz Inferno: The Testimony of a Sonderkommando*, London: Routledge and Kegan Paul Ltd., 1979, p. 65.
9 Niessner, "Preservation and Ethical Dilemmas," p. 66; Strzelecki, "The Plunder of Victims and Their Corpses," p. 260.
10 Niessner, "Preservation and Ethical Dilemmas," p. 66.
11 Ibid. Strzelecki, "The Plunder of Victims and Their Corpses," p. 261.
12 Müller, *Auschwitz Inferno*, p. 65.

matter involving dehumanization, it is however, critical to recall that a formal, legalized understanding of human rights was not in place at the time of their camp experiences. The United Nations had not drafted nor adopted The Universal Declaration of Human Rights until after the war, in December of 1948; in fact, it was the experience of the Second World War, including the Holocaust, that inspired it. As such, when a survivor describes their Holocaust experiences, the understanding they had at the time of the event could not have been informed by a legal sense of human rights because a formalized language did not exist at the time for these experiences. A formal grasp of human rights could only be coupled with their original understanding from the position of hindsight, an authorial choice that survivor-authors do not necessarily make, irrespective of their time of writing. Rather, word choices cue our present-day sense of survivors' own value-judgments in the wake of indescribable violations of what would only years later be recognized as their inalienable human rights and freedoms.

Survivor Stefan Petelycky writes, "We were *herded* into the morning *cold* like *sheep* and taken to a bathhouse where *our heads and faces were shaved*" (emphasis added).[13] Tadeusz Sobolewicz similarly describes, "next, in a corridor *they shaved our heads* and after that *we were directed – naked* to the bathhouse" (emphasis added).[14] Further on he additionally writes of the delousing process that "in the corridor I was stopped by a barber. He *ordered* me to stand on a stool and then proceeded to *shave my head* with a *blunt instrument*" (emphasis added).[15] Elie Wiesel, too, echoes, "I let myself be *dragged* along to the barber. Their clippers *tore out our hair, shaved every hair on our bodies*" (emphasis added).[16]

13 Stefan Petelycky, *Into Auschwitz, For Ukraine*, Kyiv: The Kashtan Press, 1999, p. 24.
14 Tadeusz Sobolewicz, *But I Survived*, Oświęcim: Auschwitz-Birkenau State Museum, 2012, p. 75.
15 Ibid., p. 102.
16 Elie Wiesel, *Night*, New York: Hill and Wang, 1972, p. 35.

Memoirs written by two women, Seweryna Szmaglewska[17] and Halina Birenbaum,[18] are strikingly more detailed in their accounts of their hair being shorn. Birenbaum recalls,

> Capos in dark-blue striped dresses and beautifully sewn aprons herded us, with swearing and beating to a large hut near a bath house where we waited long hours as they counted and recounted, registered us and shaved our heads.[19]

Telling of the delousing process, Szmaglewska recounts,

> within the bathhouse itself are more men. You must stand before them, bend your head to let them examine it for lice. You must climb up on a stool, raise your arms and stand quiet while they shave the hairy parts of your body.[20]

Continuing on with descriptions of how their shaved heads affected the women in the camp, Szmaglewska further writes, "Nude, emancipated women, blue with cold, their shaved heads huddled into scrawny shoulders . . . this is the picture of the barrack in 1942".[21] "Even the closely shaved heads are cold when the wind lifts the ends of kerchiefs tied under the chin, German fashion".[22] Incidentally, however, it is the memory-based literature of a child-survivor, Bogdan Bartnikowski,[23] who had been sent to Auschwitz with his mother and who was therefore shaved along with the

---

17 Seweryna Szmaglewska, *Smoke over Birkenau*, Oświęcim: The Auschwitz-Birkenau State Museum, 2008.
18 Halina Birenbaum, *Hope is the Last to Die*, Oświęcim: Auschwitz-Birkenau State Museum in Oświęcim, 2012.
19 Ibid., p. 120.
20 Szmaglewska, *Smoke over Birkenau*, p. 74.
21 Ibid., p. 17.
22 Ibid., p. 24.
23 Bogdan Bartnikowski, *Childhood Behind Barbed Wire*, Oświęcim: Auschwitz-Birkenau State Museum, 2012.

women, that, even if obliquely, manages to capture the difference in the head-shaving process for men and for women. He describes the women having their hair cut off upon arrival at Auschwitz in the following way:

> all women are naked, but not quite identical. There are blondes, brunettes, greys and redheads. However, all the women who enter the washroom have identical heads. You would not be able to tell the difference between one woman and another . . . Heads shaved bald all look alike, ridiculous and ugly.[24]

By contrast, Bartnikowski recollects his own hair removal experience in a short passage, lacking such detail: "The woman prisoners shaves my head in a blink of an eye and then bends down . . ."[25] The description of his own head being shaved is far less detailed as compared to his recollection of the women who were shaved, and in this it lacks such aesthetic value-judgments regarding matters of beauty, in contrast to his description of the women's experience, suggesting a greater jarring or clash in the impressions Bartnikowski took with him in connection to the women being shaved. Interrogation of this internal conflict on a wider plane necessarily delves into deeper issues of identity and the personhood of prisoners's bodies. Male and female, but in particular female bodies, instantly became a site upon which the SS exercised the power to breach and devoid the prisoners of cultural and gender norms, in this way separating prisoners not simply from their hair, but from visible connections to their internal sense and outward expression of being human and being a unique individual.

In conjunction with gender norms and cultural mores, religious symbolism also factored into the meaning of having one's head shaved, albeit differently for men and for women. As an aside, we must recall that our current-day secular values inhibit, rather than help, our understanding

24 Bartnikowski, *Childhood Behind Barbed Wire*, pp. 22-23.
25 Ibid.

of this point of view and we must therefore set such vantage points on this area of interest to the side. In Jewish traditions, it is common practice for women to have their hair covered,[26] especially amongst the very religious.[27] The covering of one's hair is a practice followed typically by married women[28] both to preserve their own honor and to prevent becoming the object of a male's gaze, a phenomenon that might thereby distract him from his religious services.[29] As hair is considered to be a body part in Judaism, covering the hair is a sign of modesty, and to be uncovered would be the same for religious married women as to be naked, a sin for which one could be punished with eternal damnation in hell.[30] For men of the Jewish faith, by contrast, covering their heads is a way to show religious devotion and is not done as a way to maintain modesty.[31] For married women, having to uncover their hair and then have it shaved off would have been far more difficult than for non-religious Jewish women as their faith in the context of this event heightened their sense of immodesty and nakedness, accompanied by a feeling of religious transgression.

Remains or a Belonging?

Taking into account survivors' voices, and the cultural, religious and social markers that collectively contributed to the experience of having one's head shaved and grappling with the history of the hair in terms of the German-Nazi genocide, answering the "remains or belongings" debate clearly leans in favour of the hair being classified as remains. Still, the

---

26 Some of the very religious women have their hair cut after marriage. It is a symbol of being married.
27 Melanie Landau, "Re-Covering Women as Religious Subjects: Reflections on Jewish Women and Hair-Covering," *The Australian Journal of Jewish Studies*, 22, 2008, p. 57.
28 Ibid., p. 57.
29 Ibid.
30 Ibid., p. 60.
31 Ibid., p. 67.

Auschwitz-Birkenau State Museum has decided to display the hair.[32] The display is located on the second floor of Block 4 at Auschwitz I, in a room focusing on the exploitation of corpses. Here, a glass case runs down one wall and contains piles of the hair from Jewish women.[33] Across from this case, documents regarding corpse exploitation accompany the display, including a letter, dated January 4, 1943, from the WVHA (Main Reich Economic and Administrative Office) to the commandants of concentration camps regarding hair collection. [**PICTURE 7**][34] At the end wall of the room, next to the entrance door, there is another case which contains fabric made from the hair. The room itself is kept semi-dark with tinted windows, as a measure to protect the hair from sun damage; furthermore, visitors are not permitted to take photographs.

Those whose "sensitivity or religious convictions have been touched" believe that the hair is human remains, and therefore should be buried.[35] To them, the fact that the hair is displayed publicly is "an abuse of the intimacy due to the victims after their death", and they argue that the educational purpose of the display could be achieved through photographs and documentation just as well.[36] On the other side of the debate are those who believe that the hair is a belonging and should be shown to visitors for as long as possible.[37] The belonging side of the argument claims that the hair becomes an "almost tangible testimony to the awfulness of the Holocaust [and] conveys the true fate of the victims in an extraordinary way".[38] While the debate continues, nature itself is taking issue with the

---

32 This issue was briefly discussed in the foreword to the book by Deborah E. Lipstadt, *The Eichmann Trial*, New York: Nextbook Press/Schocken, 2011.

33 According to the signage accompanying the exhibit, the hair was obtained only from females. The signage also states that the hair on display weighs approximately 1,950 kilograms.

34 A copy of this letter (in German) on display at the Museum.

35 Niessner, "Preservation and Ethical Dilemmas," p. 67.

36 Ibid.

37 Ibid.

38 Ibid.

display by way of degradation of the hair, caused by atmospheric influences, changes in humidity, dust and light.[39] As "hair has never before been subjected to preservation work on such as large scale", there is no existing process for it at the present,[40] and obviously, in this specific case, there is no room for error.[41] Further complicating this problem is that different methods would also have to be used for the various types of hair and for the "different hair items including braids, locks, tangled clumps and individual hairs".[42] But even if a suitable technical procedure is developed, ultimately, the decision to apply it will have to be made on a moral level.

The Auschwitz-Birkenau State Museum is attempting to find a solution to the controversy that will satisfy both sides; however, the moral and statutory terms of the Museum include preserving and making available everything remaining from the camp, which would include the human hair, for as long as possible, in order to bear witness to the crimes which occurred.[43] As Niessner comments in his article, one potential option would be to find a form of display that does justice to both perceptions, treating the hair as both remains and a belonging. This could mean having a display for the hair which is in the ground and thereby reminiscent of a burial, but still accessible for visitors to the Museum to see.[44]

As interpretive communities remain divided on how to finalize and secure an appropriate designation for the hair taken from deportees, the hair, together with both the history and the questions regarding its present-day use surrounding it, remains a unique moral challenge. In grappling with its semiotic features and the array of candidate signs proposed for it, I argue that, because this classification is an exercise of power – both bio-power and linguistic power – as large a share as possible must be granted to survivors' voices and to Jewish religious traditions;

39 Ibid., p. 68.
40 Ibid.
41 Ibid.
42 Ibid.
43 Ibid.
44 Ibid., p. 69.

in so doing, the hair can then only be classified as remains. Furthermore, the wording of this debate – remains or belongings – suggests that the debate is a matter of *what* the hair is, rather than *whose* hair it is. Thereby, the name of the debate obscures the fact that ownership is a component of both sides. The word "remains" continues to acknowledge the deportees as the owners of the hair whereas the word "belonging" takes for granted the Museum's claim to inherit all physical materials of the Auschwitz concentration, death and labor complex. Replacing the question "remains or belonging" with the more fundamental question "whose hair is it?" necessarily invokes subsequent questions: "Whose dehumanization is it?" "Whose literal objectification is it?" "Whose trauma was or is it?" Doubtless, the only answer is that the hair and its semiotic content all belong to the deportees from whom it was stolen. Indeed, one must acknowledge that the "belonging" answer to the debate is strictly a product of our times as it serves to satisfy the needs of Holocaust educators, especially as they are increasingly left with the responsibility of narrating the Holocaust and educating future generations as the very last of survivors pass on. In other words, no essential feature of the hair itself classifies it as a belonging, though the biological origins of the hair essentially do classify it as belonging to those from whom it was taken, therein positing the "remains" answer as one that indeed is intrinsic to the hair itself. I therefore argue that though the hair must be treated as a belonging in order to continue to educate visitors to the Auschwitz Museum (as no other physical remnant of the German-Nazi genocide against the Jews and other groups of people provides such irrefutable evidence of and testimony to the abject atrocities of the Holocaust) it must be acknowledged as a *borrowed* belonging; that is, as remains belonging to the people whose bodies produced the hair in a biological effort to keep them warm, to keep their skin protected and to allow them a personal medium to develop themselves via cultural and gender norms as human beings, each with a unique sense of personhood and dignity.

Mikiko Galpin

A Cycle of Persecution:
Romani Culture[1] and the *Baro Porajmos*[2]

"The winter will ask what we did in the summer."
– a Welsh Roma proverb

In March of 2011, the European Court of Human Rights listened to the case of a Roma woman who claimed her doctors had coerced her into sterilization during childbirth.[3] In that same year, a mob in Turin burned down a Romani camp.[4] In 2004 and 2005, academics published journal articles alleging the coerced sterilization of more than 150 women in Slovakia and the Czech Republic, calling the actions a "quiet genocide" against Roma

---

1 I am grateful to Dr. Małgorzata Kołaczek (Jagiellonian University) for her suggestions and footnotes to this text. I am also thankful to Dr. Teresa Wontor-Cichy for all her help.
2 Baro Porajmos (also written Baro Porrajmos, O Baro Porrajmos, Porajmos, and Porraimos) is a Romani phrase used in reference to the genocide of Romani peoples. It translates to "the great devouring" of human life and also "gaping" (in horror) and "rape" (Hancock p. 34; see footnote 12 for full reference). It should be noted that Baro Porajmos shows more specificity in referencing the genocide of the Roma and Sinti people that occurred during the time of the Holocaust as, in theory, Porjamos can refer to other genocides (Ó hAodha p. 54; see footnote 24 for full reference). Additionally, there is still an ongoing debate within Roma communities over an appropriate, specific term for the Roma and Sinti genocide as the term Porajmos holds connotations that are considered taboo in Romani culture and the term is not as well recognized as Holocaust or Holocausto (Fonseca p. 253; see footnote 7 for full reference).
3 "Court Hears Claim of Forced Roma Sterilization," *The Washington Post*, 22 March 2011, web, http://www.washingtonpost.com/wp-dyn/content/article/2011/03/22/AR2011032202551.html, accessed 6 June 2016.
4 Yaron Matras, *I Met Lucky People: The Story of the Romani Gypsies*, Great Britain: Penguin Group, 2014, p. 201.

populations.[5] In 2000, 400 Italian police officers used excessive force to remove a group of several hundred Romani immigrants from the outskirts of Rome in an act that sent a message regarding the brutal manner in which Roma could be treated by law enforcement officers. In 1997, Romani asylum seekers from the Czech and Slovak Republics were denied entry into Britain on the basis of the ethnicity listed on their passports.[6] In 1995, four Romani men were killed in Austria when they attempted to remove a sign that read "Gypsies Go Back to India" and triggered a bomb that had been planted.[7]

These are just a few examples of the racially motivated acts of violence and persecution that have plagued the Roma peoples from as early as the middle of the 15th century where the Romani way of life was seen as a threat to the framework of feudal life.[8] Anti-Roma acts, some even threatening death, were passed in almost all European countries, including Spain, France, Germany, Portugal, Denmark, the Netherlands, England and Sweden.[9] Laws such as these as well as instances of Roma being put to death or murdered with no consequences continued well into the eighteenth-century where artists and intellectuals alike perpetuated racist stereotypes of the Roma as vagrants and criminals on the margins of society.[10] The rise of the modern nation-state at this time created a push for assimilation, and laws prohibiting nomadic lifestyles like that of the Roma were enforced, with some going as far as forcibly removing Roma

---

5 Dan Brame, "Slovakia Sterilization Practices Criticized," *Cultural Survival Quarterly*, 27(4), 2003, web, https://www.culturalsurvival.org/publications/cultural-survival-quarterly/slovakia-sterilization-practices-criticized, accessed 6 June 2016.
   Ed Holt, "Roma Women Reveal That Forced Sterilization Remains," *The Lancet*, 2005, 365(9463), pp. 927-928.
6 Matras, *I Met Lucky People*, p. 198.
7 Isabel Fonseca, *Bury Me Standing: The Gypsies and Their Journey*, New York: Vintage, 1995, p. 222.
8 Marek Isztok and Michał Kaczkowski, *Romowie – stan duszy czy kultura równoległa* – Katalog do wystawy – Stowarzyszenie Romów w Polsce, Oświęcim: Kolory 24, 2008, p. 9.
9 Ibid., p. 11; Matras, *I Met Lucky People*, p. 139.
10 Ibid., pp. 139-154.

children from their homes for the assimilation or enslavement of Roma peoples.[11] In the nineteenth century, the Roma, like Jews, were labeled as inferior beings by scholars as prominent as Darwin, and the early 20th century brought with it a multitude of publications citing euthanasia and "ruthless punishment" as solutions for the eradication of the Roma.[12]

The genocide of the Roma peoples during World War II, however, was the most widespread and devastating of these racially motivated persecutions. In 1941, after Robert Ritter deemed those of Romani descent "racially alien, inferior, and asocial", a view reinforced by centuries of discrimination, the Nazis slated the Roma for destruction. On August 2, 1943, nearly 3,000 Roma men, women, and children were gassed in the chambers at Birkenau, the last of the 23,000 who were imprisoned in the camp.[13] Other Roma were slaughtered in massacres across German Nazi occupied territory and still more died from disease, overwork and starvation in concentration camps.[14] During World War II, German Nazi doctors sterilized peoples of Roma descent against their will in an act of calculated policy drawn up on the basis of ethnicity.[15] Collectively, these facts beg the question, "Why, just 70 years after the most devastating genocide in Romani history (with historians setting the death toll at 500,000),[16] have

---

11 Ibid., p. 169.

12 Ian Hancock, *We Are the Romani People: Ame Sam E Rromane Dzene.* Hertfordshire: University of Hertfordshire, 2002, pp. 35-36.

13 Teresa Wontor-Cichy, "The Roma in Auschwitz Concentration Camp," *Auschwitz-Birkenau Memorial and Museum*, web, http://www.auschwitz.org/en/museum/news/the-roma-in-auschwitz-new-on-line-lesson,1109.html, accessed 6 June 2016.

14 Donald Kenrick and Grattan Puxon, *Gypsies Under the Swastika*, Bristol: University of Hertfordshire, 2009.

15 Toby Sonneman, *Shared Sorrows: A Gypsy Family Remembers the Holocaust*, Bristol: University of Hertfordshire, 2002, p. 198.

16 [ED] Figures given by historians on the number of Roma victims vary considerably: Michael Zimmermann estimates the number of victims as about one hundred thousand („Die nationalsozialistische Zigeunerverfolgung in Ost- und Südeuropa - ein Überblick", in: Felicitas Fischer von Weikersthal u.a., Der nationalsozialistische Genozid an den Roma Osteuropas. Geschichte und künstlerische Verarbeitung, Cologne-Weimar-Vienna: Böhlau, 2008, pp. 23-24, while Ian Hancock's estimate is a million and a half

present day injustices gone largely unnoticed, not just by the media, but by the general public as well?"[17] With the genocide of the Romani peoples labeled as one of the "forgotten Holocausts", Romani communities are still targeted and ostracized.

The cycle of persecution is based in part on the lack of general public acknowledgement of the Roma genocide during World War II through to present-day persecution of the Romani peoples. A question posed by Yaron Matras bears particular relevance to the question of commemoration within Romani communities: "Who speaks for the Roms?"[18] In his essay, Kapralski discusses the idea, commonly shared by those he interviewed for the "Violence and Memory" study, that proper education and remembrance of the genocide of Roma peoples could facilitate the struggle for equal rights currently being waged by Romani activists in Europe. One interviewee mentions this in detail saying, "The memory of the war could . . . play a very practical role in contributing to understanding and counteracting the marginalization of the Roma . . . This would require . . . governments to acknowledge that the Roma were persecuted during the Second World War . . . to ensure at least equal, if not privileged treatment of the Roma".[19]

Starting from this interviewee's statement, investigation of this cycle of persecution will link commemoration to the present by first looking at how the language surrounding the Roma genocide and the lack of proper terminology undermines and contributes to negative stereotypes of Roma culture. These negative representations of Roma culture lead to a dismissal of requests for remembrance. This dismissal, based primarily on primitive stereotypes, creates an atmosphere of mistrust and tension

("Uniqueness, Gipsies, Jews," in Yehuda Bauer et al., eds., *Remembering for the Future: Working Papers and Addenda, Vol. II: The Impact of the Holocaust on the Contemporary World,*" Oxford: Pergamon Press, 1989, pp. 2020-2024.

17 Sławomir Kapralski, "The Influence of Extermination on Contemporary Roma Identity," *Voices of Memory* 7, Oświęcim: Auschwitz-Birkenau Memorial and Museum, 2011, p. 33.

18 Matras, *I Met Lucky People*, p. 217.

19 Kapralski, "The Influence of Extermination on Contemporary Roma Identity," p. 50.

between Roma and non-Roma. Finally, the self-chosen isolation of Romani communities due to mistrust of outsiders contributes to a lack of acknowledgement of the Roma and Sinti genocide and the continued perpetration of racially motivated crimes against Roma peoples.

When discussing the lack of commemoration of the genocide of Romani peoples, it is of the utmost importance to use the correct terminology for the group and the event, particularly since incorrect terminology can further convolute these issues. While the Roma comprised one of the largest groups sent to Auschwitz, the majority of the world's present-day population is unaware of the existence of Roma peoples in concentration camps. In fact, many people outside of specific research groups have little to no understanding of what the name "Roma" refers to. The word "Roma", often mistakenly linked to the image of Romanians, actually means "men" or "person from humankind" in Romani, the language of the Roma peoples.[20] The more widely known name for the group is "Gypsies"; however, this term is incorrect as it comes from the belief that those of Romani descent originated from Egypt. Matras recognizes two reasons for this mistaken association. First, that those in the area historically called Byzantium associated all non-Europeans with the most famous non-European civilization at the time, Egypt, and second, that traveling Roma in the fifteenth-century carried safe-conduct letters characterizing their origin as an unknown location designated "Little Egypt".[21] Additionally, the image raised by the use of the word "Gypsies" is an unflattering one as the term carries with it a derogatory and fictitious image created by the non-Roma.[22]

As such, this essay will not employ the word "Gypsy" or "Gypsies", except in instances of direct quotations from other authors. Rather, the

20 Małgorzata Kołaczek, "The Nazi Persecution of the Roma, Holocaust Remembrance, and Contemporary Romani Identities," *Witnessing Auschwitz* seminar, lecture for the University of British Columbia, Oświęcim: Auschwitz-Birkenau Memorial and Museum, 20 May 2016.
21 Matras, *I Met Lucky People*, pp. 16-17.
22 Hancock, *We Are the Romani People*, p. xviii.

terms Roma (an ethnic group) and Romani (a descriptive adjective) will be used as these terms were selected by the First World Romani Congress in 1971 for use in political activities in order to erase the use of "Gypsy". It is of particular importance to also note that there are many different groups of Romani peoples (e.g. Roma, Sinti, Kale, Manouche), and these groups view each other as different due to unique cultural and linguistic characteristics; nevertheless, they have collectively been viewed as one and the same under such pejorative terms as "gypsies" and Zigeuner.[23]

Along with defining the term "Roma", it's important to discuss the terms used to refer to the genocide of Roma peoples during World War II. Currently, there is a discussion of whether the term "Holocaust" should be used to refer to the racially motivated extermination of the Roma. While the Council of Europe does refer to the mass killings of Roma peoples as part of the Holocaust, many Romani groups prefer to use either the term Porajmos (mentioned in more detail elsewhere in this essay) or Samudaripen,[24] as they feel they should have their own word to refer to the specific genocide of Roma, similar to the use of "Shoah" in reference to the Jewish genocide. It is commonly held that as the Roma were targeted

---

23 Like the term "Gypsy", the etymology of the German word Zigeuner is multifaceted and colored by historical connotations. Originating from the Greek atsingani, the name of a heretical sect mistakenly associated with the Roma due to their palmistry and aptitude with herbs, Zigeuner is both a general designation of lawless vagabonds and a derogatory racial label for those of Roma heritage (Kenrick p. 3, see footnote 46 for full reference; Matras, *I Met Lucky People*, p. 19; Fonseca, *Bury Me Standing*, p. 228). The term Zigeuner was used during the Porajmos by German Nazis to identify the Roma and Sinti for deportation and extermination and was represented in the Auschwitz-Birkenau prisoner tattoos with a "Z" at the beginning of a camp number. Kołaczek, "The Nazi Persecution of the Roma, Holocaust Remembrance, and Contemporary Romani Identities,"; Maria Martyniak, "The Deportation of Roma to Auschwitz before the Founding of the Zigeunerlager in the Light of the Extant Documents," *Voices of Memory* 7, Oświęcim: Auschwitz-Birkenau Memorial and Museum, 2011, pp. 7-8.

24 The term Samudaripen was created by a linguist and does not follow the rules of Romani morphology. It translates to "all + murder". Mícheál Ó hAodha and T. A. Acton, *Travellers, Gypsies, Roma: The Demonisation of Difference*, Newcastle: Cambridge Scholars, 2007/2009, p. 54.

for extermination on racial grounds, so like the Jewish population, it is beneficial to have a term that defines "their" Holocaust.[25] While both the Holocaust and the Porajmos are still used, the specificity of the term Porajmos makes it appropriate when focusing on the commemoration of the Roma genocide.

One of the larger issues in commemorating the Porajmos is that the extermination of Roma by the German Nazis was not officially acknowledged in Germany until 1982 (by Helmut Schmidt), and the first commemoration of the Porajmos in Poland was in 1991 when Professor Wacław Długoborski organized a conference on the Roma in the Auschwitz-Birkenau Concentration Camp. Even at present, the UN does not officially qualify the Porajmos as a genocide.[26] Moreover, negative stereotypes of

---

25 Kołaczek, "The Nazi Persecution of the Roma, Holocaust Remembrance, and Contemporary Romani Identities," lecture for the University of British Columbia; Fonseca, *Bury Me Standing*, pp. 274-275; István Pogány, *The Roma Café: Human Rights and the Plight of the Romani People*, Sterling: Pluto, 2004, p. 45; Joanna Talewicz-Kwiatkowska, "The Roma and Sinti in Auschwitz," *Voices of Memory 7*, Oświęcim: Auschwitz-Birkenau Memorial and Museum, 2011, p. 28. [ED]: It seems natural that Roma would have a right and a need to coin their own term, but one more thing needs to be taken into consideration: that the knowledge about Roma and Sinti Holocaust is still scarce, so that using new term right now could be confusing, especially when we think about European Parliament's resolution in April, 2015, regarding anti-gypsyism and Roma and Sinti Holocaust as an official term; see: http://www.europarl.europa.eu/sides/getDoc.do?type=TA&language=EN&reference=P8-TA-2015-0095http://www.europarl.europa.eu/sides/getDoc.do?type=TA&language=EN&reference=P8-TA-2015-0095.

26 Several controversies surround the label of genocide as it applies to the Porajmos. While researchers like Pogány argue that the actions taken against the Roma and Sinti such as forced sterilization and widespread massacres of adults and children satisfy definitions of genocide, like the one in the Genocide Convention in 1948, a lack of clear documentation makes formal recognition difficult, particularly in regards to the UN's guidelines (Pogány, *The Roma Café*, p. 45, Kołaczek, "The Nazi Persecution of the Roma, Holocaust Remembrance, and Contemporary Romani Identities"). Additionally, a lack of Roma representation has further impeded the recognition process. For example, no Roma witnesses were called at the Nuremberg Trials and only one Nazi, Ernst-August König, received a sentence specifically for crimes against the Roma (Kenrick and Puxon, *Gypsies under the Swastika*, p. 155; Fonseca, "Bury Me Standing," p. 274). This is partially

the Romani culture shift responsibility for the lack of commemoration to the Roma themselves. One of the stereotypes is that the oral culture of the Roma has led to an inability to pass down stories of survivors accurately from generation to generation. While oral tradition has affected remembrance of the Roma genocide, what is far more important is how memory is integrated into the community, for above all, this emphasizes that there is no lack of memory. Ficowski states, "Gypsies do not in general retain any memory of collective matters",[27] but Kapralski notes that while Roma might not access a collective memory, they do have "their own sort of memory" which "is encoded in a certain sense in social relations".[28] Additionally, the assumption that oral history discourages remembrance perpetuates a mistrust among non-Roma of Romani culture and traditions. In her book, *Bury Me Standing*, a Rom leader says to Isabel Fonseca, "Never before has a group been so persecuted and so unlovable", echoing the cycle of persecution that has plagued the Roma people for centuries.[29] From this line also follows the observation that commemoration and remembrance occur within parts of the Roma community that are not shown to outsiders for fear of these memories reminding gadje of how to persecute the Roma in the first place.[30]

Traditionally, the Roma people separate themselves from the gadje, non-Roma peoples, as they are deemed ritually polluted, while Roma are ritually clean.[31] This traditional culture has evolved into an "us versus

---

due to the fact that the push for recognition of the Porajmos by the Roma community began much later than the efforts of the Jewish community, further complicating the ability to label the Porajmos.

27 Ficowski, *Demony cudzego strachu* [Demons of others' fear], Warszawa: Wydawnictwo Nisza, 1986, p.24.

28 Kapralski, "The Influence of Extermination on Contemporary Roma Identity," p. 37.

29 Fonseca, *Bury Me Standing*, p. 273.

30 Kapralski, "The Influence of Extermination on Contemporary Roma Identity," p. 42.

31 Sonneman, *Shared Sorrows*, p. 32. [ED]: There are many different opinions regarding purity and non-Roma; according to many, the pollution and purity pertain only to the Romani world and the rules apply only to this world.

them" mentality within many Roma communities.[32] However, it is important not to blame the isolation of Romani families on their own culture. As Kapralski notes, "being a 'Roma' is to a large degree a defense mechanism to a hostile environment".[33] As an attempt to protect their culture and peoples from the gadje, there is a reluctance among the Roma survivors to discuss their stories with outsiders. This idea is demonstrated twice in Kapralski's essay, "The Influence of Extermination on Contemporary Roma Identity". First, by a gadje, "outsider", who states, "Roma don't like it when you remind them about it [the war] . . . fear dominates their lives . . . They feel that if they were . . . persecuted five times . . . then the sixth can happen very easily" and second by a Croatian Roma, who states, "There is still a great fear in the Roma. Fear of suffering and death that won't go away. It won't be forgotten".[34] This fear of persecution is so thoroughly gripping that many Roma hide their true ethnic identities, as shown by Matras in the first chapter of his book, *I Met Lucky People*, when he asks two Roma women what language they are speaking (knowing it is Romanes) and gets the answer that they are speaking Greek.[35] This fear

---

32 Fonseca, *Bury Me Standing*, p. 13.

33 Kapralski, "The Influence of Extermination on Contemporary Roma Identity," p. 36. Despite this fear, in recent years, through identity projects, Roma have made efforts to bring forward "a vision of Roma history, which . . . is important from the point of view of who the Roma see themselves to be and how they perceive their present and future", and to communicate this identity to outsiders to prevent further racially based persecution (Kapralski, "The Influence of Extermination on Contemporary Roma Identity," p. 38). Hancock suggests that the particular value of this approach is in showing that "the shadow cast by the wartime extermination falls on postwar times so that present-day acts of discrimination against the Roma should be seen as the continuation of earlier persecution". While understandable, the cultural isolation of the Roma continues to play a role in the remembrance of the Porajmos: it hinders a connection with outside cultures, despite the fact that increasing closeness with non-Roma has brought long-sought awareness to the issues of Roma persecution (Kapralski, "The Influence of Extermination on Contemporary Roma Identity," p. 42).

34 Ibd., p. 51 and p. 33.

35 Matras, *I Met Lucky People*, p. 1.

keeps Roma survivors from speaking out about their experiences. Sonneman noted that, in searching for survivors, those who would speak to her were those who were already identified as "Gypsies" in Germany and, as such, would suffer no backlash from their communities for disclosing their ethnic identity.[36]

The mistrust and fear of persecution prevalent in Romani communities is detrimental to the cause of remembrance, leads to a lack of testimonies and allows for the continuation of harmful stereotypes. Intentional or unintentional inaccuracies about the Roma genocide further perpetuate the cycle of discrimination and isolation the Romani people face. Misinformation about the Porajmos is caused in part by very limited documents about Roma deportation to concentration camps and to their extermination.[37] One of the common kinds of misinformation refers to factually inaccurate time-lines, particularly regarding the beginning of the Roma genocide, as well as the time at which the German Nazis began pursuing the extermination of Roma peoples on racial grounds. Fonseca shares with us an analysis of a statement by a historian Lucy Davidowicz who claims that "only in the last year of the war did Nazi ideologies begin to regard the Gypsies . . . as an undesirable racial element".[38] In fact, though most agree that February, 1943, marks the time that mass deportations of Roma to Auschwitz began, racial categorization and discrimination against Roma began much earlier, in 1937. It was at this time that German Nazi doctors and scientists, including Robert Ritter, who worked for the Office for Research on Race Hygiene and Population Biology,[39] forced Romani peoples to undergo examinations. In December of the following year Himmler issued a decree that stated the "Gypsy problem" would be treated as a "matter of race".[40] By June of 1941, the SS Einsatzgruppen

---

36 Sonneman, *Shared Sorrows*, p. 29.

37 Martyniak, "The Deportation of Roma to Auschwitz," p. 7.

38 Fonseca, *Bury Me Standing*, p. 258.

39 Ibid., p. 258.

40 Sonneman, *Shared Sorrows*, p. 55; Kołaczek, "The Nazi Persecution of the Roma, Holocaust Remembrance, and Contemporary Romani Identities."

began mass shootings of Roma people in German Nazi Occupied Territories.[41] In fact, Roma peoples were being deported to concentration camps such as Lackenbach[42] as early as November of 1940.[43]

Another set of misinformation surround the "Zigeunerlager", the camp for Roma families established in section BIIe of Birkenau in early 1943.[44] Unlike prisoners in other sections of Auschwitz-Birkenau, Roma were not separated from their families, were not forced to wear prisoner uniforms and, at first, were not forced to shave their heads. These differences in treatment have led to the assumption that the conditions of the Zigeunerlager were more favorable than the rest of the camp and, as such, the plight of the Roma was not one of extermination.[45] However, disease and starvation, as well as the unhygienic conditions that plagued the entire camp, led to a high death toll in the Zigeunerlager, particularly in children and the elderly.[46] Like most of the German Nazi concentration camps, scarce documentation makes it difficult to calculate numbers as well as gain a clear picture of the Romani prisoners' experience at Auschwitz-Birkenau, especially when only few prisoners of the Zigeunerlager survived. However, there is information about the treatment of Romani people in Auschwitz-Birkenau that strengthens the argument that the Roma were targeted for destruction because of their ethnicity. One of the more well-known topics is that of the medical experiments conducted by Mengele and his associates on prisoners of the Zigeunerlager.[47] In particular, the documentation of the Roma in Auschwitz by artist Dinah Gottliebova reveals Mengele's obsession with

41 Fonseca, *Bury Me Standing*, p. 261.
42 "Zigeuner-Anhaltelager Lackenbach."
43 Sonneman, *Shared Sorrows*, p. 55.
44 Talewicz-Kwiatkowska, "The Roma and Sinti in Auschwitz," pp. 16-17.
45 Ibid., pp. 19-20.
46 Kenrick and Puxon, *Gypsies Under the Swastika*, p. 133.
47 Wontor-Cichy, "The Roma in Auschwitz Concentration Camp," web, http://www.auschwitz.org/en/museum/news/the-roma-in-auschwitz-new-on-line-lesson,1109.html, accessed 6 June 2016.

the ethnic characteristics of the Romani prisoners. Dinah Gottliebova drew for Mengele detailed portraits of Roma prisoners from different regions of Europe and she offers testimony first to the poor conditions in the Zigeunerlager and second to Mengele's interest in the characteristics of Roma ethnicity. In an excerpt from her account of her experiences in the camp, Gottliebova recalled her encounter with a young Roma woman from France who was distraught over the loss of her two month old infant.[48] While this story might seem small, it speaks to the conditions of the Zigeunerlager and is a valuable glimpse into the concentration camp.

Further complications come from the intentionally distorted or false representations of events that were meant to lessen the value of the tragedies faced by Roma and to undermine Roma claims to reparation. One of these revolves around the deportations of Roma to Transnistria. The area of Transnistria originally belonged to the Ukraine (then a part of the Soviet Union) but was given to Romania by the Germany in 1941. Transnistria was governed by Gheorghe Alexianu, who directly answered to Marshal Ion Antonescu, and the area would become what Alexander Dallin called "the ethnic dumping ground of Romania".[49] Roma, both nomadic and settled, were deported from Romania to Transnistria where they suffered harsh conditions with no shelter or food, facing brutal retaliation from civil police if they attempted to escape or communicate with anyone outside of the barbed wire fences.[50] Typhus ran rampant in the camps of Transnistria and prisoners were subjected to inhuman conditions that eventually led to cannibalism.[51] These conditions and the massacres carried out by Romanian soldiers, the SS and other indigenous Romanian, Ukrainian and German civilians led to 36,000 Roma and at least 217,000 Jews losing their lives.[52]

---

48 Sławomir Kapralski, Maria Martyniak, and Joanna Talewicz-Kwiatkowska, "Roma in Auschwitz," *Voices of Memory 7*, Oświęcim: Auschwitz-Birkenau Memorial and Museum, 2011, pp. 94-95.

49 Radu Ioanid, *The Holocaust in Romania*, Chicago: Iran R. Dee, 2000, p. 176.

50 Kenrick and Puxon, *Gypsies Under the Swastika*, p. 117 and p. 120.

51 Ibid., p. 120; Ioanid, *The Holocaust in Romania*, p. 218.

52 Kenrick and Puxon, *Gypsies Under the Swastika*, p. 120; Ioanid, *The Holocaust in Romania*, p. 176 and p. 193.

Despite this staggering death toll and the fact that, besides Germany, Romania was the only country involved in massacres on such a wide scale during the Holocaust, when Fonseca visited Romani survivors of Transnistria in 1991, the Romanian Parliament was still honoring Ion Antonescu with a minute of silence on the anniversary of his execution.[53] Along with the minute of silence, the Romanian Parliament was also calling the deportations of Roma to Transnistria an effort by Marshal Ion Antonescu to "save the Gypsies from the death camps of Poland".[54] At his trial in 1946, Antonescu's justification played on the widespread stereotype of the Roma as "thieves and murderers", insisting that he was deporting the Roma to "protect the public".[55] Even after being found guilty of the murder of 270,000 Jews by the Romanian People's Tribunals for war criminals in 1946, Antonescu's justifications live on along with his memory.[56]

Justifications that shift blame onto the Roma, such as the one Antonescu's offers, demonstrate that the majority of negative stereotypes about the Roma have in fact carried on from the wartime period itself. The German Nazis' classification of Roma prisoners as asocials, marking them with black triangles on their clothing in camps like Auschwitz, is a reminder of the stereotype that the Roma are criminals by nature.[57] Views like the ones presented above, combined with scarce documentation and inconsistent treatment of the Roma by German Nazis, have led to a dismissal of the crimes against the Roma people by various national and international courts, the most notable being the dismissal by the Allied military government in 1948 and the UN in present day.[58] Additionally,

53 Fonseca, *Bury Me Standing*, p. 244; Ioanid, *The Holocaust in Romania*, p. 177.

54 Fonseca, *Bury Me Standing*, p. 244.

55 Ibid.

56 Ioanid, *The Holocaust in Romania*, p. 287.

57 Wontor-Cichy, "The Roma in Auschwitz Concentration Camp," web, http://www.auschwitz.org/en/museum/news/the-roma-in-auschwitz-new-on-line-lesson,1109.html, accessed 6 June 2016.

58 Matras, *I Met Lucky People*, p. 185; Kołaczek, "The Nazi Persecution of the Roma, Holocaust Remembrance, and Contemporary Romani Identities."

it is these conflicts of memories that lead to behaviors and attitudes expressed by Roma communities in the present day.[59]

Fonseca paints a vivid picture of the inequalities that the multitude of different Roma communities across Europe have faced since the war, ranging from deportations from various countries to discrimination by members of church and hospital staff. Perhaps the saddest statement is one by Bert Lloyd from the 1960s, when he says that the Roma he met "could not distinguish the war period" from the post-war period because Roma's postwar experiences have been one form of persecution after another.[60] Even fifty years after the war the Roma were still denied the services of priests and doctors and many lived in impoverished conditions.[61] In present day, public attitudes towards Roma peoples have still seen little change or progress, as exemplified by the consistent presence of racially motivated discrimination and violence. In 2008, the Italian government implemented a fingerprinting policy for Romani children which would "make it easier to identify child beggars", reiterating the idea shared by the German Nazis that ethnic minorities like the Roma were responsible for and predisposed to committing criminal activities based on their race alone.[62] In Hungary between 2008 and 2009, six Roma were brutally murdered by a group of ethnic Hungarians in attempts to incite violence between the Roma and Hungarians. In one of the attacks, a father and his five year old son were gunned down when they attempted to escape their burning home, a fate that mirrors the violence against Roma during the Porajmos, particularly the massacres of Roma that occurred outside the German Nazi concentration camps.[63] Finally, the Romani people's six-year

---

59 Kapralski, "The Influence of Extermination on Contemporary Roma Identity," p. 49.

60 Fonseca, *Bury Me Standing*, p. 252.

61 Ibid., p. 252 and p. 200.

62 Tom Kington, "Unicef among Critics of Italian Plan to Fingerprint Roma Children," *The Guardian*, 27 June 2008, web, https://www.theguardian.com/world/2008/jun/27/race.italy, accessed 2 November 2016.

63 Kenrick and Puxon, *Gypsies Under the Swastika*, p. 71; "Hungarian Gang Jailed for Racist Roma Killings," *BBC News*, 6 August 2013, web, http://www.bbc.com/news/world-europe-23586440, accessed 2 November 2016.

struggle before courts would hear their complaints of coerced sterilization in 2011 further demonstrates a continued discriminatory attitude.[64]

The dynamics caused by isolation and marginalization are part of a larger cycle of persecution of Roma peoples. Without proper commemoration of the persecution, the cycle continues to segregate the Roma, positioning them as easy targets for present-day persecution and discrimination. There are many different layers to this cycle. A quotation by Sonneman, partially borrowed from the authors of the *Declaration of Remembrance*, emphasizes the importance of commemoration: "Conscience is formed by memory, and these two strands must twist together into one. For memory is essential—but memory alone is not enough".[65] With a waning number of survivors to provide testimonies, the job of remembrance and commemoration will begin to fall unto the next generation, just as the mechanisms of isolation and segregation will pass on. In order to break a cycle, one must first step outside of it and that is what many young Romani activists are attempting to do. However, as Sonneman mentions, two strands must come together: non-Roma and Roma must both play a role in facilitating the remembrance of the Porajmos, the Roma genocide, so that the future of Romani communities will no longer be in the shadow of the "forgotten" Holocaust.

64 "Court Hears Claim of Forced Roma Sterilization," *The Washington Post*, 22 March 2011, web, http://www.washingtonpost.com/wp-dyn/content/article/2011/03/22/AR2011032202551.html, accessed 6 June 2016.
65 Sonneman, *Shared Sorrows*, p. 256.

Audrey Tong

Auschwitz-Birkenau Museum's National Exhibitions: Spaces of Histories, Memories and Identities

Auschwitz-Birkenau, a former Nazi German concentration and extermination camp, has been regarded as a symbol of the Holocaust, and is one of the most visited "tourist sites" in Poland. In 2015, over 1.72 million people from all around the world visited the Memorial Site, re-emphasizing its importance in memory and education. Yet interestingly enough, visitors do not often visit an important part of the Museum: the national exhibitions.[1] Although often overlooked and supplementary in nature, the national exhibitions uncover a deep cultural and historical understanding of the past. Created under the initiative of former prisoners from various countries and in association with the International Auschwitz Committee, these exhibitions reflect the influences of the Nazi occupation, the international makeup of deportees who were sent to Auschwitz and the fate of its citizens, and they acknowledge the mass murder of European Jews. In this paper, I will explore the multiple roles and functions of the national exhibitions as spaces of history, memory and identity, and emphasize their relevance for visitors in the modern present.

According to Genevieve Zubrzycki in *Crosses of Auschwitz: Nationalism and Religion in Post-Communist Poland*, the relationship between memory-making and institutional processes has the ability to make way for political and social changes and vice versa, especially in the arena of

---

1 I would like to give my sincerest thanks to Mr. Mirosław Obstarczyk (Exhibitions) for all his help and guidance, for sharing his expertise, knowledge and passion on the Exhibitions. It was an absolute privilege to gain such valuable insights.

cultural representations.[2] Zubrzycki's argument can be used to explain the trajectory of the Auschwitz-Birkenau Museum: the creation of the Museum in 1947 to the first national exhibition, established in 1960, represents a progressive movement towards the internationalization of the Holocaust. By granting international institutions the ability to speak and represent their own histories and messages, the national exhibitions are cultural buildings that reflect the universalization of the memorial site while presenting a country's specific histories, memories and identities that shape their past, present and future relationships with the Holocaust.

Following the end of the Second World War, the Auschwitz-Birkenau State Museum was created[3] by the Polish parliament on July 2, 1947.[4]

---

2 Genevieve Zubrzycki, *Crosses of Auschwitz: Nationalism and Religion in Post-Communist Poland*, Chicago: University of Chicago Press, p. 102.

3 [ED] In April, 1946, a group of former prisoners, nominated by the Ministry of Culture and Arts, arrived in Oświęcim to protect the former Auschwitz camp and establish the Museum. But setting up a museum exhibit at Auschwitz was not a strictly post-Holocaust phenomenon. In October of 1941, Camp Commandant Rudolf Höss ordered the first exhibit at Auschwitz to be established in Barrack 6 in Auschwitz I. The idea for the museum came from Polish artist-prisoner Franciszek Targosz, number 7626, whom Höss had caught sketching horses. As this was a punishable offence, Targosz suggested the establishment of a museum to provide SS officers with a source of culture in the camp. In March, 1942, the museum was moved to Barrack 24. Displays included art; collectables such as coins and stamps found among deportees' possessions in the storage and sorting warehouse, nicknamed Kanada in camp jargon; Jewish prayer books and shawls; and also German Nazi military items and documents. The post-war establishment of the Auschwitz-Birkenau State Museum empowered survivors to transcend this dehumanization, to process and articulate their Holocaust experiences, to honor those whose lives were taken by the German Nazis and to inform the world of what this act of machinized genocide had proved human beings capable of: both as perpetrators and as victims. As a racial order was the bulwark of Nazi ideology, prisoners of different ethnicities had different camp experiences. This made the notion of national exhibitions of primary importance in conveying the realities of the concentration, labor and death camp complex to the Museum's visitors. Converting the former grounds of the camp was not easy because a museum devoted to this subject was the first of its kind. Thus the former prisoners had no model to follow. As Kazimierz Smoleń noted, "A 'museum' was, historically speaking, not even the right concept . . . at least that which one normally understands by the concept 'museum.' This was anti-culture and not culture"

With the mission to preserve the site of the former concentration camp, memorialize and document the events[5] and educate[6] visitors, the main

(Kazimierz Smoleń quoted in Jonathan Huener, *Auschwitz, Poland, and the Politics of Commemoration, 1945-1979*, Athens: Ohio University Press, 2003, p. 69).

4 [ED] After liberation the Soviet military authorities administered the premises of the former camps, Auschwitz I and Birkenau. At the end of 1945 and the beginning of the following year the premises were taken over by the Polish authorities from the Soviets. Initially, they came under the control of the Temporary State Management [TSM], which inventoried the buildings. In February, 1946, the Central Office of TSM placed the wooden barracks at the disposal of the Ministry of Rebuilding, which decided to dismantle them. As a consequence the majority of wooden barracks were disassembled and sent to various places in Poland which had suffered wartime losses. Jacek Lachendro, "From KL Auschwitz to Auschwitz-Birkenau Museum and Memorial," *nytt blikk*, Kristiansand: Årsskrift fra Stiftelsen Arkivet, 2015, pp. 124-125.

5 [ED] In the early 1960s the Museum began to search for documents in institutional, provincial and national archives, especially those in the vicinity of former sub-camps. The Archives had been formally established as a department in 1957, but only in 1965 were its "tasks and prerogatives . . . set out in regulations issued by the Ministry of Culture and Art on June 30th, 1965" (Jadwiga Kulasza, "Archival Material from Auschwitz," *Pro Memoria*, 27, 2007, p. 51). These entailed: document gathering, preservation, inventory-taking and cataloguing of items; making these documents available to other museums and institutions, as well as to private individuals; historical research; making and archiving photocopies, photographs and microfilms; and finally, analyzing data and personal accounts in order to organize information about prisoners, including their names, numbers, camp experiences and fates. The creation of the Archives was not easy. The Soviet military authorities treated German property left in Polish territory, including the grounds of former Auschwitz camp, as their trophies of war; thus they dismantled parts of camp facilities, confiscated documents and a part of the movables and subsequently shipped the majority of these goods to the Soviet Union. However, copies of some of these documents, which were thousands of death certificates that the Civil Registry Office of Auschwitz had issued, were passed on to the Museum during the first Frankfurt Trial (1963-1965). Some documents, in the form of originals (e.g. 46 volumes of Sterbebücher, death certificates) or microfilms (e.g. documents of SS-Zentralbauleitung), were conveyed to the Museum in the first half of 1990s.

Many documents saved from destruction and found after the war remained under control of, among the others, the Main Commission for the Investigation of Nazi Crimes in Poland, The Jewish Historical Institute and The Polish Red Cross. The Museum wrote to these institutions with a request that they turn over any archival material in their possession, along with the provenance of these items, to the chancellery of the permanent exhibitions of the State Museum were introduced at Auschwitz I in 1955,[7] and several national exhibitions were facilitated in the 1960s.

Auschwitz Concentration Camp. The request met with positive responses from these institutions and they conveyed to the Museum a significant portion of the Auschwitz documents. Later, other institutions and individuals from Poland and abroad handed various documents (originals or copies) concerning the camp to the Museum archives. For more information about the archives, please see the Auschwitz-Birkenau Memorial and Museum Archives web page: http://auschwitz.org/en/museum/archives/. To learn more about the history and the present of the archives see also: Kulasza, "Archival Material from Auschwitz".

The Research Center studies the history of Auschwitz as well as many aspects of the second world war and publishes its findings in books and academic journals. Department staff members also give lectures and talks and help to answer inquiries made to the Museum. Prior to 1956, the Museum's publications consisted primarily of guidebooks, postcards, commemorative stamps and photographs published in order to raise funds. The first academic publication, *Zeszyty Oświęcimskie* (*Auschwitz Studies*), appeared in 1957; other academic publications now include faculty studies on the history of the camp and subcamps. Over the years the Museum has also published several memoirs of Auschwitz survivors.

6 [ED] The International Center for Education about Auschwitz and the Holocaust was founded in 2005 to educate visitors and readers about the Holocaust and the Auschwitz concentration and extermination camp. Educational projects are integral to the Center. All Center activities are aimed at students, and teachers as well as both professionals and those who may be marginalized in mainstream society. Study visits for young people and adults, conferences, training courses, special exhibitions and access to self-education materials on the Internet are some examples of the Center's commitments. To read more see: http://auschwitz.org/en/education/iceah-general-information/.

7 [ED]A small exhibit in the basement of Block 4 was opened in the summer of 1946. It included displays surrounded by barbed wire which presented items plundered from people deported to Auschwitz: clothing, prostheses, shoes, liturgical vestments and human hair. At the end of the hall there was an illuminated cross. Although the exhibit was modest, it impressed the visitors. In the *Polish Daily Express Wieczorny* (Nov. 6, 1946) one can read: "We enter the room and are turned to stone. The basement of the block mirrors the entire magnitude of the crimes committed in Auschwitz. In numerous alcoves are revealed the symbols of various strata of society that here found deaths. Thus, a peasant's coat next to a mountaineer's costume; liturgical vestments all of faiths. In another niche children's slippers speak for themselves, and next to them the hair of murdered women induces a shudder of horror. For a long time we are unable to depart

Expressing the wishes of the International Auschwitz Committee, the national exhibitions were created in conjunction with countries wishing to honor their citizens who were deported to Auschwitz. Countries where deportations had taken place to KL Auschwitz were authorized to establish exhibitions in assigned, original buildings of the concentration camp; however, these countries were responsible for the funding, expenses, content and design of the exhibits. They were to show the connection between the history of the occupation in a given country and the history of Auschwitz, the fate of the citizens and the story of resistance. Due to the political nature and implications of the time, historical distortions and distortions of narratives plagued the initial national exhibitions, and they soon became outdated and neglected.

Following the fall of the Iron Curtain, a new set of guidelines were created in the 1990s. Although some exhibitions closed, such as those of Germany[8] and Italy, many countries, including Belgium, France, Hungary, Netherlands, Slovakia, the Czech Republic and the former Soviet Union, began to modernize their displays and revise their content in accordance with the new general rules suggested by the Auschwitz-Birkenau Museum.

from this Sanctuary of Martyrology – we are moved to the depths of our emotions". Information about the exhibit and the quotation can be found in: Huener, *Auschwitz, Poland, and the Politics of Commemoration, 1945-1979*, pp. 69-70.

In 2008 work on the new exhibition began. The exhibition will be constructed on ground floors of six blocks of the former camp Auschwitz I, marked with numbers 4-9. It will be divided into three sections. The first will present the perpetrators, the institutional aspect of the camp and plans to transform it into a center for exterminating Jews. The second section will present the topic of the Holocaust from the perspective of the victims. The third section will be devoted to the prisoners of the concentration camp and will aim at showing the dehumanization of people planned by the Germans. See more at: *Long-Term Ministerial Program for Financing Creation of the New Main Exhibition*, Oświęcim: Auschwitz-Birkenau State Museum, 27 January 2013, web, http://auschwitz.org/en/museum/news/long-term-minsterial-program-for-financing-creation-of-the-new-main-exhibition,1140.html.

8   [ED]The Museum discontinued the GDR exhibition. Since the Auschwitz-Birkenau focuses on victims, the exhibition on Sinti and Roma Porajmos (Samudaripen) was opened in 2001 in Block 13.

As supplements to the permanent and main exhibitions, national exhibitions must be historical in nature, and cannot repeat information presented in the general exhibitions. The design, idea and scenario of an exhibition put forward by the exhibiting country must also be first discussed with, and approved by, the Museum to ensure accuracy of the subject matter. Devoted to the histories of prisoners from various national origins, they must also include information about the number of deportees and victims and discuss their fates starting from their lives before the war to their eventual deportations to KL Auschwitz and deaths. Additionally, national exhibitions must link the German occupation of particular countries with the history of the camp, and highlight well-known figures who had been deported to KL Auschwitz as well as active individuals in the camp.

At present, there are eleven national exhibitions: Jewish, Roma, Polish, Dutch, French, Belgian, Hungarian, Austrian, Slovak, Czech and Russian.[9] Although different in terms of feel, appearance and content, each of these exhibitions individualizes and personalizes the prisoners and victims, tackles issues and resonates with survivors and visitors of the Museum today. More importantly, the modern role of the national exhibitions can be seen

9 [ED] Today visitors can see the following exhibitions: "The Destruction of the European Roma" (opened 2001 in Block 13); Russian Exhibition "Tragedy, Valour, Liberation" (2013, Block 14); "The Struggle and Martyrdom of the Polish Nation 1939-1945" (1985, Block 15); "The Tragedy of Slovakian Jews" (2002, Block 16, the ground floor); "Prisoners from the Czech Lands in Auschwitz concentration camp" (2002, Block 16, the first floor); "The Citizen Betrayed: A Remembrance of Holocaust Victims from Hungary" (2004, Block 18, the first floor); "Belgium 1940-1945: The Occupation and Deportation to Auschwitz Concentration Camp" (2006, Block 20, the first floor); "Deportees from France to Auschwitz Concentration Camp. March 27, 1942 – January 27, 1945" (2005, Block 20, the ground floor); "The Persecution and Deportation of Jews from the Netherlands" (2005, Block 21, the first floor); "Shoah" (Block 27, prepared by the Yad Vashem Institute in 2013). The Austrian and Italian exhibitions are being redone, and the Greek exhibition is being prepared. To read more see: Auschwitz Memorial and Museum, *Visiting: "National exhibitions,"* Oświęcim: Auschwitz-Birkenau State Museum, 27 January 2013, web, http://auschwitz.org/en/visiting/national-exhibitions/, accessed 19 January 19 2017.

as tools used to explore themes of history, memory and identity. As such, this paper seeks to specifically explore the framing of history in the Polish national exhibition, the idea of collective national memory in the Russian exhibition and the controversy of identity in the Shoah exhibition.

In "On the Postwar History of the Auschwitz Site and its Symbolism", Jonathan Huener recognizes that one of the dilemmas surrounding the memorialization of Auschwitz is the forms and weight of representation of the uniqueness of the Jewish experience versus the story of other German Nazi crimes, oppression and murder. It can be argued that another dilemma or challenge that exists is the appropriate representation for each group in a fractured political and cultural landscape. Due to the complexity of the camp's history and diversity in commemoration, the national exhibitions are a "suitable representational synthesis" that allows for each group of individuals who were victims to be appropriately recognized, respected and memorialized.[10] Therefore each of the national exhibitions has the task of telling the history of the particular country while allowing for each country to come to terms with their own history and the Jewish past by taking ownership and responsibility.

Opened in 1985, the Polish national exhibition, "The Struggle and Martyrdom of the Polish Nation 1939-1945", sheds light on not only Polish history, but also on the understanding and framing of that history by Poles. Interestingly enough, the title of the very exhibit reveals an inner glimpse of the historical and symbolic significance of Auschwitz to the Polish nation. In "The Future of Auschwitz: Some Personal Reflections", Jonathan Webber posits that, for Polish people, Auschwitz stands for a symbol of Nazi oppression, and remains a place where Polish political prisoners were the first group sent to concentration camps.[11] Given the

---

10 Jonathan Huener, "On the Postwar History of the Auschwitz Site and its Symbolism," *The Last Expression: Art and Auschwitz*, Evanston: Northwestern University Press, 2003, p. 3.

11 Jonathan Webber, "The Future of Auschwitz: Some Personal Reflections," *Religion, State and Society*, 20(1), 1992, p. 85.

symbolic remembrance of this particular Polish history, aspects of Polish tragedy and longstanding sentiments, especially in regards to the systematic destruction of Polish culture and national identity, are threaded throughout the national exhibition.

Going through the exhibition, the articulation of the discourse of a nation establishes the understanding and framing of that history by Polish people. The exhibition begins with the start of the Second World War, with events associated with the German occupation on display. It concisely presents the division of Poland between Germany and the Soviet Union and then the further division of Polish land by the German occupation regime. There is also an explanation of the creation of the Polish underground state, as well as "terror, repression, the liquidation of the intelligentsia, expulsions, pacification, deportation to camps, the exploitation and destruction of the economy and culture, and germanization".[12] The exhibition ends with information on the role of Polish armed forces in the Allied war effort, and finally the list of names of Poles in Auschwitz based on archival records.

As seen in the example of the Polish national exhibition, the exhibition becomes a tool for acknowledging a nation's specific history and values from their local and spatial perspective. One can see that there are two separate histories at the Auschwitz-Birkenau Museum: a generalized history presented in the main exhibitions and a country's specific history that can only be seen in the national exhibitions. Both histories need to be acknowledged and studied to gain a fuller picture of the origins, effects and aftermath of the Holocaust. History is incredibly complex, but often simplified. Therefore, the national exhibitions act as extraordinary tools that reveal the different symbolic interpretations and representations of the history of Auschwitz.

National exhibitions also reflect another important topic of discussion: memory. Memory, like history, is often complex, and it often reflects the

---

12 *The Exhibition: The Struggle and Martyrdom of the Polish Nation 1939-1945*, Oświęcim: Auschwitz-Birkenau State Museum, web, http://www.auschwitz.org/en/visiting/national-exhibitions/poland/, accessed 19 January 2017.

values and norms of a society. Important to our discussion is "collective memory", a term coined by Maurice Halbwachs, that refers to the memory constructed within a group's social structures and institutions.[13] Timothy Snyder goes on to describe two types of collective memory: "mass personal memory" and "national memory". Mass personal memory refers to events of national importance that large numbers of individuals recollect upon.[14] National memory is the "organizational principle, or set of myths, by which nationally conscious individuals understand the past and its demands on the present," which is often represented as "numbers, facts and events worked into a predictable scheme that 'straightens' the national past and justifies national statehood".[15] Acting as spaces of remembrance, national exhibitions are modeled after the two types of collective memory, both the mass personal and the national.

As the "the public memory at Auschwitz [was] confronted with growing demands of a larger and international commemorative constituency" in the 1950s, the very construction of the national exhibitions not only demonstrates the need for countries to represent their own histories, but also to confront issues of conflicting and interwoven memories.[16] Groups select different memories to explain historical issues and concerns, and Pierre Nora argues that groups select certain dates and people to commemorate to further support collective memory, adding to its social meaning and significance.[17] Therefore the national exhibitions offer an interesting take on what a country determines is important in the context of the Holocaust, especially keeping in mind that the collective memory

13 Maurice Halbwachs and Lewis A Coser, *On Collective Memory*, Chicago: University of Chicago Press, 1992, p. 40.

14 Timothy Snyder, "Memory of Sovereignty and Sovereignty Over Memory: Poland, Lithunaia and Ukraine," *Memory and Power In Post-War Europe: Studies in the Presence of the Past*, Cambridge: Cambridge University Press 2002, p. 39.

15 Ibid., p. 50.

16 Huener, "On the Postwar History of the Auschwitz Site and its Symbolism," p. 2.

17 Pierre Nora, "The Era of Commemorations," *Realms of Memory: The Construction of the French Past*, New York: Columbia University Press, 1996, p. 615.

of Auschwitz was shaped by political and historical conditions in the post-war period. National context is just one way in which Holocaust memory is transmitted.

As Marc Silberman and Florence Vatan eloquently explain, "memory is not coherent, but contested, with complex articulations such as communicative, collective, cultural, and social memory, and there are important distinctions among memory communities, be they official, national, familial, or personal".[18] The Russian national exhibition is just one example that demonstrates the underlying complexities and controversies of national collective memory. The initial USSR pavilion was opened in 1961, restructured in 1977, completely changed in 1985, encountered difficulties with the redevelopment of the exhibition in 2005, and then officially re-opened in January 2013 on the 68th anniversary of the liberation of the Nazi German concentration and extermination camp Auschwitz. Dr. Piotr M. A. Cywiński, Director of the Auschwitz-Birkenau Museum, offered a few words in the January, 2013 Auschwitz-Birkenau Museum press release with the re-opening of the new Russian exhibition, "Tragedy. Valour. Liberation":

> The creation of a new Russian exhibition was a long process, it is true. This reflects the profound differences in historical memory. Therefore, it was good that the talks went finally well and we succeeded in the opening of the exhibition. I think that if there is an event in our common history that should not divide us, it is the tragedy of victims who suffered and died in Auschwitz.[19]

---

18 Marc Silberman and Florence Vatan, *Memory and Postwar Memorials: Confronting the Violence of the Past*, New York: Palgrave Macmillan, 2013, p. 216.

19 Dr. Piotr M. A. Cywiński quoted in: *"Tragedy. Valour. Liberation," New Russian Exhibition at the Auschwitz Memorial*, Oświęcim: Auschwitz-Birkenau State Museum, 27 January 2013, web, http://www.auschwitz.org/en/museum/news/tragedy-valour-liberation-new-russian-exhibition-at-the-auschwitz-memorial-982.html, accessed 19 January 2017.

Although history is usually written by the victor, this version of events is often confronted by emerging discourses that challenge national accounts and call for the re-examination of historical issues. This truth explains the circumstances that led to the attempt to create a new Russian exhibition in 2005, but also explains its delay. According to the Auschwitz-Birkenau Museum, "the divergences concern[ed] the nomenclature used in relation to the population and territories, which – due to the USSR activities resulting from the Ribbentropp-Molotov pact – came under its control in the years 1939-1941".[20] Although the exhibition was officially re-opened in 2013, with scenarios and content now confirmed with the Museum, it still echoes a specific Soviet memory, where war is an integral part of its revolutionary legacy. Ultimately, the four parts of the exhibition, "The Tragedy of Soviet Prisoners of War", "Occupation Regime", "The Civilian Population from the Territories of the USSR in Auschwitz", and "Liberation" reflect the Russian attitude towards the topic of the Holocaust and Auschwitz. Although it could be argued that a militaristic approach to and preoccupation with heroic staging is irrelevant to the devotion to the Soviet victims and even inappropriate at a memorial site, the Russian national exhibition remains an interesting place of research on how a country relates itself to the Holocaust based on national memory.

Memory, when gradually internalized, becomes part of identity, and this is the next topic of interest with regards to the national exhibitions. Identity, stemming from social and historical memories, is a phenomenon of belonging and socialization that links one to a social category or community. More important to our discussion is national identity; like history and memory, identity also invites various and disputed readings

---

20 Jerzy Malczyk, *Martyrdom of the USSR Nations During the Great Patriotic War in the Years 1941-1945*, Oświęcim: Auschwitz-Birkenau State Museum, 27 January 2013, web, http://www.auschwitz.org/en/museum/news/martyrdom-of-the-ussr-nations-during-the-great-patriotic-war-in-the-years-1941-1945,463.html, accessed 19 January 2017.

of the national exhibitions. National identity can be seen as the recognition of collective memories, beliefs, symbols and codes of behavior that connect the past, present and future of a nation. The sense of solidarity that stems from national identity articulates national interests, values and understandings. But given the difficulty in forging collective national identities, how do groups come to terms with their own identities, challenging them and reclaiming them, while still allowing visitors to identify with them all within the context of the Holocaust and Auschwitz-Birkenau? This question becomes evident in the Shoah exhibition in Block 27.

In 2005, the Government of Israel, on behalf of the Jewish people, entrusted the Yad Vashem Institute to create a new Jewish exhibition that will allow for reflection on and remembrance of the Shoah victims. Stepping through the entrance, visitors are immediately welcomed into a multisensory experience. A melody of prayer lingers before the visitor steps into the next room where a 360-degree montage of Jewish life in prewar Europe is projected onto the walls. The next gallery is devoted to Nazi racist ideology and the extermination of Jews within Nazi-occupied Europe, which provides the context and background for the next section on the genocide and murder of the Jewish people. One room is dedicated to the children murdered during the Holocaust, with authentic drawings sketched by Jewish children copied onto the walls. The exhibition ends with the "Book of Names", which contains the names of the millions murdered during the Holocaust, as collected by the Yad Vashem Institute. There is also a Reflection Centre, where visitors can reflect upon some important questions surrounding the Holocaust that are answered by figures from around the world.

As history and memory are combined at an institutional level, the Shoah exhibition forges one common Jewish identity and contributes to modern identity formation. Avner Shalev, director of the Yad Vashem Institute, comments: "[the exhibition] show[s] the most important topics related to the Holocaust, which is not necessarily a historical narrative, but rather a presentation of the very deep ethical and cultural dimensions of the memory of the Holocaust".[21] Like the other national exhibitions, the Shoah exhibition personalizes the individual victims of the camp and offers educational opportunities that cannot be obtained in the main exhibitions. However, it is important to also note its location within Auschwitz-Birkenau; situated across from the "Death Block", the Shoah exhibition serves as an appropriate place of remembrance and tribute to the victims. Given the emotional nature of the exhibition, it gives rise to an individual, but also collective, Holocaust consciousness and remembrance. This is becoming more central to not only the identity of those with Jewish backgrounds, but to all those who internalize the knowledge gained and depart with new insights and continue the dialogue.

In conclusion, the national exhibitions play a much needed and important role at the Auschwitz-Birkenau Museum. In addition to informing and educating about and commemorating the Holocaust, national exhibitions present a condensed but purposeful history of their respective countries, revealing specific collective memories and redefining modern identities. The national exhibitions also personalize and tell the historical facts of what happened in each respective country that is not found in the main exhibitions, but is still important in presenting a well-rounded understanding of the Holocaust and trajectories towards reconciliation. Taking a closer look at the national exhibitions and their potential to connect themes and engage people in new social discussions and discourses, their multiple roles and functions contribute to the layering and intensification of knowledge for visitors and the exceptional comprehension and diversity of information at Auschwitz-Birkenau.

---

21 *"Shoah": New Exhibition in Block 27: Light of Remembrance for Avner Shalev,* Oświęcim: Auschwitz-Birkenau State Museum, 27 January 2013, web, http://www.auschwitz.org/en/museum/news/shoah-new-exhibition-in-block-27-light-of-remembrance-for-avner-shalev-,1016.html, accessed 19 January 2017.

Jae Hyun Kim

The Holocaust in South Korea's Public History

When the survivors of the Holocaust and its concentration camps gathered at the Auschwitz-Birkenau State Museum in 2005 and composed the "Act of Foundation" for the International Center for Education about Auschwitz and the Holocaust, it was a text which reflected their hopes of a continued Holocaust education for future generations. Education for them meant to strive towards "[saving] the man, Europe and the world of today" in response to what they saw as the resurgence of hatred. In the survivors' acknowledgement that there will be "fewer and fewer of [them]" as the years pass, they in turn placed their hope in "historians, researchers, teachers and educators" to continue to convey the memories of the victims and their effort to recognize and prevent such atrocity from occurring again.[1] For such a group, be it scholars of the Holocaust or members of museums, to perpetuate the memories of the victims and ensure their importance for generations to come is a great undertaking. While the ways in which such a task could be achieved is a subject of important discussion, this paper seeks to present another phenomenon within the public history of the Holocaust: the fact that societies outside of the so-called "western world" would perceive its events through the lens of their own history and modern day issues.

Considering the wealth of diversity in the world not part of the western world, this paper will specifically focus on one country as an example

---

1   "Act of Foundation," *Auschwitz-Birkenau State Museum*, web, http://auschwitz.org/en/education/iceah-general-information/act-of-foundation, accessed 19 January 2017.

of how an event which occurred in the so-called "west" is perceived.[2] It is important to note that this paper is discussing a particular society's perception; it is meant to represent an individual's view, but that which is reflected by the mainstream media, its government, public organizations and most importantly, public education. It is therefore, a focus on a society's public history. In this spirit, on the topic of education concerning the Holocaust and Auschwitz, this paper suggests that understanding how a different society perceives what had occurred may enable educators and historians to tackle misconceptions and even politicizations of suvivors' experiences.

The country in focus for this paper is the Republic of Korea (South Korea), an East Asian country situated at the southern end of the Korean peninsula, and a society which has a unique history of being a colony of a non-western country, Japan.[3] For most of its history, spanning more than two millennia, Korea's location at one of the most eastern points of Eurasia ensured its isolation from the affairs of Europe as well as from having any Jewish communities within its society. In spite of this historical distance, South Korean visitors to the Auschwitz-Birkenau State Museum as of 2015 numbered up to 34,600 visitors annually. In context, this not only makes the country home to the largest number of visitors from East Asia, but this number of visitors is also higher than other European states such as Austria and Denmark.[4] Although not all of these visitors could have been in Poland solely for a visit to a museum about the Holocaust and Auschwitz, this phenomenon can be seen as a reflection of the special attention the Holocaust receives within South Korea's public history. This paper will begin with observations of two South Korean tour groups (termed Group A and B) which visited the

2   I am grateful to Dr. Donald Baker (UBC, Department of Asian Studies) for his comments and academic support.
3   Carter J. Eckert, Ki-baik Lee, Young Ick Lew, Michael Robinson, and Edward W. Wagner, *Korea Old and New: A History*, Seoul: Ilchokak Publishers, 1990, p. 256.
4   Bartosz Bartyzel and Paweł Sawicki, *Auschwitz-Birkenau State Museum: 2015*, Oświęcim: Auschwitz-Birkenau State Museum, 2016, p. 28.

State Museum in May of 2016. The goals of these observations are to identify the methods employed by South Korean tour guides to convey the history of the Holocaust and Auschwitz to their groups, their terminology in describing the event and the groups' reactions to their surroundings. In the later parts of this paper, these observations will ultimately be linked back to the nature of South Korea's public history of the Holocaust, which will allow for exploration of how such perceptions formed, along with exploration of some of the implications for education concerning the Holocaust and Auschwitz.

While members of both Group A and B come from a variety of both educational and occupational backgrounds, they all shared one commonality, which was that their visit to the State Museum was one part of their larger tour in Eastern Europe. Due to their strict schedules, their visits were less than an hour and restricted to Auschwitz I, specifically to the exhibitions in Block 4 (which focus on the various groups of prisoners and the methods of extermination)[5] and Block 5 (which displays everyday items which had been seized from the Jewish victims),[6] as well as Gas Chamber I. Both tour guides were one of more than a dozen South Korean guides residing in Eastern Europe, and their job required them to have a general knowledge about the region and its history.

This general, not expert, knowledge about the Holocaust and Auschwitz became clear in how the information throughout the exhibitions was conveyed. The tour guides mostly acted as translators of the contents in the exhibitions, and when describing certain situations a prisoner may face in the camp (an example being the selection process after arrival), these descriptions were done by using an abstract storytelling narrative or by alluding to scenes from Holocaust films such as *Schindler's List* and

---

5 "Auschwitz I, Block 4 – Extermination," *Auschwitz-Birkenau State Museum*, web, http://auschwitz.org/en/visiting/permanent-exhibition/extermination, accessed 19 January 2017.

6 "Auschwitz I, Block 5 – Physical Evidence of Crime," *Auschwitz-Birkenau State Museum*, http://auschwitz.org/en/visiting/permanent-exhibition/evidence-of-crime, accessed 19 January 2017.

the *Son of Saul*. In terms of mentioning any stories of any specific survivor, neither guide did so, with the minor exception of when Group A's guide, in the conclusion of the tour, recited a quote from a survivor, Władysław Bartoszewski, which was the exact quote found in the 32-page Museum guidebook, *Auschwitz-Birkenau: The Past and the Present*.[7] Ignoring the fact that these tour guides are no experts of the Holocaust, an observation that one may draw from this case is that for South Koreans, this past is a subject which they do know about generally, in part thanks to popular media, but about which they know very little regarding the specific experiences of the survivors and victims. This is reflected in South Korea's existing literature about the Holocaust and Auschwitz. To contextualize, Primo Levi's *If This is a Man* had its first Korean translation in 2007 and *The Drowned and the Saved* in 2014. In the latter's translator's note, Dr. Lee Soo Young stated that she had felt that it was long overdue for Levi's text to be accessible for Koreans ever since her first read in a Japanese translation in 1980. She expressed her hope that her work would be a catalyst for more texts by survivors to be translated. Indeed, Dr. Lee's hope is understandable, considering that texts by other survivors such as Halina Birenbaum and Seweryna Szmaglewska are non-existent in South Korea.[8] In the State Museum alone, there are only three Korean translations of its publications: a brochure, a DVD documentary and the book *Auschwitz-Birkenau: The Past and the Present*.[9]

This lack of exposure was further evident in the terminology employed by the tour guides to convey what had occurred in Auschwitz. There were

7   "Millions of people around the world know what Auschwitz was but it is that basic that we retain in our minds and memories awareness that it is humans who decide whether such a tragedy will ever take place again. This is the work of humans and it is humans alone who can prevent any such return." From: Teresa Świebocka, Jadwiga Pinderska-Lech, and Jarko Mensfelt, *Auschwitz-Birkenau: The Past and the Present*, trans. Adam Czasak, Oświęcim: Auschwitz-Birkenau State Museum, 2016, p. 29.

8   Primo Levi, *The Drowned and the Saved*, trans. Lee Soo Young, Seoul: Dolbaegae Publishers, 2014, p. 278.

9   "한국어," *Auschwitz-Birkenau State Museum*, web, http://auschwitz.org/en/language/koreanski, accessed 19 January 2017.

a few terms which were common and noticeable. One is that the victims were collectively referred as "people," saram, in recognition that there were different groups of victims in Auschwitz. However, the guides only conveyed the experience of the Jewish victims. Though the Museum tended to use the term Sinti and Roma, the tour guides used the more commonly known Gypsies, and only used this term when talking about the variety of victims in the camps. The most notable terminology referred to the perpetrators, specifically the SS camp guards. Both tour guides either used the term for "German" or "German soldier". Aside from the historical inaccuracy of such term (the SS was not part of the German Wehrmacht but rather a paramilitary wing of the Nazi party), these terms completely ignored the role and existence of the Sonderkommandos. Both guides mentioned the Sonderkommando only in Block 5 where the exhibition specifically mentions that the photos of the victims as they were undressing and as their bodies were being burnt were secretly taken by members of the Sonderkommando. Other than that, no further explanation was provided, nor was it conveyed that the camp guards had forcibly made these specific prisoners a labor force to maintain the exterminations within Auschwitz. In the abstract narratives that the tour guides provided, there is a clear line between perpetrator and victim; upon arrival there was only interaction between the words for a "German" and a "person"; the path of a "person's" death in the gas chamber was led by a "German", and so on. This problematic term which the guides applied to the perpetrators is also reflected in the Korean translations of texts about the Holocaust and Auschwitz. One example can be found in the Korean translation of *Auschwitz-Birkenau: The Past and the Present*. While it does mention the perpetrators as "camp guards" or the "S.S.", it also has instances when it uses the term "German army", Togil-gun, and when compared to the English translation, it is clear that the meaning of the narrative is completely different. For example, in a section regarding the liberation of Auschwitz by the Red Army, the English version refers to the "camp authorities" attempting to cover up evidence of the crimes, while the Korean version calls them the "German army".[10] Also, in a section in the Korean version, regarding the different groups of prisoners (a section which the English translation does not have), the "German army" is once again the perpetrator that had brought the victims all across Europe to Auschwitz.[11]

Within South Korea's history textbooks for middle school and high school, terms for perpetrators are generalized further by referring to the perpetrators as "Germany" or "Nazi Germany". The implications of this terminology within South Korean society are far more than a mere problematic choice of words, or even the marginalizing of victims. To use such terms to describe the perpetrators is ultimately to declare a verdict of guilty on the people belonging to such an identity, misplacing blame, responsibility and accountability. Within South Korea today, the issue of the accountability of a perpetrator in the form of a nation-state is one that holds great interest because of their neighbour, a former colonial overlord, and one of the Axis powers of the Second World War, Japan. Importantly, it is not only the horrors that befell the victims of the Holocaust that inspire interest, in South Korea, but, rather, how a perpetrator-as-country may be held accountable for its actions.

When Group B was about to finish their tour with a visit to Auschwitz I's gas chamber, they encountered a group of Japanese tourists in front of the execution site of Rudolf Höss. The tour guide, upon noticing this group, expressed their surprise at the presence of a Japanese group and pondered for what reason they would visit the museum. Soon after, as the group began to leave the museum, the tour guide continued to comment on the matter, including how it was uncommon to see Japanese visitors, in their experience, and that they were still uncertain of the reason behind their visit. The supposed uncommonness of Japanese visitors is

---

10 Świebocka, Pinderska-Lech, Mensfelt, *The Past and the Present*, trans. Adam Czesak, p. 12. Teresa Świebocka, Jadwiga Pinderska-Lech, and Jarko Mensfelt, *Auschwitz-Birkenau: The Past and the Present*, trans. Magda Jung, Seong-woong Jung, and Chang-hyun Nam, Oświęcim: Auschwitz-Birkenau State Museum, 2016, p. 12.

11 Świebocka, Pinderska-Lech, and Mensfelt, *The Past and the Present*, trans. Jung, Jung and Nam, p. 12.

an incorrect observation, because while their numbers are indeed fewer than South Koreans, they still number up to 19,500 visitors annually.[12] The question of why Japanese people would visit is in itself an unusual question to ponder, but when viewed through the lens of South Korea's public history about the Holocaust, doing so focuses the issue of how the perpetrators and their country of origin should be held accountable and live up to their past. Ultimately, it is linked with how South Korean public history perceives the experience of the Koreans in the periods before and during the Second World War while they were a colony of the Empire of Japan, and their dispute with today's Japan regarding accountability for the crimes committed then. Within this realm of public history which deals with the past and the present in East Asia, the Holocaust is treated as an event comparable to the atrocities committed by the Imperial Japanese army during the Second-Sino Japanese War (1937-1945) and the Pacific War (1941-1945), despite the fact that they occurred in different parts of the world. One reason why the two events are compared is to consider how the two former perpetrator countries, Germany and Japan, have been held accountable and apologized for their pasts.

This paper's position is not in favor of this comparison; comparing the Holocaust to the crimes committed by the Imperial Japanese army borders on oversimplification. However, this paper will conceptualize why this comparison, however simplified, has been made. The most obvious factor is geography; the Korean Peninsula's isolation from Europe means that it had never directly experienced the German Nazis, and due to its proximity to Japan, it became a colony in 1910, which was three decades prior to the beginning of the Second World War. The focus on Japan also is not unwarranted since Korea, after being an independent kingdom for five centuries, was annexed and turned into the newly modernized Japan's colony.[13] While political and cultural repressions were to continue for the next two decades, 1931 marked the beginning of wanton aggression from

12 Bartyzel and Sawicki, *State Museum*, p. 28.
13 Eckert, et al., *Korea Old and New*, p. 254.

Japan, with its civilian government increasingly under the influence of the military factions. After arbitrarily engineering a pretext for expansion into Manchuria (the Mukden Incident), the army managed to establish a puppet state called Manchukuo (1932-1945), and with the home government's failure and inability to punish their insubordination, its political influence was to dictate Japan's behavior towards its neighbours. Under this nationalist and militaristic government, Japan continued its bellicose stance against China as well as the west, with results which manifested themselves from the beginning of the Second Sino-Japanese War (1937-1945), to Japan's resignation from the League of Nations in 1933, and eventually, to establishing the Tripartite Pact in 1940 following Nazi Germany's military successes. Within this period, Koreans, as Japan's colonial subjects, were also to be affected by the wars. They were used as forced laborers, conscripts (from 1944), and targets of terror campaigns from the military police (kempeitai) to curb dissent.[14] Therefore, before the Second World War had begun with Germany's invasion of Poland, Koreans, and by and large East Asia, had become embroiled in conflict which had been started by the Empire of Japan. It is within this period that many of the crimes occured which South Korea's public history equates with the Holocaust.

There are three crimes committed by the Imperial Japanese army which are discussed in South Korean history textbooks. The first is the three-week long massacre (and mass rape) of Chinese civilians in the city of Nanjing in late 1937 (known as "The Rape of Nanking").[15] The sheer number of civilian deaths in this massacre, the higher estimates ranging in the hundreds of thousands (which are the ones accepted by South Korean textbooks), has made it a subject of comparison to Auschwitz. The second is the Imperial Japanese army's biological and chemical weapons research

---

14 Ibid., pp. 321-322; Herbert P. Bix, *Hirohito and the Making of Modern Japan*, New York: Harper Collins Publishers, 2000, p. 375.

15 Timothy Brook, *Documents on the Rape of Nanking*, Ann Arbor: The University of Michigan Press, 1999, p. 2.

unit known as Unit 731.[16] The unit conducted human experiments, much as the SS physicians in the camps did so; thus this was another point of comparison between the Holocaust and Imperial Japanese army's crimes. Third and lastly there was the plight of the so-called "Comfort Women": women and girls who were forced into sexual slavery. While the textbooks treat the Comfort Women as an event of its own, Japan's acknowledgement of these womens' plight, alongside the Nanking massacre and Unit 731, has been the subject of comparison to Germany's acknowledgement of the Holocaust.

In the context of this paper, it is important to recognize the nuances that distinguish these events from what occurred during the Holocaust and within Auschwitz, though this of course should not underplay the human suffering that occurred in both situations. What occurred in Nanjing in 1937 was not an isolated case in the context of the Second Sino-Japanese War; the Imperial Japanese army perpetrated various war crimes against both Chinese civilians and soldiers alike. However rare this event may have been overall, there is a documented case in which Japanese soldiers maintained order and prevented harm to Chinese civilians.[17] Within camps such as Auschwitz, no such instances have been found. It must also be noted that while there was the perpetuation of the attitude that the Japanese were superior to other Asians, such policies generally did not translate into that of the need to exterminate them to have a Lebensraum of their own in China (or Korea for that matter).[18] However propagandic it may have been, the establishment of the idea of the so-called "Greater Asian Co-Prosperity Sphere" was based on an anti-colonialist idea of freeing Asians from the western powers, and its

16 Peter Williams and David Wallace, *Unit 731: Japan's Secret Biological Warfare in World War II*, New York: The Free Press, 1989, pp. 19-20.

17 Brook, *Documents*, p. 136.

18 Eckert, et al., *Korea Old and New*, pp. 315-316, 318-319. Though there was an attempt to assimilate the Koreans via forcing them to adopt Japanese names and language, it still did not translate into mass killings nor did it allow those who assimilated to be treated as a Japanese.

success depended on Japan as its leader.[19] The victims of Unit 731 were not selected solely based on their race or genetic traits as with Josef Mengele in Auschwitz; ratherm they were composed of non-Japanese enemy combatants and political prisoners. Since the goal of research was to test and develop potent chemical and biological weapons, it cannot be argued that it was the same as, for example, Mengele's research on twins and dwarves.[20] However, unlike the victims of the crimes mentioned above, the women and girls who were forced into becoming Comfort Women were indeed non-Japanese. In the end, however, it is difficult to argue that the nature of the Imperial Japanese army's crimes are the same as the Holocaust, in which its goal by the time of the Wannsee Conference in 1942 was that of extermination.[21] Within South Korea's public history, however, such nuances are not recognized.

Ultimately, the reason why Group B pondered for what reason a Japanese person would visit a museum about the Holocaust is, in actuality, not due to genuine concern about intentions. Rather, the reason reflects South Korea's public history of the government of Japan, which, unlike its Germany counterpart, has failed to live up to its past or even apologize. Thereby, many South Koreans question whether the Japanese, as a society, know about their so-called "own" crimes, which had concurrently happened with the Holocaust. This is an issue, and perhaps hypocritically, of memorializing one past while being unknowingly or intentionally ignorant of another. This perception is reflected in South Korea's mainstream media and public school history textbooks. When the current Japanese Prime Minister Shinzō Abe visited the U.S. Holocaust Memorial Museum on April 27, 2016, the response of the South Korean media was critical of

---

19 John Toland, *The Rising Sun: The Decline and Fall of the Japanese Empire 1936-1945*, New York: Random House, 1970, p. 447; James L. McClain, *Japan, A Modern History*, New York: W. W. Norton and Company, 2002, p. 494; Bix, *Making of Modern Japan*, p. 397.

20 Irena Strzelecka, *Voices of Memory 2: Medical Crimes: The Experiments in Auschwitz*, Oświęcim: Auschwitz-Birkenau State Museum, 2001, p. 76.

21 Doris L. Bergen, *War and Genocide: A Concise History of the Holocaust*, New York: Rowman and Littlefield Publishers Inc., 2009, pp. 164-165.

what they viewed as utter hypocrisy.[22] This is because Prime Minister Abe, alongside several other Japanese politicians, are or have been accused of underplaying or denying events such as the Rape of Nanking,[23] or of being two-faced when they apologized for the past.[24] The latter point is exacerbated by a controversial Shintō Shrine called the Yasukuni Shrine, where visits from Japanese politicians are seen as proof of Japan's failure to live up to its past. The shrine, which was established in 1869 by Emperor Meiji, was intended to inter the "spirit", kami, of those who had died in service to Japan. The same privilege is also extended to the soldiers and civilians during the Second Sino-Japanese War and the Pacific War, which also included military leaders who were deemed to be war criminals.[25] Thus visits from Japanese politicians are seen as a commemoration of such perpetrators[26] instead of commemoration for the soldiers and civilians who perished during and beyond this period. South Korea's media conveys the conviction that Prime Minister Abe, as with some other Japanese politicians, is acting hypocritically by visiting such sites, recognizing the

22 "일본국회의원 'A급전범합사 야스쿠니신사 참배," *Yonhapnews.co.kr*, web, http://www. yonhapnews.co.kr/bulletin/2015/10/20/0200000000AKR20151020031400073.html, accessed 19 January 2017;

Yun Jung-ho, "[美·日 新밀월시대] 과거史 사죄없이 홀로코스트 박물관 방문 . . . 아베, '일본판 쉰들러' 내세워 '역사 세탁'," *News.chosun.com*, web, http://news.chosun.com/site/data/html_dir/2015/04/29/2015042900332.html, accessed 19 January 2017;

23 Hiroko Tabuchi, "Japan's Abe: No Proof of WWII Sex Slaves," *Washingtonpost. com*, web, http://www.washingtonpost.com/wpdyn/content/article/2007/03/01/AR2007030100578.html, accessed 19 January 2017.

24 "Abe may have changed his wording, but his attitude is still the same," *Hani.co.kr*, web, http://english.hani.co.kr/arti/english_edition/e_editorial/684595.html, accessed 19 January 2017.

25 Akiko Takenaka, *Yasukuni Shrine: History, Memory, and Japan's Unending Postwar*, Honolulu: University of Hawai'i Press, 2015, pp. 2-8. War criminals were not interred into the shrine until 1959.

26 "Japanese MPs make provocative visit to Tokyo's Yasukuni war shrine," *The Guardian. com*, web, https://www.theguardian.com/world/2015/apr/22/japanese-mps-make-provocative-visit-to-tokyos-yasukuni-war-shrine, accessed 19 January 2017.

victims of the Holocaust while apparently not recognizing the victims of their country's crimes during the Second World War.[27]

This view is reflected within South Korean history textbooks as well. Typically, the goal of these history textbooks is to provide a general and wide variety of information on world history. To achieve this, each period or set of events are to be covered in roughly fewer than ten pages, and the pages are filled with texts, questions, and photos to help students gain some general knowledge, but never in great detail as a result. The Holocaust in particular is taught to different degrees depending on the publisher, ranging from an entire page to merely one photo with a short description. In general, the only points about the Holocaust that are consistently conveyed are that it was the result of the notion of racial superiority perpetuated by the Nazis (and Fascists in general), of the existence of the Auschwitz concentration camps, and of the death of millions of Jews in the gas chambers. Depending on the textbook, the human experiments conducted within the camps are also mentioned, but without specifying for what purpose or even who did so. Other particulars about the Holocaust and Auschwitz, such as the existence of the ghettos or the prisoners being subjected to force labor, are never mentioned. The most important concept within these textbooks is that the Holocaust is not a subject to be discussed alone, but must be considered alongside the crimes committed by the Imperial Japanese army. Such statements make it clear that these events are to be equated with crimes committed by the Axis powers, not separately as the Nazi's depraved perception of race versus the abject brutality of the Imperial Japanese army, but as one and the same. It also causes the readers to start comparing the former perpetrators not as individuals but as countries to see how they dealt with their past. In comparison to Japan, Germany is represented as a country which lived up to its past. This perception is not at all implicit in a textbook published

27 "아베, 홀로코스트 박물관 가는 까닭은... 과거사 교묘한 물타기?," Yonhapnews. co.kr, web, http://www.yonhapnews.co.kr/bulletin/2015/04/26/0200000000A KR20150426001200071.html, accessed 19 January 2017.

by Kumsung Publishing, where the famous photo of West Germany's Prime Minister Brandt kneeling in front of the Monument to the Ghetto Heroes in 1970 (Warschauer Kniefall) occupies a spot within a two-page section on the Cold War.[28] Another textbook published by Jihaksa is very explicit in equating the events discussed in this paper and in comparing the attitudes of the former perpetrator countries. It dedicates an entire page to this endeavour, titled "Lessons from the Second World War", which consists of four photos accompanied by brief descriptions and two questions at the end. The first photo is of the selections occurring in Auschwitz-Birkenau, and the description simply conveys that the victims, Jewish people, were all being sent to die in a gas chamber, despite the fact that some in the photos were being permitted to live as laborers. The second photo is of a group of Comfort Women, and the text states that the "Japanese" (the Imperial Japanese army) subjected these women to sexual slavery. The third photo shows the members of Unit 731, and it mentions that both Axis powers had conducted human experiments. The fourth photo is actually two placed side by side to be compared. The left is the photo of Prime Minister Brandt kneeling in Warsaw, and the right is of former Japanese Prime Minister Jun'ichirō Koizumi visiting the Yasukuni Shrine. The first question asks the students to consider how to prevent such atrocities from happening again. The second question asks the students to compare and contrast the attitudes of the two former perpetrator countries; the correct answer is, as conveyed by the textbook, that Japan as a country is not living up to its crime against people such as the Comfort Women, while Germany did live up to its crime during the Holocaust.[29] In the media, this perception of Germany is quite clear; see, for example, the title of a news article by *Dong-a Ilbo*: "Chancellor Merkel

28 Yi Byeong-hui, Kim Sŏgu, Yi Seong-je, Kim Hyeong-deok, Choi Hyun-sam, Kim Kyŏng-ho, Park Min-yŏk, Yi Yong-seok and Kim Kyŏng-jin, 고등학교 역사 부도, Seoul: Kumsung Publishing, 2014, p. 329.

29 Jung Jae-jung, Kim Tae-shik, Park Kun-chil, Choi Byŏng-taek, Kang Shin-tae, Ku Bon-hyŏng, Jang Jong-kun, Park Chan-sŏk, Kang Seong-ju, Kim Jong-hyun, and Kim Ji-hyun, 중학교 역사 2, Seoul: Jihaksa, 2012, p. 189.

apologizes once more about Nazi crimes".[30] Thus it can be deduced that, within South Korea's public history, the Holocaust and Auschwitz are not events to be discussed on their own, but are rather to be reconciled with South Korea's perception of the past and their current dispute with Japan about *their* past.

Though South Korean public history does recognize the Holocaust as an atrocity and an inhumane experience for its victims, it is ultimately an object of comparison; it is compared to the history both Korea and Japan share, where Koreans were the victims and Japan the sole perpetrator. It is understandable that South Korea, distant from Europe and therefore the Holocaust, by trying to equate this distant event to their own, has fallen into the trap of generalization, leading to a limited understanding of what occurred. This is reflected in the history textbooks which always compare the Holocaust to atrocities committed by the Imperial Japanese army, the lack of indigenous scholarly texts on the Holocaust and even a general absence of testimonials from actual survivors. Also, contrasting Germany's so-called "repentant" attitude concerning the Holocaust with Japan's so-called "unrepentant" nature is an act that diminishes the importance of the victim's perspective in the Holocaust. This is so because when South Korea's media and history textbooks are critical of Japanese politicians who underplay or deny the experience of the victims such as the Comfort Women, it is in the end done to ensure that the experience of those victims be remembered. However, in the process, by turning the Holocaust into a concurrent atrocity for which the perpetrator country had been repentant, there is in the end not a victim oriented perspective, but rather the perspective of the perpetrator country, along with their merit for recognizing their past. Overall, the Holocaust's place in South Korea's public history has been both of great relevance and of obscurity at the same time. It is an event that is equated by South Korea with South

---

30 Hwang In-chan, "나치의 만행 또 사죄한 메르캘 총리," *News.donga.com*, web, http://news.donga.com/List/3/0218/20160127/76151116/1, accessed 17 January 2017.

Korea's own victimhood, and thereby, while also understood fundamentally as a horrible experience for the Holocaust victims, it is, at the same time, an event which has become engrained in South Korea's relations with Japan.

Helena Bryn-McLeod

Remembrance and Reality:
The Holocaust and Social Media

Social media are a new and evolving kind of platform upon which Holocaust memory and commemoration have found expression since October
14, 2009, when the Auschwitz Memorial made their first "post" on the
social media site Facebook.[1] To gain some insight into the ever-chang-
ing representation of collective traumatic memory, I will explore the
discrepancies between ex-prisoners' experiences and the way modern
society chooses to inherit this information. The experience of the Holocaust is now prolifically represented online through the most popular
social sharing services: Facebook, Instagram, Twitter and YouTube. The
space between what physically happened in Auschwitz and what is being
continued into cyber space requires a discussion about representation,
perception and reality. It requires us to discuss what is being disseminated
into people's minds and poses various important ethical questions. How
do social media create awareness of the Holocaust? Does this facilitate
the education of its history? What truth is one interacting with when
one posts or sees posts about the Holocaust? Are we creating a "forgetful
memory" of the event?[2]

---

1   Paweł Sawicki, "Historical Train Car on the Ramp at Birkenau," *Facebook: Auschwitz
    Memorial / Muzeum Auschwitz*, 14 October 2009, web, https://www.facebook.com/
    auschwitzmemorial, accessed July 15, 2015; Paweł Sawicki, Public Relations Depart-
    ment, the Auschwitz-Birkenau State Museum, Personal interview, 17 May 2015.
2   Michael F. Bernard-Donals, *Forgetful Memory: Representation and Remembrance in the
    Wake of the Holocaust*, Albany: State University of New York, 2009.

The Auschwitz-Birkenau State Museum has approached some ethical walls in the last half decade in terms of how to use the force of social media to complete their educational and commemorative mission.[3] One of these ethical concerns is respecting the will and comfort level of survivors. Evidently, the Museum has recognized what Stephanie Benzaquen points out in her 2014 contribution to *Auschwitz Heute*: that "social media are part of our daily environment. They shape the way we relate to a wide range of situations, from the most banal one (having a coffee) to the most challenging one (visiting a former death camp)".[4] Remembering is one of the most definitive traits of being human. Thus, it goes without saying that while channels and methods of remembrance are changing, "bearing witness to Nazi crimes in Auschwitz remains an essential task for generations to come".[5]

The spectrum of remembrance is enormous and varied. We remember because it brings us emotion to know we existed in certain special situations. But most poignantly, we remember because it hurt us, because something had such a strong impact that it will never go away. In terms of the Holocaust, this is definitive. As the event itself is distanced from us temporally, the remembrance grows spatially; "the physical reality of the Holocaust exists now only in its consequences, its effects and simulations: the rest is memory, itself increasingly shaped by the reality of our simulations".[6]

3 Sawicki, Personal interview, 18 May 2015.
4 Stephanie Benzaquen, "Post, Update, Download: Social Media and the Future of Auschwitz Remembrance," *Auschwitz Heute - Dzisiaj -Today*, Berlin: Hentrich and Hentrich, 14 September 2014, p. 136.
5 Ibid., p. 137.
6 James Edward Young, *At Memory's Edge: After-Images of the Holocaust in Contemporary Art and Architecture*, New Haven: Yale University Press: 2000, p. 44.
7 Dr. Bożena Karwowska, "CENS 303A: Representations of the Holocaust - Introduction," lecture, University of British Columbia, Vancouver, 3 January 2017 and "CENS 303A: Representations of the Holocaust – What is the Camp?," lecture, University of British Columbia, Vancouver, 2 February 2015.

After considering this, we all must remain appreciative of the inability to know.[7] We will never know. Our memory is our own invention in our own reality. The complete knowledge of the Holocaust died with the death of each individual who passed through the gas chamber door between the first use of Zyclon B in Crematorium I in late 1941, and the last in late 1944 in crematoria in Auschwitz II.

Fascinatingly, humans will always invent a new way to capture memory. Although it is intangible, it is inarguably one of our most valued resources. And in the last half decade, the memory of the Holocaust has become readily apparent and accessible online through social sharing sites. Previously, this information had been preserved most profoundly in the physical spaces around Poland: Auschwitz, Treblinka, Chelmno, Sobibor and Majdanek; or in historical books or accounts. But now, the Auschwitz-Birkenau Memorial Museum itself has their own Facebook page, Twitter account, Instagram account and YouTube account. Each one is a tool which operates within this new mode of remembrance, a modern stage where pictures, stories and news blend with multiple personal identities, anyone who wishes to so-incorporate themselves. This is an enormous new way to preserve history, and there are many facets of the situation which bring the horror of the past to the forefront in unpredictable ways.

To answer the first question, concerning how social media facilitate the education and awareness of the Holocaust, we turn to the 2010 New York Times article "Brave New World of Digital Remembrance". The author, Clive Thompson, writes that "psychologists have long known that people can engage in 'parasocial' relationships with fictional characters, like those on TV shows or in books, or with remote celebrities we read about in magazines".[8] In the case of the Holocaust being remembered on social media, however, this issue may take a new form. This "new

8   Clive Thompson, "Brave New World of Digital Intimacy," *The Time's Magazine: New York Times*, 5 September 2008.
9   Ibid.

class of relationships", [9] manifested through a distancing of the subject with his or her computer screen, could be more harmful when applied to remembering such an event. Upon searching "hashtags" involved in Instagram posts (where subjects can use a picture of a physical site to depict a photographic journey of where they are and what they are doing), one can find examples of complete detachment from the actual reality of what took place. For instance, on one young man's Instagram post (user name: "loupjunior"), you see him with his tongue out at Birkenau with the description "Photobombing in Auschwitz" followed by the hashtags: #nazi #ss #birkenau #aushwitz #auschwitz and three emoticons: fire, a train, and another fire image. This person is engaging with what can be seen as a "new class of relationships", not with people, but with historical sites themselves. Another young man (user name: "karol_pitu") poses with his girlfriend, both smiling in front of the gate to Birkenau, with the hashtags #thedoorofthedeath #krakow #poland #verano #vacaciones2015 as captions. Apparently, the stopover at this tragic site is a place for this person to add to their 2015 vacation list and show to their friends that "they were there". If they did learn about an ex-prisoner's horrifying fate, they do not share it. Such posts are fixated on their own personality. Both these examples depict parasocial relationships, in which a person feels they *know* the person they "follow" on social media. But in this study, these people appear be parasocially connecting to the physical site of Auschwitz II itself, glossing over the gargantuan presence they stand upon.

In these cases, of which there are plenty more, there is little evidence to suggest that the user is emotionally attached to respecting what happened in the place they are standing, where 1.1 million human beings were murdered. Secondly, in the example of the first man, the hashtags suggest that he venerates the perpetrator and not the victims. Now when

10 Benzaquen, "Post, Update, Download," p. 141, quoting Gary Weissman, *Fantasies of Witnessing: Postwar Efforts to Experience the Holocaust*, Ithaca: Cornell University Press, 2004.

somebody will search "#ss" or "#nazi" on Instagram, his "photobombing" face will show up with the ominous barracks in the background, giving energy to those who created them, not those who suffered and died in them due to malnutrition, beatings, lack of hygiene, typhus and direct murder. Of course, one cannot make an assumption about what this Instagramer's story is, and how he actually feels about the Holocaust, but in terms of representing the memory of the space the victims lived and died in on the Internet, his decision to "photobomb" and use perpetrators in his caption of the image makes him part of the problem, not part of the solution.

One should strive to know *who did what to whom* when one posts about such an event on their online sharing platform. And if one does not care, it is the action of someone who is letting the perpetrators win at violently snuffing out their own kind. It is saying, "I do not care enough to know", and moreover "it does not matter". As Benzaquen points out, posting images and stories "provide a space where we can enact and display our 'fantasies of witnessing'",[10] Discussing this portrays the great potential of social media to produce a detrimental disconnection from the past, and especially from acts of human cruelty throughout history where our kin are murdered without a voice.

However, although "many people try now to evade the conformity of the standard record of a museum visit",[11] wherein the danger of parasocial connection lies, the Auschwitz-Birkenau Press Office head, Paweł Sawicki, has another perspective. In our May 20, 2015, interview, he underlined the incredible power of the various social media they can employ as educators. When the Memorial joined Facebook in 2009, it was very much a puzzle. Sawicki worried that since social media were all about entertainment, having "fans" or "likers" would be problematic. The Museum was ready to shut down the page at any inkling of people demanding respect, but the "result was amazing".[12] They asked members, "should we be on

11 Benzaquen, "Post, Update, Download," p. 143.
12 Sawicki, Personal interview, 20 May 2015.

Facebook?", to which they had very positive and supportive replies. As he said in October, 2009, when the site launched, "if our mission is to educate the younger generation to be responsible in the contemporary world, what better tool can we use to reach them than the tools they use themselves?"[13] The next step was to have a strict set of rules, to which they have remained committed. When there is an inappropriate discussion, it is targeted as soon as possible by one of the staff in the press office, who are monitoring the site constantly, and the inappropriate discussion is removed.[14] Above all, "the survivors are the voice we listen to and respect at all times", says Sawicki; "we need to be assertive and protect the site from people who want to use it as a stage".[15]

The main benefit of Facebook is that it extends the physical place of Auschwitz and Birkenau into cyberspace. For those who cannot afford to travel to Auschwitz, they consider the online version "a living memory".[16] As Sawicki pointed out, there are over 1.5 million people visiting each year, meaning there are six billion who are not. Money might not be the only issue, too. Some may choose not to go for personal reasons; therefore social media are "providing . . . a hand which is reached to people who want to learn, but who can't come here".[17] The brilliance of extending the Memorial into an online space is that it provides access to millions around the world who wish to commemorate and engage with history. Furthermore, it is a potential solution for future remembrance of the Holocaust. The seas of testimonies, videos and art from the no-longer living survivors will be preserved at the Memorial, and on the Internet. Thus the Facebook page of the Memorial is a place where pictures, facts and discussions begin, where the Museum can uphold various moments

---

13 Ibid.; also quoted in: Berg, Raffi, "Auschwitz Launches Facebook Site," *BBC News*, 14 October 2009, web, http://news.bbc.co.uk/2/hi/europe/8307162.stm, accessed 24 January 2017.

14 Sawicki, Personal interview, 20 May 2015.

15 Ibid.

16 Ibid.

17 Ibid.

between 1940-1945, share testimonial truth and records, and have people from around the world engage with it from this day forwards. Below is an example of how a Facebook post functions. On July 2, 2015, the Memorial testified on their Facebook page that,

> on July 2, 1942, 11 Jewish prisoners died during work at Buna-Werke unit (construction works of the IG Farbenindustrie chemical plant). These were: Adalbert Weiss, Wilhelm Schloss, Moritz Abrannovitch, Samuel Fridmann, Abram Grinberg, Felix Nirenstein, Wally Schaffier, Moritz Waserstein, Moses Daum, Mordka Wengerow and Luzian Dreyfus. On the same day 10 Poles were shot at the execution wall on the yard of Block 11. These were: Karol Turczak, Jan Drożdż, Stefan Janik, Emil Mentel, Michał Jakubiec, Józef Kufel, Michał Zuziak, Wincenty Biegun, Władysław Matlak and Jan Moczek.[18]

This post constitutes a very distinct act of remembrance. By zooming in on the names of the victims of one particular day, the vastness of the crime is individualized: it is brought to a very concrete standstill that asks for our recognition. Also, it is a fascinating new way of sharing archival information. People may now bypass the research they may or may not have invested in (which has the possibility of producing inaccurate data), and they have, instead, an insight into a real and important moment in time (in this case, precisely 73 years ago). It shows exact spelling of names and specific dates – concisely put and easily accessible. Now it appears there is very little excuse to get the facts wrong. If you want to know something for sure or have a question, like the name of an ex-prisoner, for example, you can send the Auschwitz-Birkenau State Museum a message on Facebook. Also, if you are a history enthusiast, you can use the page to engage with other like-minded individuals around the globe who wish to discuss or debate various perspectives on the facts. People can

---

18 Paweł Sawicki, *Facebook: Auschwitz Memorial / Muzeum Auschwitz*, 2 July 2015, web, https://www.facebook.com/auschwitzmemorial, accessed 15 July 2015.

count on the Facebook page of the Museum as a standard of Holocaust representation, and this is invaluable for the modern learning community.

Interviewing Press Office official and Auschwitz-Birkenau guide Łukasz Lipiński provided key information about the Museum's use of Twitter. Since its inception in 2012, whenever people, newscasters or historical channels make a mistake when posting or sharing information, the Memorial can use Twitter to immediately call them out. No corporation or individual wants a bad reputation, and since Twitter functions within such a fast-acting online community, it does not take long for the mistake to become apparent. For instance, Dutch television and Belgian newspapers last year used the term "Polish Concentration Camp". The Museum immediately called them out on their mistake, that Auschwitz was certainly German Nazi death camps, on Polish soil, which does not make them Polish. Additionally, a history channel who labelled the camp kitchens at Auschwitz I as the crematorium can be reprimanded accordingly for getting their facts wrong.[19] A final example is a tweet in which an author (Twitter name: @Arisoffer1) misrepresented who killed whom with Zyklon B, to which the Memorial tweeted "@AriSoffer1 People who killed with Zyklon cans in German Nazis camps were in fact Germans. Please correct your article!" to which the author responded, "Reference has been duly corrected. Apologies for any offense, and thanks for bringing it to my attention" (Twitter.com, 07.02.2015). As Lipiński said, "it is a big issue when people teach things wrong. Therefore, Twitter is a strong tool".[20] Compared to previous years before social media, when the discussion of crucial mistakes was done on the Auschwitz.org website, the corrections today are more efficient, assertive and widely-read. The Memorial's voice is heard and respected in the online community. As always, as Lipiński reminded me, the main goal of the Auschwitz-Birkenau Museum staff is to make sure the dissemination of history and fact is done correctly and respectfully.[21]

19 Łukasz Lipiński, Public Relations Department, the Auschwitz-Birkenau State Museum, Personal interview, 15 May 2015.
20 Ibid.
21 Ibid.

However, many issues remain with the personal use of these online platforms. As Danah Boyd (fellow at Harvard's Berkman Center for Internet and Society) mentions in Thompson's article, people on social media "can observe you, but it's not the same as *knowing* you".[22] After a quick search of the hashtags #auschwitz, #auschwitzbirkenau and #auschwitzselfie on Instagram, this comment proves true. There are hundreds of thousands who are observing the physical sites in Poland and letting the world know about what they see and feel there. The grounds of the concentration and death camp are being documented every day. But far from representing what truly happened, the result is simply constant additional pictures of the most "popular" perspectives (the "Arbeit macht frei" gate, the train tracks into Birkenau, and the long row of distant barracks, for example) with the personality of the subject injected into the scene. When followers see these images, it is because they are "friends" of the person on Instagram. By "liking" the image, are they recognizing the reality of those murdered there, are they contemplating those individual stories? Or are they stimulating the ego of the "historical Instagramer"? Actually knowing what happened takes genuine effort, as does being someone's real friend (to apply the "Friend-ing" social media metaphor). Furthermore, knowing what happened requires a deeply empathic study, even after which one cannot fully understand.

Bernard-Donals' term "Forgetful Memory", based off the philosophy of Yosef Yerushalmi, epitomizes this issue. Yerushalmi calls us to understand how breaks in history, which rupture our understanding of existence, incline us to retrieve at times "exceedingly selective, sometimes careless or mightily subjective" information.[23] Consequently, this leads readers, writers, thinkers: us, to creating "something other than memory, something new, and something perhaps tenuously related to what took place".[24] Arguably, this is precisely what occurs in the online sphere of

---

22 Thompson, "Brave New World of Digital Intimacy."
23 Yosef Yerushalmi, quoted in Bernard-Donals, *Forgetful Memory*, p. 3.
24 Ibid.

remembrance. Bernard-Donals explores this phenomenon, saying that those who are disconnected from veritably witnessing an event, be it second-hand witnesses, or even third or fourth-hand witnesses, produce a material in their minds which is "a kind of 'excess' of the event".[25] The plenitude of people "photobombing" at Auschwitz, Birkenau, Treblinka, Sobibor, Chelmo etc. on Instagram, or those using Facebook to illustrate their journeys backpacking across Europe (in which Auschwitz may be a quick stopover to procure a picture depicting their historical fascination) is a poignant example of this excess. And as Bernard-Donals explains "Forgetful Memory":

> I want to make the case that memory and forgetfulness are facets of the same phenomenon of understanding; the occurrence of events begins interminably to recede into an inaccessible past at the very moment of occurrence, while the event's passage into language—into any knowledge that we might formulate of the occurrence—makes of the occurrence something (narrative, testimony, history) *other* than the event . . . The Holocaust, as a break, functions doubly . . . in Blanchot's words, [it] "ruined everything", [it] forced us to decisively change how we think of history and its relation to memory; and it also haunts our accounts of how memory and its object—our representation of events and the events themselves—come into contact with one another since 1945.[26]

This is a powerful notion that shapes the world of remembrance itself, but takes on an even more profound shape when applied to social media and those who use it as a way to connect to the past. Are we inevitably fated to produce something other than the event, from each day forwards, in each moment that we share something about the Holocaust on the Internet? Is it a step further away from being a new witness than the already extant distance before Facebook and Instagram? Or is it simply that we

25 Ibid.
26 Bernard-Donals, *Forgetful Memory*, pp. 3-4.

must work in a new medium where we have to become conscious of the way we permit events to "recede" into the inaccessible past?

One could probably say that forgetfulness is the other side of the memory coin. The event of the Holocaust itself, the actual experience of being in the concentration or death camp, remains in the minds of either those who were there, or disappeared the moment the person was murdered. From then on, everything is a new perspective, a changed perspective. Carl Friedman's novel *Nightfather* is an impeccable illustration of this:

> My father sings every evening. When we leave the table, one by one, after supper, he stays in his chair. He opens his mouth a little and rocks backward and forward, as if pumping his voice up from very deep down. It takes a little while for the sound to come out. We don't understand his songs. He learned them from fellow-sufferers drawn from every corner of Europe, people who shared barracks or bunks with him, or perhaps a piece of bread. They are dead, they can no longer speak, and they can't hear him. Yet it is for them that he sings. His long, drawn-out Slav vowels float over our heads, but they're not meant for us.[27]

The young daughter of the Holocaust survivor grows up experiencing her father's dark memory, but the memory itself is his, expressed for those whose spirits no one will hear from again.

Ernst van Alphen supports this, explaining that the nature of *remembering* the Holocaust and growing up experiencing *other people's story* of the Holocaust are different. "Children of survivors can be traumatized, but their trauma does not consist of the Holocaust experience, not even in a direct or mitigated form. Their trauma is cause by being raised by a traumatized Holocaust survivor".[28] Read further, we can see how his work

---

27 Carl Friedman, *Nightfather*, New York: Persea, 1994, p. 28f. as quoted in: Ernst van Alphen, "Second-Generation Testimony, Transmission of Trauma, and Postmemory," *Poetics Today* 27(2), 2006, p. 481.
28 van Alphen, "Second-Generation Testimony," p. 482.

applies to remembrance in the present social media sphere, where the testimonies are mostly several generations removed from the true witnesses of the Holocaust, the complete witness of which we must remember is the dead victim.[29] When the trauma of a Holocaust survivor raises the next generation to experience their suffering, they are passing on not the dark secrets of their mind, but a narrative with which this new human will frame the story of pain. Their own pain becomes a new experience, one which is removed from the inside of the camp, because it is through a personal filter and a personal dream. Van Alphen continues: "public accounts of the Holocaust [enable] personal memories to be narratable. They provide the narrative framework in which memory fragments can be integrated".[30] These memory fragments combine to create an ever-evolving idea of what the Holocaust was, based on who shares them.

Seeing this notion flourish on social media speaks to the paradox of this generation, in which subjects are connected more than ever, yet very much disconnected—in this case from the survivors' personal memories of the Holocaust. Considering the fact that a small number of survivors remain and that the future of remembrance will exist, other than at the Memorial Museum itself, in an active way on the World Wide Web preserved in video, interview and story, the question remains: are we who engage in social media while commemorating the Holocaust creating our own version of the Holocaust? Has popular online culture let the truth recede so deeply into the inaccessible past, as Bernard-Donals suggests, that the forgetfulness becomes the only side of the coin? This situation surely indicates "not only a loss of life or of culture or of family, but also a site where the event is replaced by a representation that bears a vexed relation to the event itself".[31]

29 Primo Levi, *The Drowned and the Saved,* New York: Random House, 1989, p. 83f.; Giorgio Agamben, *Remnants of Auschwitz: The Witness and the Archive,* New York: Zone Books, 1999, p. 33.
30 van Alphen, "Second-Generation Testimony," p. 485.
31 Bernard-Donals, *Forgetful Memory,* p. 5.

Since 1945, all peoples aware of the Holocaust (and arguably unaware, but that is a different study) have been dealing with their versions of Holocaust remembrance as second-hand witnesses. Most of the people alive today, except for a sliver of approximately three hundred survivors, do not know what it was like within the concentration and death camp walls in Auschwitz. Furthermore, no one knows what the experience of the gas chamber was. And yet, the pain of the event will never dissipate, and we know that because we, too, are human, and we, too, feel the mercilessness and desperation seeping from the spaces themselves in Germany and Poland, and the haunting sadness and despair which characterizes the stories of those victimized there. As Martin Blatt testifies in "Holocaust Remembrance and Heidelberg", in which he shares the experience of returning with his mother to her birth town (one of many reconciliation trips to Germany, sponsored by the town's government for former Jewish citizens expulsed by German Nazis in the late 1930s) each person's grasp on reality is unique, but shared:

> My mother remembered the people and the places. My memory and consciousness, which had been based solely on her accounts and those of my maternal grandmother, had been transformed and enhanced by our visit.[32]

As in each situation, humans are existing within a co-constructed, shared memory. We are all collecting partial elements of the history, of the event itself, and together we interpret it, re-tell it and carry it forwards as best as possible, focusing on our own perception of what is important. As Young points out in "At Memory's Edge", "when an artist like David Levinthal sets out "to remember" the Holocaust, all he can actually remember are the numberless images passed down to him in books, films and photographs. When he sets out "to photograph" the Holocaust, therefore, he takes pictures of *his* Holocaust experiences".[33]

32 Blatt, "Holocaust Remembrance and Heidelberg," p. 95.
33 Young, *At Memory's Edge*, p. 44.

In conclusion, while social media are an excellent tactical tool to support the educational and commemorative goals of the Auschwitz-Birkenau Museum, and a great online representation of the physicality of the Memorial, there are many downfalls in how popular culture uses them. The "forgetful memory" of human-kind has bound us in a form of permanent separation from the event of the Holocaust, no matter what we do to reverse it. Furthermore, a staggering number of those who engage with the platforms available on the Internet consent to letting the reality of Auschwitz or Birkenau remain in the past because redefining it or trivializing it seem to be prioritized in the sixty seconds they have to make a "post" about it. Therefore, unless one engages in philosophical and testimonial literature, explicitly representative fiction or connects with the information shared by the Auschwitz-Birkenau State Memorial on their Facebook, Instagram, Twitter or YouTube feeds about the peoples who lived and died in the concentration and death camps in Poland, one will loose a sense of what occurred. Bernard-Donals would argue that as soon as it happened, it became impossible to authentically remember, and it seems pertinent in this study to agree. But, as our humanity sustains our desire to continue remembering, and to continue spreading awareness, we are inevitably trapped within a cycle of perpetuating the past as a construct of our own awareness, unconsciously and consciously picking and choosing what history to create each and every day. Social media are simply the extension of our nature as forgetful rememberers.